Books
by
Norman
Mailer

The Naked and the Dead
Barbary Shore
The Deer Park
The White Negro
Advertisements for Myself
Deaths for the Ladies (and Other Disasters)
The Presidential Papers
An American Dream
Cannibals and Christians
Why Are We in Vietnam?
The Deer Park — A Play
The Armies of the Night
Miami and the Siege of Chicago
Of a Fire on the Moon
The Prisoner of Sex
Maidstone
Existential Errands

EXISTENTIAL ERRANDS

EXISTENTIAL ERRANDS

NORMAN MAILER
LITTLE, BROWN AND COMPANY — BOSTON — TORONTO

818

*To Barbara, to Susan,
to Adeline, and to Al*

Preface

This collection covers pieces written almost entirely in the last five years, a period in which *The Deer Park* as a play was given its last draft and then produced, *Why Are We in Vietnam?* was written and then *The Armies of the Night, Miami and the Siege of Chicago, Of a Fire on the Moon* and *The Prisoner of Sex.* Three movies were also made. So it is a period when, with every thought of beginning a certain big novel which had been promised for a long time, the moot desire to have one's immediate say on contemporary matters kept diverting the novelistic impulse into journalism. Such passing books began to include many of the themes of the big novel. On the way, shorter pieces were also written for a variety of motives and occasions, written in a general state of recognition that if one had a philosophy it was being put together in many pieces. Still a view of life was expressed in those books and those years. Perhaps it was also expressed in the movies which were made and in the campaign to get the Democratic nomination for Mayor of New York. In any case, it was reasonable to think that people who liked my work might be interested in this collection since many a passing remark in the longer books became a chapter of investigation here, and more than one empty space in the high winds of other rhetoric settled into a serious discussion in these pages. So the merit of this assembly may be in the main for people who are sufficiently intrigued with a few of my ideas to try out a few more. If the emphasis is then less personal than *Advertisements for Myself, The Presidential Papers,* or *Cannibals and Christians,* it ought also to be said before too many apologies are upon us that this book may have a particular merit the others do not possess. Its parts are more even. It is more coherent. The ends of one piece are likely to buttress the ideas in the next. What is said about film has its relation to boxing, and to theatre and to bullfight; the pieces side by side offer elucidation of one another — besides, what is said about politics comes out of much obsession and some unfiltered experience. Even what is said about literature in the middle of this book is related to the rest, for the remarks on the Establishment and the put-on in "Up the Family Tree" have their reflection in every piece which follows, and carry by extension into the sinister even vertiginous notions of politics and Establishment which the work, and lack of work, of the Warren Commission aroused in us. The put-on is perhaps the spirit elixir of technology. In that future world where children will be raised by professional nurses who will be guided by directives determined in the main by the ruminative processes of computers, the notion of mother and father

[x]

itself will take on the same aspects of High Camp we used to recognize in politicians' voices when they spoke of fighting for freedom in Southeast Asia. It is one thing to think of an Establishment as evil, (it is equivalent in its sense of bitter tragic security to the gloom of the theologian who decides God is not good) but to come to that slippery slope where one knows that the Establishment is not good, not evil, but a put-on even to itself is to cross that plastic curtain which separates the world of the past from the futures of technology. So these pieces, one may suppose, are the abstract journal of a trip from the relative certainty of boxing and bullfighting to that cubist state of the psyche where one runs for mayor with one's heart in one's mouth and is congratulated for the éclat in the put-on. It is no wonder this is a miscellany of writings on existential themes. For in our world of gesture, role, costume, supposition, and borrowed manner which is all of the air that is left to the graces of our city, in that perpetual transformation of moral axes which is the inner life of the drug, there is except for attrition no way out but by way of that moment which proves deeper than any of our pretenses, that stricken existential moment in which Camp is stripped of its marks of quotation, and put-ons shrivel in the livid air. What better way then to begin than by a description of a fight between heavyweight champions for fifteen rounds?

Contents

[xiii]

[xiv]

PART
ONE

CLUES
TO
THE
AESTHETIC
OF
THE
ARENA

Boxing

King of the Hill

Ego! It is the great word of the twentieth century. If there is a single word our century has added to the potentiality of language, it is ego. Everything we have done in this century, from monumental feats to nightmares of human destruction, has been a function of that extraordinary state of the psyche which gives us authority to declare we are sure of ourselves when we are not.

Muhammad Ali begins with the most unsettling ego of all. Having commanded the stage, he never pretends to step back and relinquish his place to other actors — like a six-foot parrot, he keeps screaming at you that he is the center of the stage. "Come here and get me, fool," he says. "You can't, 'cause you don't know who I am. You

don't know *where* I am. I'm human intelligence and you
don't even know if I'm good or evil." This has been his
essential message to America all these years. It is intolerable to our American mentality that the figure who is
probably most prominent to us after the President is simply not comprehensible, for he could be a demon or a
saint. Or both! Richard Nixon, at least, appears comprehensible. We can hate him or we can vote for him, but at
least we disagree with each other about him. What kills
us about Cassius Clay is that the disagreement is
inside us. He is *fascinating* — attraction and repulsion
must be in the same package. So, he is obsessive. The
more we don't want to think about him, the more we are
obliged to. There is a reason for it. He is America's Greatest Ego. He is also, as I am going to try to show, the
swiftest embodiment of human intelligence we have had
yet, he is the very spirit of the twentieth century, he is
the prince of mass man and the media. Now, perhaps
temporarily, he is the fallen prince. But there still may
be one holocaust of an urge to understand him, or try to,
for obsession is a disease. Twenty little obsessions are
twenty leeches on the mind, and one big obsession can
become one big operation if we refuse to live with it. If
Muhammad Ali defeats Frazier in the return bout, then
he'll become the national obsession and we'll elect him
President yet — you may indeed have to vote for any
man who could defeat a fighter as great as Joe Frazier
and still be Muhammad Ali. That's a combination!

Yes, ego — that officious and sometimes efficient exercise of ignorance-as-authority — must be the central
phenomenon of the twentieth century, even if patriotic
Americans like to pretend it does not exist in their
heroes. Which, of course, is part of the holy American
horseball. The most monstrous exhibition of ego by a
brave man in many a year was Alan Shepard's three
whacks at a golf ball while standing on the moon. There,
in a space suit, hardly able to stand, he put a club head

on an omnipurpose tool shaft, and, restricted to swinging with one arm, dibbled his golf ball on the second try. On the third it went maybe half a mile — a non-phenomenal distance in the low gravitational field of the lunar sphere.

"What's so unpleasant about that?" asked a pleasant young jet-setter.

Aquarius, of the old book, loftily replied, "Would you take a golf ball into St. Patrick's and see how far you can hit it?"

The kid nodded his head. "Now that you put it that way, I guess I wouldn't, but I was excited when it happened. I said to my wife, 'Honey, we're playing golf on the moon.' "

Well, to the average fight fan, Cassius Clay has been golf on the moon. Who can comprehend the immensity of ego involved? Every fighter is in a whirligig with his ego. The fight game, for example, is filled with legends of fighters who found a girl in an elevator purposefully stalled between floors for two minutes on the afternoon of a main-event fight. Later, after he blew the fight, his irate manager blew his ears. "Were you crazy?" the manager asked. "Why did you do it?"

"Because," said the fighter, "I get these terrible headaches every afternoon, and only a chick who knows how, can relieve them."

Ego is driving a point through to a conclusion you are obliged to reach without knowing too much about the ground you cross between. You suffer for a larger point. Every good prizefighter must have a large ego, then, because he is trying to demolish a man he doesn't know too much about, he is unfeeling — which is the ground floor of ego; and he is full of techniques — which are the wings of ego. What separates the noble ego of the prize-fighters from the lesser ego of authors is that the fighter goes through experiences in the ring which are occasionally immense, incommunicable except to fighters who

[5]

have been as good, or to women who have gone through every minute of an anguish-filled birth, experiences which are finally mysterious. Like men who climb mountains, it is an exercise of ego which becomes something like soul — just as technology may have begun to have transcended itself when we reached to the moon. So, two great fighters in a great fight travel down subterranean rivers of exhaustion and cross mountain peaks of agony, stare at the light of their own death in the eye of the man they are fighting, travel into the crossroads of the most excruciating choice of karma as they get up from the floor against all the appeal of the sweet swooning catacombs of oblivion — it is just that we do not see them this way, because they are not primarily men of words, and this is the century of words, numbers, and symbols. Enough.

We have come to the point. There are languages other than words, languages of symbol and languages of nature. There are languages of the body. And prizefighting is one of them. There is no attempting to comprehend a prizefighter unless we are willing to recognize that he speaks with a command of the body which is as detached, subtle, and comprehensive in its intelligence as any exercise of mind by such social engineers as Herman Kahn or Henry Kissinger. Of course, a man like Herman Kahn is by report gifted with a bulk of three hundred pounds. He does not move around with a light foot. So many a good average prizefighter, just a little punchy, does not speak with any particular éclat. That doesn't mean he is incapable of expressing himself with wit, style, and an aesthetic flair for surprise when he boxes with his body, any more than Kahn's obesity would keep us from recognizing that his mind can work with strength. Boxing is a dialogue between bodies. Ignorant men, usually black, and usually next to illiterate, address one another in a set of *conversational* exchanges which go deep into the heart of each other's matter. It is just that they converse with their physiques. But unless you believe that you cannot receive a mortal wound from an incisive remark, you may be forced to accept the novel idea that men doing friendly boxing have a conversation on which they can often thrive. William Buckley and I in a discussion in a living room for an evening will score points on one another, but enjoy it. On television, where the stakes may be more, we may still both enjoy it. But put us in a debating hall with an argument to go on without cease for twenty-four hours, every encouragement present to humiliate each other, and months of preparation for such a debate, hooplas and howlers of publicity, our tongues stuck out at one another on TV, and repercussions in Vietnam depending on which one of us should win, then add the fatigue of harsh lights, and a moderator who keeps interrupting us, and we are at the beginning of a conversation in which at least one of us will be hurt, and maybe both. Even hurt seriously. The example is picayune, however, in relation to the demands of a fifteen-round fight — perhaps we should have to debate nonstop for weeks under those conditions before one of us was carried away comatose. Now the example becomes clearer: Boxing is a rapid debate between two sets of intelligence. It takes place rapidly because it is conducted with the body rather than the mind. If this seems extreme, let us look for a connection. Picasso could never do arithmetic when he was young because the number 7 looked to him like a nose upside down. So to learn arithmetic would slow him up. He was a future painter — his intelligence resided somewhere in the coordination of the body and the mind. He was not going to cut off his body from his mind by learning numbers. But most of us do. We have minds which work fairly well and bodies which sometimes don't. But if we are white and want to be comfortable we put our emphasis on learning to talk with the mind. Ghetto cultures, Black, Puerto Rican and Chicano cultures, having less expectation of comfort, tend to stick with the wit their bodies provide. They speak to each other with their bodies, they signal with their clothes. They talk with many a silent telepathic intelligence. And doubtless feel the frustration of being unable to express the subtleties of their states in words, just as the average middle-class white will feel unable to carry out his dreams of glory by the uses of his body. If Black people are also beginning to speak our mixture of formal English and jargon-polluted American with real force, so white corporate America is getting more sexual and more athletic. Yet to begin to talk about Ali and Frazier, their psyches, their styles, their honor, their character, their greatness and their flaws, we have to recognize that there is no way to comprehend them as men like ourselves — we can only guess at their insides by a real jump of our imagination into the science Ali invented — he was the first psychologist of the body.

Okay. There are fighters who are men's men. Rocky Marciano was one of them. Oscar Bonavena and Jerry Quarry and George Chuvalo and Gene Fullmer and Carmen Basilio, to name a few, have faces which would give a Marine sergeant pause in a bar fight. They look like they could take you out with the knob of bone they have left for a nose. They are all, incidentally, white fighters. They have a code — it is to fight until they are licked, and if they have to take a punch for every punch they give, well, they figure they can win. Their ego and their body intelligence are both connected to the same source of juice — it is male pride. They are substances close to rock. They work on clumsy skills to hone them finer, knowing if they can obtain parity, blow for blow with any opponent, they will win. They have more guts. Up to a far-gone point, pain is their pleasure, for their character in combat is their strength to trade pain for pain, loss of faculty for loss of faculty.

One can cite Black fighters like them. Henry Hank and Reuben Carter, Emile Griffith and Benny Paret. Joe Frazier would be the best of them. But Black fighters tend to be complex. They have veins of unsuspected strength and streaks when they feel as spooked as wild horses. Any fight promoter in the world knew he had a good fight if Fullmer went against Basilio, it was a proposition as certain as the wages for the week. But Black fighters were artists, they were relatively moody, they were full of the surprises of Patterson or Liston, the virtuosities of Archie Moore and Sugar Ray, the speed, savagery, and curious lack of substance in Jimmy Ellis, the vertiginous neuroses of giants like Buster Mathis. Even Joe Louis, recognized by a majority in the years of his own championship as the greatest heavyweight of all time, was surprisingly inconsistent with minor fighters like Buddy Baer. Part of the unpredictability of their performances was due to the fact that all but Moore and Robinson were heavyweights. Indeed, white champions in the top division were equally out of form from fight to fight. It can, in fact, be said that heavyweights are always the most lunatic of prizefighters. The closer a heavyweight comes to the championship, the more natural it is for him to be a little bit insane, secretly insane, for the heavyweight champion of the world is either the toughest man in the world or he is not, but there is a real possibility he is. It is like being the big toe of God. You have nothing to measure yourself by. Lightweights, welterweights, middleweights can all be exceptionally good, fantastically talented — they are still very much in their place. The best lightweight in the world knows that an unranked middleweight can defeat him on most nights, and the best middleweight in the world will kill him every night. He knows that the biggest strongman in a tough bar could handle him by sitting on him, since the power to punch seems to increase quickly with weight. A fighter who weighs two-forty will punch more than twice as hard as a fighter who weighs one-twenty. The figures have no real basis, of course, they are only there to indicate the law of the ring: a good big man beats a good little man. So the notion of prizefighters as hardworking craftsmen is most likely to be true in the light and middle divisions. Since they are fighters who know their limitations, they are likely to strive for excellence in their category. The better they get, the closer they have come to sanity, at least if we are ready to assume that the average fighter is a buried artist, which is to say a *body* artist with an extreme amount of violence in him. Obviously the better and more successful they get, the more they have been able to transmute violence into craft, discipline, even body art. That is human alchemy. We respect them and they deserve to be respected.

But the heavyweights never have such simple sanity. If they become champions they begin to have inner lives like Hemingway or Dostoyevsky, Tolstoy or Faulkner, Joyce or Melville or Conrad or Lawrence or Proust. Hemingway is the example above all. Because he wished to be the greatest writer in the history of literature and still be a hero with all the body arts age would yet grant him, he was alone and he knew it. So are heavyweight champions alone. Dempsey was alone and Tunney could never explain himself and Sharkey could never believe himself nor Schmeling nor Braddock, and Carnera was sad and Baer an indecipherable clown; great heavyweights like Louis had the loneliness of the ages in their silence, and men like Marciano were mystified by a power which seemed to have been granted them. With the advent, however, of the great modern Black heavyweights, Patterson, Liston, then Clay and Frazier, perhaps the loneliness gave way to what it had been protecting itself against — a surrealistic situation unstable beyond belief.

Being a Black heavyweight champion in the second half of the twentieth century (with Black revolutions opening all over the world) was now not unlike being Jack Johnson, Malcolm X and Frank Costello all in one. Going down the aisle and into the ring in Chicago was conceivably more frightening for Sonny Liston than facing Patterson that night — he was raw as uncoated wire with his sense of retribution awaiting him for years of prison pleasures and underworld jobs. Pools of paranoia must have reached him like different washes of color from different sides of the arena. He was a man who had barely learned to read and write — he had none of the impacted and mediocre misinformation of all the world of daily dull reading to clot the antenna of his senses — so he was keen to every hatred against him. He knew killers were waiting in that mob, they always were, he had been on speaking terms with just such subjects himself — now he dared to be king — any assassin could strike for his revenge upon acts Liston had long forgot; no wonder Liston was in fear going into the ring, and happier once within it.

And Patterson was exhausted before the fight began. Lonely as a monk for years, his daily gym work the stuff of his meditation, he was the first of the Black fighters to be considered, then used, as a political force. He was one of the liberal elite, an Eleanor Roosevelt darling, he was political mileage for the NAACP. Violent, conceivably, to the point of murder if he had not been a fighter, he was a gentleman in public, more, he was a man of the nicest, quietest, most private good manners. But monastic by inclination. Now, all but uneducated, he was appealed to by political Blacks to win the Liston fight for the image of the Negro. Responsibility sat upon him like a comic cutback in a silent film where we return now and again to one poor man who has been left to hold a beam across his shoulders. There he stands, hardly able to move. At the end of the film he collapses. That was the weight put on Patterson. The responsibility to beat Liston was too great to bear. Patterson, a fighter of incorruptible honesty, was knocked out by punches hardly anybody saw. He fell in open air as if seized by a stroke. The age of surrealistic battles had begun. In the second fight with Liston, Patterson, obviously more afraid of a repetition of the first nightmare than anything else, simply charged his opponent with his hands low and was knocked down three times and out in the first round. The age of body psychology had begun and Clay was there to conceive it.

A kid as wild and dapper and jaybird as the president of a down-home college fraternity, bow tie, brown-and-white shoes, sweet, happy-go-lucky, *raucous,* he descended on Vegas for the second Patterson-Liston fight. He was like a beautiful boy surrounded by doting aunts. The classiest-looking middle-aged Negro ladies were always flanking him in Vegas as if to set up a female field of repulsion against any evil black magnetic forces in the offing. And from the sanctuary of his ability to move around crap tables like a kitten on the frisk, he taunted black majestic king-size Liston before the fight and after the fight. "You're so ugly," he would jeer, crap table safely between them, "that I don't know how you can get any uglier."

"Why don't you sit on my knee and I'll feed you your orange juice," Liston would rumble back.

"Don't insult me, or you'll be sorry. 'Cause you're just an ugly slow bear."

They would pretend to rush at one another. Smaller men would hold them back without effort. They were building the gate for the next fight. And Liston was secretly fond of Clay. He would chuckle when he talked about him. It was years since Liston had failed to knock out his opponent in the first round. His charisma was majestic with menace. One held one's breath when near him. He looked forward with obvious amusement to the happy seconds when he would take Clay apart and see the expression on that silly face. In Miami he trained for a three-round fight. In the famous fifth round when Clay came out with caustic in his eyes and could not see, he waved his gloves at Liston, a look of abject horror on his face, as if to say, "Your younger brother is now an old blind beggar. Do not strike him." And did it with a peculiar authority. For Clay looked like a ghost with his eyes closed, tears streaming, his extended gloves waving in front of him like a widow's entreaties. Liston drew back in doubt, in bewilderment, conceivably in concern for his new great reputation as an ex-bully; yes, Liston reacted like a gentleman, and Clay was home free. His eyes watered out the caustic, his sight came back. He cut Liston up in the sixth. He left him beaten and exhausted. Liston did not stand up for the bell to the seventh. Maybe Clay had even defeated him earlier that day at the weigh-in when he had harangued and screamed and shouted and whistled and stuck his tongue out at Liston. The Champ had been bewildered. No one had been able ever to stare him in the eyes these last four years. Now a boy was screaming at him, a boy reported to belong to Black Muslims, no, stronger than that, a boy favored by Malcolm X who was braver by reputation than the brave, for he could stop a bullet any day. Liston, afraid only, as he put it, of crazy men, was afraid of the Muslims for he could not contend with their allegiance to one another in prison, their puritanism, their discipline, their martial ranks. The combination was too complex, too unfamiliar. Now, their boy, in a pain of terror or in a mania of courage, was screaming at him at the weigh-in. Liston sat down and shook his head, and looked at the press, the press now become his friend, and wound his fingers in circles around his ear, as if saying, Whitey to Whitey, "That Black boy is nuts." So Clay made Liston Tom it, and when Liston missed the first jab he threw in the fight by a foot and a half, one knew the night would not be ordinary in the offing.

For their return bout in Boston, Liston trained as he had never before. Clay got a hernia. Liston trained again. Hard training as a fighter grows older seems to speak of the dull deaths of the brightest cells in all the favorite organs; old fighters react to training like beautiful women to washing floors. But Liston did it twice, once for Clay's hernia, and again for their actual fight in Maine, and the second time he trained, he aged as a fighter, for he had a sparring partner, Amos Lincoln, who was one of the better heavyweights in the country. They had wars with one another every afternoon in the gym. By the day before the fight, Liston was as relaxed and sleepy and dopey as a man in a steam bath. He had fought his heart out in training, had done it under constant pressure from Clay who kept telling the world that Liston was old and slow and could not possibly win. And their fight created a scandal, for Liston ran into a short punch in the first round and was counted out, unable to hear the count. The referee and timekeeper missed signals with one another while Clay stood over fallen Liston screaming, "Get up and fight!" It was no night for the fight game, and a tragedy for Clay since he had trained for a long and arduous fight. He had developed his technique for a major encounter with Liston and was left with a horde of unanswered questions including the one he could never admit — which was whether there had been the magic of a real knockout in his punch or if Liston had made — for what variety of reasons! — a conscious decision to stay on the floor. It did him no good.

He had taken all the lessons of his curious life and the outrageously deep comprehension he had of the motivations of his own people — indeed, one could even approach the beginnings of a Psychology of the Blacks by studying his encounters with fighters who were Black — and had elaborated that into a technique for boxing

[*14*]

which was almost without compare. A most cultivated technique. For he was no child of the slums. His mother was a gracious pale-skinned lady, his father a bitter wit pride-oriented on the family name of Clay — they were descendants of Henry Clay, the orator, on the white side of the family, nothing less, and Cassius began boxing at twelve in a police gym, and from the beginning was a phenomenon of style and the absence of pain, for he knew how to use his physical endowment. Tall, relatively light, with an exceptionally long reach even for his size, he developed defensive skills which made the best use of his body. Working apparently on the premise that there was something obscene about being hit, he boxed with his head back and drew it further back when attacked like a kid who is shy of punches in a street fight, but because he had a waist which was more supple than the average fighter's neck, he was able to box with his arms low, surveying the fighter in front of him, avoiding punches by the speed of his feet, the reflexes of his waist, the long spoiling deployment of his arms which were always tipping other fighters off-balance. Added to this was his psychological comprehension of the vanity and confusion of other fighters. A man in the ring is a performer as well as a gladiator. Elaborating his technique from the age of twelve, Clay knew how to work on the vanity of other performers, knew how to make them feel ridiculous and so force them into crucial mistakes, knew how to set such a tone from the first round — later he was to know how to begin it a year before he would even meet the man. Clay knew that a fighter who had been put in psychological knots before he got near the ring had already lost half, three-quarters, no, all of the fight could be lost before the first punch. That was the psychology of the body.

Now, add his curious ability as a puncher. He knew that the heaviest punches, systematically delivered, meant little. There are club fighters who look like armadillos and alligators — you can bounce punches off them forever and they never go down. You can break them down only if they are in a profound state of confusion, and the bombardment of another fighter's fists is never their confusion but their expectation. So Clay punched with a greater variety of mixed intensities than anyone around, he played with punches, was tender with them, laid them on as delicately as you put a postage stamp on an envelope, then cracked them in like a riding crop across your face, stuck a cruel jab like a baseball bat held head on into your mouth, next waltzed you in a clinch with a tender arm around your neck, winged away out of reach on flying legs, dug a hook with the full swing of a baseball bat hard into your ribs, hard pokes of a jab into the face, a mocking soft flurry of pillows and gloves, a mean forearm cutting you off from coming up on him, a cruel wrestling of your neck in a clinch, then elusive again, gloves snake-licking your face like a whip. By the time Clay defeated Liston once and was training for the second fight, by the time Clay, now champion and renamed Muhammad Ali, and bigger, grown up quickly and not so mysteriously (after the potent ego-soups and marrows of his trip through Muslim Africa) into a Black Prince, Potentate of his people, new Poombah of Polemic, yes, by this time, Clay — we will find it more natural to call him Ali from here on out (for the Prince will behave much like a young god) — yes, Muhammad Ali, Heavyweight Champion of the World, having come back with an amazing commitment to be leader of his people, proceeded to go into training for the second Liston fight with a commitment and then a genius of comprehension for the true intricacies of the Science of Sock. He alternated the best of sparring partners and the most ordinary, worked rounds of dazzling speed with Jimmy Ellis — later, of course, to be champion himself before Frazier knocked him out — rounds which displayed the high aesthetic of boxing at its best, then lay against the ropes with other sparring partners, hands at his sides as if it were the eleventh or thirteenth round of an excruciating and exhausting fight with Liston where Ali was now so tired he could not hold his hands up, could just manage to take punches to the stomach, rolling with them, smothering them with his stomach, absorbing them with backward moves, sliding along the ropes, steering his sparring partner with passive but off-setting moves of his limp arms. For a minute, for two minutes, the sparring partner — Shotgun Sheldon was his name — would bomb away on Ali's stomach much as if Liston were tearing him apart in later rounds, and Ali weaving languidly, sliding his neck for the occasional overhead punch to his face, bouncing from the rope into the punches, bouncing back away from punches, as if his torso had become one huge boxing glove to absorb punishment, had penetrated through into some further conception of pain, as if pain were not pain if you accepted it with a relaxed heart, yes, Ali let himself be bombarded on the ropes by the powerful bull-like swings of Shotgun Sheldon, the expression on his face as remote and as searching for the last routes into the nerves of each punch going in as a man hanging on a subway strap will search into the meaning of the market quotations he has just read on the activities of a curious stock. So Ali relaxed on the ropes and took punches to the belly with a faint disdain, as if, curious punches, they did not go deep enough and after a minute of this, or two minutes, having offered his body like the hide of a drum for a mad drummer's solo, he would snap out of his communion with himself and flash a tattoo of light and slashing punches, mocking as the lights on water, he would dazzle his sparring partner, who, arm-weary and punched out, would look at him with eyes of love, complete was his admiration. And if people were ever going to cry watching a boxer in training, those were the moments, for Ali had the far-off concentration and disdain of an artist who simply cannot find anyone near enough or good enough to keep him and his art engaged, and all the while was perfecting the essence of his art which was to make the other fighter fall secretly, helplessly, in love with him. Bundini, a special trainer, an alter ego with the same harsh, demoniac, witty, nonstop powers of oration as Ali himself — he even looked a little like Ali — used to weep openly as he watched the workouts.

Training session over, Ali would lecture the press, instruct them — looking beyond his Liston defense to what he would do to Patterson, mocking Patterson, calling him a rabbit, a white man's rabbit, knowing he was putting a new beam on Patterson's shoulders, an outrageously helpless and heavy beam of rage, fear, hopeless anger and secret Black admiration for the all-out force of Ali's effrontery. And in the next instant Ali would be charming as a movie star on the make speaking tenderly to a child. If he were Narcissus, so he was as well the play of mood in the water which served as mirror to Narcissus. It was as if he knew he had disposed of Patterson already, that the precise attack of calling him a rabbit would work on the weakest link — wherever it was — in Patterson's tense and tortured psyche and Patterson would crack, as indeed, unendurably for himself, he did, when their fight took place. Patterson's back gave way in the early rounds, and he fought twisted and in pain, half crippled like a man with a sacroiliac for eleven brave and most miserable rounds before the referee would call it and Ali, breaking up with his first wife then, was unpleasant in the ring that night, his face ugly and contemptuous, himself well on the way to becoming America's most unpopular major American. That, too, was part of the art — to get a public to the point of hating him so much the burden on the other fighter approached the metaphysical — which is where Ali wanted it. White fighters with faces like rock embedded in cement would trade punch for punch, Ali liked to get the boxing where it belonged — he would trade meta-physic for metaphysic with anyone.

So he went on winning his fights and growing forever more unpopular. How he inflamed the temper of boxing's White Establishment, for they were for most part a gaggle of avuncular drunks and hard-bitten hacks who were ready to fight over every slime-slicked penny, and squared a few of their slippery crimes by getting fighters to show up semblance-of-sober at any available parish men's rally and charity church breakfast — "Everything I am I owe to boxing," the fighter would mumble through his dentures while elements of gin, garlic, and goddess-of-a-girlie from the night before came off in the bright morning fumes.

Ali had them psyched. He cut through moribund coruscated dirty business corridors, cut through cigar smoke and bushwah, hypocrisy and well-aimed kicks to the back of the neck, cut through crooked politicians and patriotic pus, cut like a laser, point of the point, light and impersonal, cut to the heart of the rottenest meat in boxing, and boxing was always the buried South Vietnam of America, buried for fifty years in our hide before we went there, yes, Ali cut through the flag-dragooned salutes of drunken dawns and said, "I got no fight with those Vietcongs," and they cut him down, thrust him into the three and a half years of his martyrdom. Where he grew. Grew to have a little fat around his middle and a little of the complacent muscle of the clam to his world-ego. And grew sharper in the mind as well, and deepened and broadened physically. Looked no longer like a boy, but a sullen man, almost heavy, with the beginnings of a huge expanse across his shoulders. And developed the patience to survive, the wisdom to contemplate future nights in jail, grew to cultivate the suspension of belief and the avoidance of disbelief — what a rack for a young man! As the years of hope for reinstatement, or avoidance of prison, came up and waned in him, Ali walked the tightrope between bitterness and apathy, and had enough left to beat Quarry and beat Bonavena, beat Quarry in the flurry of a missed hundred punches, ho! how his timing was off! beat him with a calculated whip, snake-lick whip, to the corrugated sponge of dead flesh over Quarry's Irish eyes — they stopped it after the third on cuts — then knocked out Bonavena, the indestructible, never stopped before, by working the art of crazy mixing in the punches he threw at the rugged — some of the punches Ali threw that night would not have hurt a little boy — the punch he let go in the fifteenth came in like a wrecking ball from outer space. Bonavena went sprawling across the ring. He was a house coming down.

Yet it may have been the blow which would defeat him later. For Ali had been tired with Bonavena, lackluster, winded, sluggish, far ahead on points but in need of the most serious work if he were to beat Frazier. The punch in the last round was obliged, therefore, to inflame his belief that the forces of magic were his, there to be called upon when most in need, that the silent leagues of Black support for his cause — since their cause was as his own — were like some cloak of midnight velvet, there to protect him by Black blood, by Black sense of tragedy, by the Black consciousness that the guilt of the world had become the hinge of a door that they would open. So they would open the way to Frazier's chin, the Blacks would open the aisle for his trip to the gods.

Therefore he did not train for Frazier as perhaps he had to. He worked, he ran three miles a day when he could have run five, he boxed some days and let a day and perhaps another day go, he was relaxed, he was confident, he basked in the undemanding winter sun of Miami, and skipped his rope in a gym crowded with fighters, stuffed now with working fighters looking to be seen, Ali comfortable and relaxed like the greatest of movie stars, he played a young fighter working out in a corner on the heavy bag — for of course every eye was on him — and afterward doing sit-ups in the back room and having his stomach rubbed with liniment, he would talk to reporters. He was filled with confidence there was no Black fighter he did not comprehend to the root of the valve in the hard-pumping heart, and yes, Frazier, he assured everybody, would be easier than they realized. Like a little boy who had grown up to take on a mountain of responsibility, he spoke in the deep relaxation of the wise, and teased two of the reporters who were present and fat. "You want to drink a lot of water," he said, "good cold water instead of all that liquor rot-your-gut," and gave the smile of a man who had been able to intoxicate himself on water (although he was, by repute, a fiend for soft sweet drinks), "and fruit and good clean vegetables you want to eat and chicken and steak. You lose weight then," he advised out of kind secret smiling thoughts, and went on to talk of the impact of the fight upon the world. "Yes," he said, "you just think of a stadium with a million people, ten million people, you could get them all in to watch, they would all pay to see it live, but then you think of the hundreds of millions and the billions who are going to see this fight, and if you could sit them all down in one place, and fly a jet plane over them, why that plane would have to fly for an hour before it would reach the end of all the people who will see this fight. It's the greatest event in the history of the world, and you take a man like Frazier, a good fighter, but a simple hardworking fellow, he's not built for this kind of pressure, the eyes," Ali said softly, "of that many people upon him. There's an experience to pressure which I have had, fighting a man like Liston in Miami the first time, which he has not. He will cave in under the pressure. No, I do not see any way a man like Frazier can whup me, he can't reach me, my arms are too long, and if he does get in and knock me down I'll never make the mistake of Quarry and Foster or Ellis of rushing back at him, I'll stay away until my head clears, then I begin to pop him again, pop! pop!" — a few jabs — "no there is no way this man can beat me, this fight will be easier than you think."

There was one way in which boxing was still like a street fight and that was in the need to be confident you would win. A man walking out of a bar to fight with another man is seeking to compose his head into the confidence that he will certainly triumph — it is the most mysterious faculty of the ego. For that confidence is a sedative against the pain of punches and yet is the sanction to punch your own best. The logic of the spirit would suggest that you win only if you deserve to win: the logic of the ego lays down the axiom that if you don't think you will win, you don't deserve to. And, in fact, usually don't; it is as if not believing you will win opens you to the guilt that perhaps you have not the right, you are too guilty.

So training camps are small factories for the production of one rare psychological item — an ego able to bear huge pain and administer drastic punishment. The flow of Ali's ego poured over the rock of every distraction, it was an ego like the flow of a river of constant energy fed by a hundred tributaries of Black love and the love of the white left. The construction of the ego of Joe Frazier was of another variety. His manager, Yancey "Yank" Durham, a canny foxy light-skinned Negro with a dignified mien, a gray head of hair, gray moustache and a small but conservative worthy's paunch, plus the quick-witted look of eyes which could spot from a half-mile away any man coming toward him with a criminal thought, was indeed the face of a consummate jeweler who had worked for years upon a diamond in the rough until he was now and at last a diamond, hard as the transmutation of black carbon from the black earth into the brilliant sky-blue shadow of the rarest shining rock.

What a fighter was Frazier, what a diamond of an ego had he, and what a manager was Durham. Let us look.

Sooner or later, fight metaphors, like fight managers, go sentimental. They go military. But there is no choice here. Frazier was the human equivalent of a war machine. He had tremendous firepower. He had a great left hook, a left hook frightening even to watch when it missed, for it seemed to whistle; he had a powerful right. He could knock a man out with either hand — not all fighters can, not even very good fighters. Usually, however, he clubbed opponents to death, took a punch, gave a punch, took three punches, gave two, took a punch, gave a punch, high speed all the way, always working, pushing his body and arms, short for a heavyweight, up through the middle, bombing through on force, reminiscent of Jimmy Brown knocking down tacklers, Frazier kept on coming, hard and fast, a hang-in, hang-on, go-and-get-him, got-him, got-him, slip and punch, take a punch, wing a punch, whap a punch, never was Frazier happier than with his heart up on the line against some other man's heart, let the bullets fly — his heart was there to stand up at the last. Sooner or later, the others almost all fell down. Undefeated like Ali, winner of twenty-three out of twenty-six fights by knockout, he was a human force, certainly the greatest heavyweight force to come along since Rocky Marciano. (If those two men had ever met, it would have been like two Mack trucks hitting each other head on, then backing up to hit each other again — they would have kept it up until the wheels were off the axles and the engines off the chassis.) But this would be a different kind of fight. Ali would run, Ali would keep hitting Frazier with long jabs, quick hooks and rights while backing up, backing up, staying out of reach unless Frazier could take the punishment and get in. That was where the military problem began.

For getting in against the punishment he would take was a question of morale, and there was a unique situation in this fight — Frazier had become the white man's fighter, Mr. Charley was rooting for Frazier, and that meant Blacks were boycotting him in their heart. That could be poison to Frazier's morale, for he was twice as black as Clay and half as handsome, he had the rugged decent life-worked face of a man who had labored in the pits all his life, he looked like the deserving modest son of one of those Negro cleaning women of a bygone age who worked from six in the morning to midnight every day, raised a family, endured and occasionally elicited the exasperated admiration of white ladies who would kindly remark, "That woman deserves something better in her life." Frazier had the mien of the son, one of many, of such a woman, and he was the hardest-working fighter in training many a man had ever seen, he was conceivably the hardest-working man alive in the world, and as he went through his regimen, first boxing four rounds with a sparring partner, Kenny Norton, a talented heavyweight from the coast with an almost unbeaten record, then working on the heavy bag, then the light bag, then skipping rope, ten to twelve rounds of sparring and exercise on a light day, Frazier went on with the doggedness, the concentration, and the pumped-up fury of a man who has had so little in his life that he can endure torments to get everything, he pushed the total of his energy and force into an absolute abstract exercise of will so it did not matter if he fought a sparring partner or the heavy bag, he lunged at each equally as if the exhaustions of his own heart and the clangor of his lungs were his only enemies, and the head of a fighter or the leather of the bag as it rolled against his own head was nothing but some abstract thunk of material, not a thing, not a man, but thunk! thunk! something of an obstacle, thunk! thunk! thunk! to beat into thunk! oblivion. And his breath came in rips and sobs as he smashed into the bag as if it were real, just that heavy big torso-sized bag hanging from its chain — but he attacked it as if it were a bear, as if it were a great fighter and they were in the mortal embrace of a killing set of exchanges of punches in the middle of the eighth round, and rounds of exercise later, skipping rope to an inhumanly fast beat for this late round in the training day, sweat pouring like jets of blood from an artery, he kept swinging his rope, muttering, "Two-million-dollars-and-change, two-million-dollars-and-change," railroad train chugging into the terminals of exhaustion. And it was obvious that Durham, jeweler to his diamond, was working to make the fight as abstract as he could for Frazier, to keep Clay out of it — for they would not call him Ali in their camp — yes, Frazier was fortifying his ego by depersonalizing his opponent, Clay was, thunk! the heavy bag, thunk! and thunk! — Frazier was looking to get no messages from that cavern of velvet when Black people sent their good wishes to Ali at midnight, no, Frazier would insulate himself with prodigies of work, hardest-working man in the hell-hole of the world, and on and on he drove himself into the depressions each day of killing daily exhaustion.

That was one half of the strategy to isolate Frazier from Ali, hard work and thinking of thunking on inanimate Clay; the other half was up to Durham who was running front relations with the Blacks of North Philly who wandered into the gym, paid their dollar, and were ready to heckle on Frazier. In the four rounds he boxed with Norton, Frazier did not look too good for a while. It was ten days before the fight and he was in a bad mood when he came in, for the word was through the gym that they had discovered one of his favorite sparring partners, just fired that morning, was a Black Muslim and had been calling Ali every night with reports, that was the rumor, and Frazier, sullen and cold at the start, was bopped and tapped, then walloped by Norton moving fast with the big training gloves in imitation of Ali, and Frazier looked very easy to hit until the middle of the third round when Norton, proud of his something like twenty wins and one loss, beginning to get some ideas himself about how to fight champions, came driving in to mix it with Frazier, have it out man to man and caught a right which dropped him, left him looking limp with that half-silly smile sparring partners get when they have been hit too hard to justify any experience or any money they are going to take away. Up till then the crowd had been with Norton. Restricted to one end of the Cloverlay gym, a street-level storefront room which could have been used originally by an automobile dealer, there on that empty, immaculate Lysol-soaked floor, designed when Frazier was there for only Frazier and his partners (as opposed to Miami where Ali would rub elbows with the people) the people, since they were here kept to the end off the street, jeered whenever Norton hit Frazier, they laughed when Norton made him look silly, they called out, "Drop the mother," until Durham held up a gentlemanly but admonishing finger in request for silence. Afterward, however, training completed, Durham approached them to answer questions, rolled with their sallies, jived the people back, subtly enlisted their sympathy for Frazier by saying, "When I fight Clay, I'm going to get him somewhere in the middle rounds," until the Blacks quipping back said angrily, "You ain't fighting him, Frazier is."

"Why you call him Clay?" another asked. "He Ali."

"His name is Cassius Clay to me," said Durham.

"What you say against his religion?"

"I don't say nothing about his religion and he doesn't say anything about mine. I'm a Baptist."

"You going to make money on this?"

"Of course," said Durham, "I got to make money. You don't think I work up this sweat for nothing."

They loved him. He was happy with them. A short fat

man in a purple suit wearing his revival of the wide-brim bebop hat said to Durham, "Why don't you get Norton to manage?" He was beating up on your fighter," and the fat man cackled for he had scored and could elaborate the tale for his ladies later how he had put down Yank who was working the daily rite on the edge of the Black street for his fighter, while upstairs, dressed, and sucking an orange, sweat still pouring, gloom of excessive fatigue upon him, Frazier was sitting through his two-hundredth or two-thousandth interview for this fight, reluctant indeed to give it at all. "Some get it, some don't," he had said for refusal, but relented when a white friend who had done roadwork with him interceded, so he sat there now against a leather sofa, dark blue suit, dark T-shirt, mopping his brow with a pink-red towel, and spoke dispiritedly of being ready too early for the fight. He was waking up an hour too early for roadwork each morning now. "I'd go back to sleep but it doesn't feel good when I do run."

"I guess the air is better that hour of the morning."

He nodded sadly. "There's a limit to how good the air in Philly can get."

"Where'd you begin to sing?" was a question asked.

"I sang in church first," he replied, but it was not the day to talk about singing. The loneliness of hitting the bag still seemed upon him as if in his exhaustion now, and in the thoughts of that small insomnia which woke him an hour too early every day was something of the loneliness of all Blacks who work very hard and are isolated from fun and must wonder in the just-awakened night how large and pervasive was the curse of a people. "The countdown's begun," said Frazier, "I get impatient about now."

For the fight, Ali was wearing red velvet trunks, Frazier had green. Before they began, even before they were called together by the referee for instructions, Ali went dancing around the ring and glided past Frazier with a sweet little-boy smile, as if to say, "You're my new playmate. We're going to have fun." Ali was laughing. Frazier was having nothing of this and turned his neck to embargo him away. Ali, having alerted the crowd by this big first move, came prancing in again. When Frazier looked ready to block him, Ali went around, evading a contact, gave another sweet smile, shook his head at the lack of high spirit. "Poor Frazier," he seemed to say.

At the weigh-in early that afternoon Ali looked physically resplendent; the night before in Harlem, crowds had cheered him; he was coming to claim his victory on the confluence of two mighty tides — he was the mightiest victim of injustice in America and he was also — the twentieth century was nothing if not a tangle of opposition — he was also the mightiest narcissist in the land. Every beard, dropout, homosexual, junkie, freak, swinger, and plain simple individualist adored him. Every pedantic liberal soul who had once loved Patterson now paid homage to Ali. The mightiest of the Black psyches and the most filigreed of the white psyches were ready to roar him home, as well as every family-loving hardworking square American who genuinely hated the war in Vietnam. What a tangle of ribbons he carried on his lance, enough cross-purposes to be the knight-resplendent of television, the fell hero of the medium, and he had a look of unique happiness on television when presenting his program for the course of the fight, and his inevitable victory. He would be as content then as an infant splashing the waters of the bathinette. If he was at once a saint and a monster to any mind which looked for category, any mind unwilling to encounter the thoroughly dread-filled fact that the twentieth-century breed of man now in birth might be no longer half good and half evil — generous and greedy by turns — but a mutation with Cassius Muhammad for the first son — then that mind was not ready to think about Twentieth-Century Man. (And indeed Muhammad Ali had twin poodles he called Angel and Demon.) So now the ambiguity of his presence filled the Garden before the fight was fairly begun, it was as if he had announced to that plural billion-footed crowd assembled under the shadow of the jet which would fly over them that the first enigma of the fight would be the way he would win it, that he would initiate his triumph by getting the crowd to laugh at Frazier, yes, first premise tonight was that the poor Black man in Frazier's soul would go berserk if made a figure of roll-off-your-seat amusement.

The referee gave his instructions. The bell rang. The first fifteen seconds of a fight can be the fight. It is equivalent to the first kiss in a love affair. The fighters each missed the other. Ali blocked Frazier's first punches easily, but Ali then missed Frazier's head. That head was bobbing as fast as a third fist. Frazier would come rushing in, head moving like a fist, fists bobbing too, his head working above and below his forearm, he was trying to get through Ali's jab, get through fast and sear Ali early with the terror of a long fight and punches harder than he had ever taken to the stomach, and Ali in turn, backing up, and throwing fast punches, aimed just a trifle, and was therefore a trifle too slow, but it was obvious Ali was trying to shiver Frazier's synapses from the start, set waves of depression stirring which would reach his heart in later rounds and make him slow, deaden nerve, deaden nerve went Ali's jab flicking a snake tongue, whoo-eet! whoo-eet! but Frazier's head was bobbing too fast, he was moving faster than he had ever moved before in that bobbing nonstop never-a-backward step of his, slogging and bouncing forward, that huge left hook flaunting the air with the confidence it was enough of a club to split a tree, and Ali, having missed his jabs, stepped nimbly inside the hook and wrestled Frazier in the clinch. Ali looked stronger here. So by the first forty-five seconds of the fight, they had each surprised the other profoundly. Frazier was fast enough to slip through Ali's punches, and Ali was strong enough to handle him in the clinches. A pattern had begun. Because Ali was missing often, Frazier was in under his shots like a police dog's muzzle on your arm, Ali could not slide from side to side, he was boxed in, then obliged to go backward, and would end on the ropes again and again with Frazier belaboring him. Yet Frazier could not reach him. Like a prestidigitator Ali would tie the other's punches into odd knots, not even blocking them yet on his elbows or his arms, rather throwing his own punches as defensive moves, for even as they missed, he would brush Frazier to the side with his forearm, or hold him off, or clinch and wrestle a little of the will out of Frazier's neck. Once or twice in the round a long left hook by Frazier just touched the surface of Ali's chin, and Ali waved his head in placid contempt to the billions watching as if to say, "This man has not been able to hurt me at all."

The first round set a pattern for the fight. Ali won it and would win the next. His jab was landing from time to time and rights and lefts of no great consequence. Frazier was hardly reaching him at all. Yet it looked like Frazier had established that he was fast enough to get in on Ali and so drive him to the ropes and to the corners, and that spoke of a fight which would be determined by the man in better condition, in better physical condition rather than in better psychic condition, the kind of fight Ali could hardly want for his strength was in his pauses, his nature passed along the curve of every dialectic, he liked, in short, to fight in flurries, and then move out, move away, assess, take his time, fight again. Frazier would not let him. Frazier moved in with the snarl of a wolf, his teeth seemed to show through his mouthpiece, he made Ali work. Ali won the first two rounds but it was obvious he could not continue to win if he had to work all the way. And in the third round Frazier began to get to him, caught Ali with a powerful blow to the face at the bell. That was the first moment where it was clear to all that Frazier had won a round. Then he won the next. Ali looked tired and a little depressed. He was moving less and less and calling upon a skill not seen since the fight with Chuvalo when he had showed his old ability, worked on all those years ago with Shotgun Sheldon, to lie on the ropes and take a beating to the stomach. He had exhausted Chuvalo by welcoming attacks on the stomach but Frazier was too incommensurable a force to allow such total attack. So Ali lay on the ropes and wrestled him off, and moved his arms and waist, blocking punches, slipping punches, countering with punches — it began to look as if the fight would be written on the ropes, but Ali was getting very tired. At the beginning of the fifth round, he got up slowly from his stool, very slowly. Frazier was beginning to feel that the fight was his. He moved in on Ali jeering, his hands at his side in mimicry of Ali, a street fighter mocking his opponent, and Ali tapped him with long light jabs to which Frazier stuck out his mouthpiece, a jeer of derision as if to suggest that the mouthpiece was all Ali would reach all night.

There is an extortion of the will beyond any of our measure in the exhaustion which comes upon a fighter in early rounds when he is already too tired to lift his arms or take advantage of openings there before him, yet the fight is not a third over, there are all those rounds to go, contractions of torture, the lungs screaming into the dungeons of the soul, washing the throat with a hot bile that once belonged to the liver, the legs are going dead, the arms move but their motion is limp, one is straining into another will, breathing into the breath of another will as agonized as one's own. As the fight moved through the fifth, the sixth and the seventh, then into the eighth, it was obvious that Ali was into the longest night of his career, and yet with that skill, that research into the pits of every miserable contingency in boxing, he came up with odd somnambulistic variations, holding Frazier off, riding around Frazier with his arm about his neck, almost entreating Frazier with his arms extended, and Frazier leaning on him, each of them slowed to a pit-a-pat of light punches back and forth until one of them was goaded up from exhaustion to whip and stick, then hook and hammer and into the belly and out, and out of the clinch and both looking exhausted, and then Frazier, mouth bared again like a wolf, going in and Ali waltzing him, tying him, tapping him lightly as if he were a speed bag, just little flicks, until Frazier, like an exhausted horse finally feeling the crop, would push up into a trot and try to run up the hill. It was indeed as if they were both running up a hill. As if Frazier's offensive was so great and so great was Ali's defense that the fight could only be decided by who could take the steepest pitch of the hill. So Frazier, driving, driving, trying to drive the heart out of Ali, put the pitch of that hill up and up until they were ascending an unendurable slope. And moved like somnambulists slowly working and rubbing one another, almost embracing, next to locked in the slow moves of lovers after the act until, reaching into the stores of energy reaching them from cells never before so used, one man or the other would work up a contractive spasm of skills and throw punches at the other in the straining slow-motion hypnosis of a deepening act. And so the first eight rounds went by. The two judges scored six for Frazier, two for Ali. The referee had it even. Some of the press had Ali ahead — it was not easy to score. For if it were an alley fight, Frazier would win. Clay was by now hardly more than the heavy bag to Frazier. Frazier was dealing with a man, not a demon. He was not respectful of that man. But still! It was Ali who was landing the majority of punches. They were light, they were usually weary, but some had snap, some were quick, he was landing two punches to Frazier's one. Yet Frazier's were hardest. And Ali often looked as tender as if he were making love. It was as if he could now feel the whole absence of that real second fight with Liston, that fight for which he had trained so long and so hard, the fight which might have rolled over his laurels from the greatest artist of pugilism to the greatest brawler of them all — maybe he had been prepared on that night to beat Liston at his own, be more of a slugger, more of a man crude to crude than Liston. Yes, Ali had never been a street fighter and never a whorehouse knock-it-down stud, no, it was more as if a man with the exquisite reflexes of Nureyev had learned to throw a knockout punch with either hand and so had become champion of the world without knowing if he were the man of all men or the most delicate of the delicate with special privilege endowed by God. Now with Frazier, he was in a sweat bath (a mud pile, a knee, elbow, and death-thumping chute of a pit) having in this late year the fight he had sorely needed for his true greatness as a fighter six and seven years ago, and so whether ahead, behind or even, terror sat in the rooting instinct of all those who were for Ali for it was obviously Frazier's fight to win, and what if Ali, weaknesses of character now flickering to the surface in a hundred little moves, should enter the vale of prizefighting's deepest humiliation, should fall out half-conscious on the floor and not want to get up. What a death to his followers.

The ninth began. Frazier mounted his largest body attack of the night. It was preparations-for-Liston-with-Shotgun-Sheldon, it was the virtuosity of the gym all over again, and Ali, like a catcher handling a fast-ball pitcher, took Frazier's punches, one steamer, another steamer, wing! went a screamer, a steamer, warded them, blocked them, slithered them, winced from them, absorbed them, took them in and blew them out and came off the ropes and was Ali the Magnificent for the next minute and thirty seconds. The fight turned. The troops of Ali's second corps of energy had arrived, the energy for which he had been waiting long agonizing heartsore vomit-mean rounds. Now he jabbed Frazier, he snake-licked his face with jabs faster than he had thrown before, he anticipated each attempt of Frazier at counterattack and threw it back, he danced on his toes for the first time in rounds, he popped in rights, he hurt him with hooks, it was his biggest round of the night, it was the best round yet of the fight, and Frazier was beginning to move into that odd petulant concentration on other rituals besides the punches, tappings of the gloves, stares of the eye, that species of mouthpiece-chewing which is the prelude to fun-strut in the knees, then Queer Street, then waggle on out, drop like a steer.

It looked like Ali had turned the fight, looked more like the same in the tenth, now reporters were writing another story in their mind where Ali was not the magical untried Prince who had come apart under the first real pressure of his life but was rather the greatest heavy-weight champion of all time for he had weathered the purgatory of Joe Frazier.

But in the eleventh, that story also broke. Frazier caught him, caught him again and again, and Ali was near to knocked out and swayed and slid on Queer Street himself, then spent the rest of the eleventh and the longest round of the twelfth working another bottom of Hell, holding off Frazier who came on and on, sobbing, wild, a wild hermit of a beast, man of will reduced to the common denominator of the will of all of us back in that land of the animal where the idea of man as a tool-wielding beast was first conceived. Frazier looked to get Ali forever in the eleventh and the twelfth, and Ali, his legs slapped and slashed on the thighs between each round by Angelo Dundee, came out for the thirteenth and incredibly was dancing. Everybody's story switched again. For if Ali won this round, the fourteenth and the fifteenth, who could know if he could not win the fight? . . . He won the first half of the thirteenth, then spent the second half on the ropes with Frazier. They were now like crazy death-march-maddened mateys coming up the hill and on to home, and yet Ali won the fourteenth, Ali looked good, he came out dancing for the fifteenth, while Frazier, his own armies of energy finally caught up, his courage ready to spit into the eye of any devil black or white who would steal the work of his life, had equal madness to steal the bolt from Ali. So Frazier reached out to snatch the magic punch from the air, the punch with which Ali topped Bonavena, and found it and hit Ali a hell and a heaven of a shot which dumped Muhammad into fifty thousand newspaper photographs — Ali on the floor! Great Ali on the floor was out there flat singing to the sirens in the mistiest fogs of Queer Street (same look of death and widowhood on his far-gone face as one had seen in the fifth blind round with Liston) yet Ali got up, Ali came sliding through the last two minutes and thirty-five seconds of this heathen holocaust in some last exercise of the will, some iron fundament of the ego not to be knocked out, and it was then as if the spirit of Harlem finally spoke and came to rescue and the ghosts of the dead in Vietnam, something held him up before arm-weary triumphant near-crazy Frazier who had just hit him the hardest punch ever thrown in his life and they went down to the last few seconds of a great fight, Ali still standing and Frazier had won.

The world was talking instantly of a rematch. For Ali had shown America what we all had hoped was secretly true. He was a man. He could bear moral and physical torture and he could stand. And if he could beat Frazier in the rematch we would have at last a national hero who was hero of the world as well, and who could bear to wait for the next fight? Joe Frazier, still the champion, and a great champion, said to the press, "Fellows, have a heart — I got to live a little. I've been working for ten long years." And Ali, through the agency of alter-ego Bundini, said — for Ali was now in the hospital to check on the possible fracture of a jaw — Ali was reported to have said, "Get the gun ready — we're going to set traps." Oh, wow. Could America wait for something so great as the Second Ali-Frazier?

Bullfighting

Homage to El Loco

The mind returns to the comedy and the religious dedication of the bullfight. Late afternoons of color — hues
of lavender, silver, pink, orange silk and gold in the *traje
de luces* — now begin to play in one's mind against the
small sharp impact on the eyes of horseballs falling like
eggs between the frightened legs of the horse, and the
flanks of the bull glistening with the sheen of a dark wet
wood. And the blood. The bullfight always gets back to
the blood. It pours in gouts down the forequarters of the
bull, it wells from the hump of his *morrillo,* and moves
in waves of bright red along the muscles of his chest and
the heaving of his sides. If he has been killed poorly and

the sword goes through his lung, then the animal dies in vomitings of blood. If the matador is working close to the animal, the suit of lights becomes stained — the dark bloodstain is honorable, it is also steeped in horror. Should the taste of your favorite herb come from the death of some rare love, so the life of the bright red blood of an animal river pouring forth becomes some other life as it darkens down to the melancholy hues of an old dried blood which speaks in some lost primitive tongue about the mysteries of death, color, and corruption. The dried blood reminds you of the sordid glory of the bull-fight, its hint of the Renaissance when noble figures stated their presence as they paraded through the marketplace and passed by cripples with stumps for legs, a stump for a tongue, and the lewdest grin of the day. Yes, the spectrum of the bullfight goes from courage to gangrene.

In Mexico, the hour before the fight is always the best hour of the week. It would be memorable not to sound like Hemingway, but in fact you would get happy the night before just thinking of that hour next day. Outside the Plaza Mexico, cheap cafés open only on Sunday, and huge as beer gardens, filled with the public (us tourists, hoodlums, pimps, pickpurses and molls, Mexican variety — which is to say the whores had headdresses and hindquarters not to be seen elsewhere on earth, for their hair rose vertically twelve inches from the head, and their posteriors projected horizontally twelve inches back into that space the rest of the whore had just marched through). The mariachis were out with their romantic haunting caterwauling of guitar, violin, songs of carnival and trumpet, their song told of hearts which were true and hearts which were broken, and the wail of the broken heart went right into the trumpet until there were times when drunk the right way on tequila or Mexican rum, it was perhaps the best sound heard this side of

Miles Davis. You hear a hint of all that in the Tijuana Brass.

You see, my friends, the wild hour was approaching. The horrors of the week in Mexico were coming to term. Indeed, no week in Mexico is without its horrors for every last Mexican alive — it is a city and a country where the bones of the dead seem to give the smell of their char to every desert wind and auto exhaust and frying tortilla. The mournfulness of unrequited injustice hangs a shroud across the centuries. Every Mexican is gloomy until the instant he becomes happy, and then he is a maniac. He howls, he whistles, smoke of murder passes off his pores, he bullies, he beseeches friendship, he is a clown, a brigand, a tragic figure suddenly merry. The intellectuals and the technicians of Mexico abominate their national character because it is always in the way. It puts the cracks in the plaster of new buildings, it forgets to cement the tiles, it leaves rags in the new pipes of new office buildings and forgets to put the gas cap back on the tank. So the intellectuals and the technicians hate the bullfight as well. You cannot meet a socialist in Mexico who approves of the running of the bulls. They are trying to turn Mexico into a modern country, and thus the same war goes on there that goes on in three-quarters of the world — battlefront is the new highways to the suburbs, and the corporation's office buildings, the walls of hospital white, and the myopic sheets of glass. In Mexico, like everywhere else, it is getting harder and harder to breathe in a mood through the pores of the city because more and more of the city is being covered with corporation architecture, with surgical dressing. To the vampires and banshees and dried blood on the curses of the cactus in the desert is added the horror of the new technology in an old murder-ridden land. And four o'clock on Sunday is the beginning of release for some of the horrors of the week. If many come close to feeling the truth only by telling a lie, so Mexicans come close to love by watching the flow of blood on an animal's flanks and the certain death of the bull before the bravery and/or humiliation of the bullfighter.

I could never have understood it if someone tried to explain ahead of time, and in fact, I came to love the bullfight long before I comprehended the first thing about why I did. That was very much to the good. There are not too many experiences a radical American intellectual could encounter in those days (when the youngest generation was called the silent generation) which invaded his sure sense of his own intellectual categories. I did not like the first bullfights I saw, the formality of the ritual bored me, the fights appeared poor (indeed they were) and the human content of the spectacle came out atrocious. Narcissistic matadors, vain when they made a move, pouting like a girl stood up on Saturday night when the crowd turned on them, clumsy at killing, and the crowd, brutal to a man. In the Plaza Mexico, the Indians in the cheap seats buy a paper cup of beer and when they are done drinking, the walk to the W.C. is *miles* away, and besides they are usually feeling sullen, so they urinate in their paper cup and hurl it down in a cascade of harvest gold, Indian piss. If you are an American escorting an American girl who has blond hair, and you have tickets in *Sol*, you buy your girl a cheap sombrero at the gate, for otherwise she will be a prime target of attention. Indeed, you do well not to sit near an American escorting a blond whose head is uncovered, for the aim of a drunken Indian is no better than you when your aim is drunk. So no surprise if one's early detestation of the bullfight was fortified in kidney brew, Azteca.

Members of a minority group are always ready to take punishment, however, and I was damned if I was going to be excluded from still another cult. So I persisted in going to bullfights, and they were a series of lousy bullfights, and then the third or fourth time I got religion. It was a windy afternoon, with threats of rain, and now and then again ten minutes of rain, poisonous black clouds overhead, the chill gloom of a black sky on Sundays in Mexico, and the particular torero (whose name I could not recall for anything) was a clod. He had a nasty build. Little spindly legs, too big a chest, a butt which was broad and stolid, real peasant ass, and a vulgar worried face with a gold tooth. He was engaged with an ugly bull who kept chopping at the muleta with his horns, and occasionally the bull would catch the muleta and fling it in the air and trample it and wonder why the object was either dead or not dead, the bull smelling a hint of his own blood (or the blood of some cousin) on the blood of the muleta, and the crowd would hoot, and the torero would go over to his sword handler at the barrera, and shake his head and come out with a new muleta, and the bull would chop, and the wind would zig the muleta out of control, and then the matador would drop it and scamper back to the barrera, and the crowd would jeer and the piss would fly in yellow arcs of rainbow through the rain all the way down from the cheap seats, and the whores would make farting sounds with their spoiled knowledgeable mouths, while the aficionados would roll their eyes, and the sound of Mexican laughter, that operative definition of the echo of total disgust, would shake along like jelly-gasoline through the crowd.

I got a look at the bullfighter who was the center of all this. He was not a man I could feel something for. He had a cheap pimp's face and a dull, thoroughgoing vanity. His face, however, was now in despair. There was something going on for him more humiliating than humiliation — as if his life were going to take a turn into something more dreadful than anything it had encountered until now. He was in trouble. The dead dull fight he was giving was going to be death for certain hopes in his psyche. Somehow it was going to be more final than the average dead dull fight to which he was obviously all too accustomed. I was watching the despair of a profoundly mediocre man.

Well, he finally gave up any attempt to pass the bull, and he worked the animal forward with jerks of his muleta to left and right, a competent rather than a beautiful technique at best, and even to my untutored eye he was a mechanic at this, and more whistles, and then desperation all over that vain incompetent pimp's face, he profiled with his sword, and got it halfway in, and the animal took a few steps to one side and the other and fell over quickly.

The art of killing is the last skill you learn to judge in bullfighting, and the kill on this rainy afternoon left me less impressed than the crowd. Their jeers were replaced by applause (later I learned the crowd would always applaud a kill in the lung — all audiences are Broadway audiences) and the approbation continued sufficiently for the torero to take a tour of the ring. He got no ears, he certainly didn't deserve them, but he had his tour and he was happy, and in his happiness there was something suddenly likable about him, and I sensed that I was passing through some interesting emotions since I had felt contempt for a stranger and then a secret and most unsocialistic desire to see this type I did not like humiliated a little further, and then in turn I was quietly but most certainly overcome by his last-minute success sufficiently to find myself liking a kind of man I had never considered near to human before. So this bad bullfight in the rain had given a drop of humanity to a very dry area of my heart, and now I knew a little more and had something to think about which was no longer altogether in category.

We have presented the beginning of a history then — no, say it better — the origin of an addiction. For a drug's first appeal is always existential — our sense of life (once it is made alert by the sensation of its absence) is thereupon so full of need as the desire for a breath of air. The sense of life comes alive in the happy days when the addict first encounters his drug. But all histories of addiction are the same — particularly in the beginning. They fall into the larger category of the history of a passion. So I will spare each and every one of us the titles of the books I read on the running of the bulls, save to mention the climactic purchase of a three-volume set in leather for fifty 1954 dollars (now doubtless in value one hundred) of *Los Toros* by Cossío. Since it was entirely in Spanish, a language I read with about as much ease and pleasure as Very Old English, *Los Toros* remains in my library as a cornerstone of my largest mental department — *The Bureau of Abandoned Projects:* I was going to write *the* novel about bullfight, dig!

Nor will I reminisce about the great bullfighters I saw, of the majesties of Arruza and the *machismo* of Procuna, the liquidities of Silverio and the solemnity of César Girón, no, we will not micturate the last of such memory to tell a later generation about El Ranchero and Ortiz of the Orticina, and Angel Peralta the Rejoneador, nor of Manolete, for he was dead long before I could with confidence distinguish a bull from a heifer or a steer, and no more can I talk of Luis Miguel and Antonio, for neither of them have I seen in a fight, so that all I know of Ordóñez is his reputation, and of Dominguín his style, for I caught his work in a movie once and it was not work the way he made it look. No, enough of these qualifications for *afición.* The fact is that I do not dwell on Arruza and Procuna and Silverio and Girón and Peralta and Ranchero because I did not see them that often and in fact most of them I saw but once. I was always in Mexico in the summer, you see, and the summer is the *temporada de novillos,* which is to say it is the time when the *novilladas* are held, which is to say it is the time of the novices.

Now the fellow who is pushing up this preface for you is a great lover of the bullfight — make on it no mistake.

For a great bullfight he would give up just about any other athletic or religious spectacle — the World Series in a minute, a pro football championship, a mass at the Vatican, perhaps even a great heavyweight championship — which, kids, is really saying it. No love like the love for four in the afternoon at the Plaza Mexico. Yet all the great matadors he saw were seen only at special festivals when they fought very small bulls for charity. The novillada is, after all, the time of the novilleros, and a novillero is a bullfighter approximately equal in rank to a Golden Gloves fighter. A very good novillero is like a very good Golden Gloves finalist. The Sugar Ray Robinsons and the Rocky Marcianos of the bullfighting world were glimpsed by me only when they came out of retirement long enough to give the equivalent of a snappy two-round exhibition. My love of bullfighting, and my experience of it as a spectator, was founded then by watching novilleros week after week over two separate summers in Mexico City. So I know as much about bullfighting as a man would know about boxing if he read a lot and heard a lot about great fighters and saw a few movies of them and one or two exhibitions, and also had the intense, if partial, fortune to follow two Golden Gloves tournaments all the way and to follow them with some lively if not always dependable instinct for discerning what was good and what was not so good in the talent before him.

After a while I got good at seeing the flaws and virtues in novilleros, and in fact I began to see so much of their character in their style, and began to learn so much about style by comprehending their character (for nearly everything good or bad about a novice bullfighter is revealed at a great rate) that I began to take the same furious interest and partisanship in the triumph of one style over another that is usually reserved for literary matters (is Philip Roth better than John Updike? — you know) or what indeed average Americans and some not so average might take over political figures. To watch a

bullfighter have an undeserved triumph on Sunday afternoon when you detest his style is not the worst preparation for listening to Everett Dirksen nominate Barry
Goldwater or hearing Lyndon Johnson give a lecture on
TV about Amurrican commitments to the free universe.
Everything bad and God-awful about the style of life got
into the style of bullfighters, as well as everything light,
delightful, honorable and good.

At any rate, about the time I knew a lot about bullfighting, or as much as you could know watching nothing but novilleros week after week, I fell in love with a
bullfighter. I never even met this bullfighter, I rush to tell
you. I would not have wanted to meet him. Meeting him
could only have spoiled the perfection of my love, so pure
was my affection. And his name — not one in a thousand of you out there, dear general readers, can have
heard of him — his name was El Loco. El Loco, the
Crazy One. It is not a term of endearment in Mexico,
where half the populace is crazy. To amplify the power
of nomenclature, El Loco came from the provinces, he
was God's own hick, and his real name was Amado
Ramírez, which is like being a boy from Hicksville,
Georgia, with a name like Beloved Remington. Yet there
was a time when I thought Beloved Remington, which is
to say Amado Ramírez, would become the greatest bullfighter in the whole world, and there were critics in Mexico City hoary with *afición* who held the same opinion
(if not always in print). He came up one summer a
dozen years ago like a rocket, but a rocket with one tube
hot and one tube wet and he spun in circles all over the
bullfighting world of Mexico City all through the summer and fall.

But we must tell more of what it is like to watch novilleros. You see, novice bullfighters fight bulls who are
called *novillos,* and these bulls are a year younger and
two to four hundred pounds lighter than the big fighting
bulls up around a thousand pounds which matadors

must face. So they are less dangerous. They can still kill a man, but not often does that happen — they are more likely to pound and stomp and wound and bruise a novillero than to catch him and play him in the air and stab him up high on the horns the way a terrible full-grown fighting bull can do. In consequence, the analogy to the Golden Gloves is imperfect, for a talented novillero can at his best look as exciting as, or more exciting than, a talented matador — the novice's beast is smaller and less dangerous, so his lack of experience is compensated for by his relative comfort — he is in less danger of getting killed. (Indeed, to watch a consummate matador like Carlos Arruza work with a new young bull is like watching Norman Mailer box with his three-year-old son — absolute mastery is in the air.)

Novilleros possess another virtue. Nobody can contest their *afición*. For every novillero who has a manager, and a rich man to house and feed him, and influential critics to bring him along on the sweet of a bribe or two, there are a hundred devoted all but unknown novilleros who hitch from *poblado* to *poblado* on back dirt roads for the hint of a chance to fight at some fiesta so small the results are not even phoned to Mexico City. Some of these kids spend years in the provinces living on nothing, half-starved in the desire to spend a life fighting bulls and they will fight anything — bulls who are overweight, calves who are under the legal limit, beasts who have fought before and so are sophisticated and dangerous. These provincial novilleros get hurt badly by wounds which show no blood, deep bruises in the liver and kidney from the flat of a horn, deep internal bleedings in the gut, something lively taken off the groin — a number of them die years later from malnutrition and chronic malfunctions of some number of those organs — their deaths get into no statistics on the fatalities of the bullfight.

A few of these provincial novilleros get enough fights

and enough experience and develop enough talent, however, to pick up a reputation of sorts. If they are very lucky and likable, or have connections, or hump themselves — as some will — to rich homosexuals in the capital, then they get their shot. Listen to this. At the beginning of the novillada, six new bullfighters are brought in every Sunday to fight one bull each in the Plaza Mexico. For six or eight weeks this goes on. Perhaps fifty fighters never seen before in Mexico City have their chance. Maybe ten will be seen again. The tension is enormous for each novillero. If he fails to have a triumph or attract outstanding attention, then his years in the provinces went for nothing. Back again he will go to the provinces as a punishment for failing to be superb. Perhaps he will never fight again in the Plaza Mexico. His entire life depends on this one fight. And even this fight depends on luck. For any novillero can catch a poor bull, a dull mediocre cowardly bull. When the animal does not charge, the bullfighter, unless possessed of genius, cannot look good.

Once a novillero came into the Plaza on such an occasion, was hit by the bull while making his first pass, a veronica, and the boy and cape sailed into the air and came down together in such a way that when the boy rolled over, the cape wrapped around him like a tortilla, and one wit in *Sol*, full of the harsh wine of Mexico's harsh grapes, yelled out, *"Suerte de Enchiladas."* The young bullfighter was named The Pass of the Enchiladas. His career could never be the same. He went on to fight that bull, did a decent honorable job — the crowd never stopped laughing. Suerte de Enchiladas. He was branded. He walked off in disgrace. The one thing you cannot be in any land where Spanish is spoken is a clown. I laughed with the rest. The bullfight is ninetenths cruelty. The bullfight brews one's cruelty out of one's pores — it makes an elixir of cruelty. But it does something else. It reflects the proportions of life in

[47]

Latin lands. For in Mexico it does not seem unreasonable that a man should spend years learning a dangerous trade, be rapped once by a bull, and end up ruined, a Suerte de Enchiladas. It is unfair, but then life is monstrously unfair, one knows that, one of the few gleams in the muck of all this dubious Mexican majesty called existence is that one can on occasion laugh bitterly with the gods. In the Spanish-Indian blood, the substance of one's dignity is found in sharing the cruel vision of the gods. In fact, dignity can be found nowhere else. For courage is seen as the servant of the gods' cruel vision.

On to Beloved Remington. He arrived in Mexico City at the end of the beginning of the novillada in the summer of 1954. He was there, I think, on the next to last of the early Sundays when six bulls were there for six novilleros. (In the full season of the novillada, when the best new young men have been chosen, there are six bulls for only three toreros — each kid then has two bulls, two chances.) I was not yet in Mexico for Amado Ramírez's first Sunday, but I heard nothing else from my bullfighting friends from the day I got in. He had appeared as the last of six novilleros. It had been a terrible day. All of the novilleros had been bad. He apparently had been the last and the worst, and had looked so clumsy that the crowd in derision had begun to applaud him. There is no sign of displeasure greater among the Mexican bullfighting public than to turn their ovations upside down. But Ramírez had taken bows. Serious solemn bows. He had bowed so much he had hardly fought the bull. The Plaza Mexico had rung with merriment. It took him forever to kill the beast — he received a tumultuous ovation. He took a turn of the ring. A wit shouted *"Ole, El Loco."* He was named. When they cheer incompetence they are ready to set fire to the stadium.

El Loco was the sensation of the week. A clown had fought a bull in the Plaza Mexico and gotten out alive. The promoters put him on the following week as a seventh bullfighter, an extra added attraction. He was not considered worth the dignity of appearing on the regular card. For the first time that season, the Plaza was sold out. It was also the first fight I was to see of my second season.

Six young novilleros fought six mediocre bulls that day, and gave six mediocre fights. The crowd grew more and more sullen. When there is no good bullfight, there is no catharsis. One's money has been spent, the drinks are wearing down, and there has been no illumination, no moment to burn away all that spiritual sewer gas from the horrors of the week. Dull violence breeds, and with it, contempt for all bullfighters. An ugly Mexican bullfighting crowd has the temper of an old-fashioned street corner in Harlem after the police wagon has rounded up the nearest five studs and hauled them away.

Out came the clown, El Loco. The special seventh bullfighter. He was an apparition. He had a skinny body and a funny ugly face with little eyes set close together, a big nose, and a little mouth. He had very black Indian hair, and a tuft in the rear of his head stood up like the spike of an antenna. He had very skinny legs and they were bent at the knee so that he gave the impression of trudging along with a lunchbox in his hand. He had a comic ass. It went straight back like a duck's tail feathers. His suit fit poorly. He was some sort of grafting between Ray Bolger and Charlie Chaplin. And he had the sense of self-importance to come out before the bull, he was indeed given a turn of the ring before he even saw the bull. An honor granted him for his appearance the week before. He was altogether solemn. It did not seem comic to him. He had the kind of somber extravagant ceremoniousness of a village mayor in a mountain town come out to greet the highest officials of the government. His knees stuck out in front and his buttocks in back. The Plaza rocked and rocked. Much applause followed by circulating zephyrs of laughter. And under it all, like a croaking of frogs, the beginnings of the biggest thickest Bronx raspberry anybody living ever heard.

Amado Ramírez went out to receive the bull. His first pass was a yard away from the animal, his second was six feet. He looked like a fifty-five-year-old peon ready to retire. The third pass caught his cape, and as it flew away on the horns, El Loco loped over to the barrera with a gait like a kangaroo. A thunderstorm of boos was on its way. He held out his arm horizontally, an injunction to the crowd, fingers spread, palm down, a mild deprecatory peasant gesture, as if to say, "Wait, you haven't seen nothing yet." The lip-farters began to smack. Amado went back out. He botched one pass, looked poor on a basic veronica. Boos, laughter, even the cops in the aisle were laughing. *Que payaso!*

His next pass had a name, but few even of the *afición* knew it, for it was an old-fashioned pass of great intricacy which spoke of the era of Belmonte and El Gallo and Joselito. It was a pass of considerable danger, plus much formal content (for a flash it looked like he was inclining to kiss a lady's hand, his cape draped over his back, while the bull went roaring by his unprotected ass). If I remember, it was called a *gallicina*, and no one had seen it in five years. It consisted of whirling in a reverse *serpentina* counterclockwise into the bull, so that the cape was wrapped around your body just like the Suerte de Enchiladas, except you were vertical, but the timing was such that the bull went by at the moment your back was to him and you could not see his horns. Then the whirling continued, and the cape flared out again. Amado was clumsy in his approach and stepped on his cape when he was done, but there was one moment of lightning in the middle when you saw clear sky after days of fog and smelled the ozone, there was an instant of heaven — finest thing I had yet seen in the bullfight — and in a sob of torture and release, "Olé" came in a panic of disbelief from one parched Mexican throat near to me. El Loco did the same pass one more time and then again. On the second pass, a thousand cried "Olé," and on the third, the Plaza exploded and fifty thousand men and women gave up the word at the same time. Something merry and corny as a gypsy violin flowed out of his cape.

After that, nothing but comedy again. He tried a dozen fancy passes, none worked well. They were all wild, solemn, courtly, and he was there with his peasant bump of an ass and his knobby knees. The crowd laughed with tears in their eyes. With the muleta he looked absurd, a man about to miss a train and so running with his suitcase. It took him forever to kill and he stood out like an old lady talking to a barking dog, but he could do no wrong now for this crowd — they laughed, they applauded, they gave him a tour of the ring. For something had happened in those three passes which no one could comprehend. It was as if someone like me had gotten in the ring with Cassius Clay and for twenty seconds had clearly outboxed him. The only explanation was divine intervention. So El Loco was back to fight two bulls next week.

If I remember, he did little with either bull, and killed the second one just before the third *aviso*. In a good season, his career would have been over. But it was a dreadful season. A couple of weeks of uneventful bullfights and El Loco was invited back. He looked awful in his first fight, green of face, timid, unbelievably awkward with the cape, morose and abominably prudent with the muleta. He killed badly. So badly in fact that he was still killing the bull when the third *aviso* sounded. The bull was let out alive. A dull sullen silence riddled with Mexican whistles. The crowd had had a bellyful of laughs with him. They were now getting very bored with the joke.

But the second bull he liked. Those crazy formal courtly passes, the *gallicinas*, whirled out again, and the horns went by his back six inches away. Olé. He went to put the banderillas in himself and botched the job, had to run very fast on the last pair to escape the bull and looked like a chicken as he ran. The catcalls tuned up again. The crowd was like a bored lion uncertain whether to eat entrails or lick a face. Then he came out with the muleta and did a fine series of *derechazos*, the best seen in several weeks, and to everyone's amazement, he killed on the first *estocada*. They gave him an ear. He was the *triunfador* of the day.

This was the afternoon which confirmed the beginning of a career. After that, most of the fights are mixed in memory because he had so many, and they were never without incident, and they took place years ago. All through the summer of 1954, he fought just about every week, and every week something happened which shattered the comprehension of the most veteran bullfighting critic. They decided after this first triumph that he was a mediocre novillero with nothing particular to recommend him except a mysterious flair for the *gallicina*, and a competence with the *derechazo*. Otherwise, he was uninspired with the cape and weak with the muleta. So the following week he gave an exhibition with the muleta. He did four *pases de pecho* so close and luminous (a pass is luminous when your body seems to lift with breath as it goes by) that the horns flirted with his heart. He did *derechazos* better than the week before, and finished with *manoletinas*. Again he killed well. They gave him two ears. Then his second bull went out alive. A *fracaso*.

Now the critics said he was promising with the muleta but weak with the cape. He could not do a veronica of any value. So in one of the following weeks he gave five of the slowest, most luminous, most soaring veronicas anyone had ever seen.

Yet, for three weeks in a row, if he cut ears on one bull, he let the other go out alive. A bullfighter is not supposed to let his animal outlive three avisos. Indeed if the animal is not killed before the first aviso, the torero is in disgrace already. Two avisos is like the sound of the knell of the bell in the poorhouse, and a bullfighter who hears the third aviso and has to let his bull go out alive is properly ready for hara-kiri. No sight, you see, is worse. It takes something like three to five minutes from the first aviso to the last, and in that time the kill becomes a pigsticking. Because the torero has tried two, three, four, five times, even more, to go in over the horns, and he has hit bone, and he has left the sword half in but in some abominable place like the middle of the back or the flank, or he has had a perfect thrust and the bull does not die and minutes go by waiting for it to die and the peons run up with their capes and try to flick the sword out by swirling cloth around the pommel guard and giving a crude Latin yank — nothing is cruder than a peon in a sweat for his boss. Sometimes they kick the bull in the nuts in the hope it will go down, and the crowd hoots. Sometimes the bull sinks to its knees and the puntillero comes in to sever its neck with a thrust of his dagger, but the stab is off-center, the spinal cord is not severed. Instead it is stimulated by the shock and the dying bull gets up and wanders all over the ring looking for its *querencia* while blood drains and drips from its wounds and the bullfighter, looking ready to cry, trots along like a farmer accompanying his mule down the road. And the next aviso blows. Such scenes are a nightmare for the torero. He will awaken from dreams where he is stabbing and stabbing over the horns with the *descabellar* and the bull does not drop but keeps jerking his head. Well, you receive this communication, I'm sure. A bull going out alive because the torero was not able to kill him in the allotted time is a sight about as bloody and attractive as a victim getting out of a smashed car and stumbling down the road, and the matador is about as popular as the man who caused the accident. The average torero can afford less than one occasion a year when three avisos are heard. El Loco was allowing an average of one bull a week to go out unkilled. One may get an idea of how good he was when he was good, if you appreciate a prize-fighter who is so good that he is forgiven even if every other fight he decides to climb out of the ring and quit.

For a period, criticism of El Loco solidified. He had brilliant details, he was able on occasion to kill with inspiration, he had huge talent, but he lacked the indispensable ingredient of the bullfighter, he did not know how to get a good performance out of a bad bull. He lacked tenacity. So Ramírez created the most bizarre *faena* in anyone's memory, a fight which came near to shattering the rules of bullfighting. For on a given Sunday, he caught a very bad bull, and worked with him in all the dull, technical, unaesthetic ways a bullfighter has to work with an unpromising beast, and chopped him to left and to right, and kept going into the bull's querencia and coaxing him out and this went on for minutes, while the public demonstrated its displeasure. And El Loco paid no attention and kept working with the bull, and then finally got the bull to charge and he made a few fine passes. But then the first aviso sounded and everyone groaned. Because finally the bull was going good, and yet Amado would have to kill him now. But Amado had his bull in shape and he was not going to give him up yet, and so with everyone on the scent of the loss of each second, he made derechazos and the pass with the muleta which looks like the *gaonera* with the cape, and he did a deliberate *adorno* or two and the second aviso sounded and he made an effort to kill and failed, but stayed very cool and built up the crowd again by taking the bull through a series of *naturales,* and with twenty seconds left before the third aviso and the Plaza in pandemonium he went in to kill and had a perfect estocada and the bull moved around softly and with dignity and died about ten seconds after the third aviso, but no one could hear the trumpet for the crowd was in a delirium of thunder, and every white handkerchief in the place was out. And Amado was smiling, which is why you could love him, because his pinched ugly little peasant face was full of a kid's decent happiness when he smiled. And a minute later there was almost a riot against the judges for they were not going to give him tail or two ears or even an ear — how could they if the bull had died after the third aviso? — and yet the tension of fighting the bull on the very edge of his time had given a quality to this fight which had more than a hint of the historic, for new emotions had been felt. The bullfighting public has a taste for new emotions equaled only by the lust of a lady for new pleasures.

This record of triumphs is in danger of becoming as predictable as any record of triumphs since Caesar. Let us keep it alive with an account of the fiascos. Amado was simply unlike any bullfighter who had ever come along. When he had a great fight, or even a great pass, it was unlike the passes of other fine novilleros — the passes of El Loco were better than anything you had ever seen. It was as if you were looking at the sky and suddenly a bird materialized in the air. And a moment later disappeared again. His work was frightening. It was simple, lyrical, light, illumined, but it came from nowhere and then was gone. When El Loco was bad, he was not mediocre or dull, he was simply the worst, most inept, and most comical bullfighter anyone had ever seen. He seemed to have no technique to fall back on. He would hold his cape like a shroud, his legs would bend at the knees, his sad ass seemed to have an eye for the exit, his expression was morose as Fernandel, and his feet kept tripping. He looked like a praying mantis on its hind legs. And when he was afraid he had a nerveless incapacity to kill which was so hopeless that the moment he stepped out to face his animal you knew he could not go near this particular bull. Yet when he was good, the comic body suddenly straightened, indeed took on the camber of the best back any Spanish aristocrat chose to display, the buttocks retired into themselves like a masterpiece of poise, and the cape and the muleta moved slowly as full sails, or whirled like the wing of that mysterious bird. It was as if El Loco came to be every comic Mexican who ever breathed the finest Spanish grace into his pores. For five odd minutes he was as completely transformed as Charlie Chaplin's tramp doing a consummate impersonation of the one and only Valentino, long-lost Rudolph.

Let me tell then of Amado's best fight. It came past the middle of that fine summer when he had an adventure every week in the Plaza and we had adventures watching him, for he had fights so mysterious that the gods of the bulls and the ghosts of dead matadors must have come with the mothers and the witches of the centuries, homage to Lorca! to see the miracles he performed. Listen! One day he had a sweet little bull with nice horns, regular, pleasantly curved, and the bull ran with gaiety, even abandon. Now we have to stop off here for an imperative explanation. I beg your attention, but it is essential to discuss the attitudes of *afición* to the natural. To them the natural is the equivalent of the full parallel turn in skiing or a scrambling T-formation quarterback or a hook off a jab — it cannot be done well by all athletes no matter how good they are in other ways, and the natural is, as well, a dangerous pass, perhaps the most dangerous there is. The cloth of the muleta has no sword to extend its width. Now the cloth is held in the left hand, the sword in the right, and so the target of the muleta which is presented for the bull's attraction is half as large as it was before and the bullfighter's body is thus so much bigger and so much more worthy of curiosity to the beast — besides the bull is wiser now, he may be ready to suspect it is the man who torments him and not the swirling sinister chaos of the cloth in which he would bury his head. Moreover — and here is the mystique of the natural —

the bullfighter has a psychic communion with the bull. Obviously. People who are not psychic do not conceive of fighting bulls. So the torero fights the bull from his psyche first. And with the muleta he fights him usually with his right hand from a position of authority. Switching the cloth to the left hand exposes his psyche as well as his body. He feels less authority — in compensation his instinct plays closer to the bull. But he is so vulnerable! So a natural inspires a bullfighting public to hold their breath, for danger and beauty come closest to meeting right here.

It was naturales Amado chose to perform with this bull. He had not done many this season. The last refuge of his detractors was that he could not do naturales well. So here on this day he gave his demonstration. Watch if you can.

He began his faena by making no exploratory pass, no *pase de muerte,* no derechazos, he never chopped, no, he went up to this sweet bull and started his faena with a series of naturales, with a series of five naturales which were all linked and all beautiful and had the Plaza in pandemonium because where could he go from there? And Amado came up sweetly to the bull, and did five more naturales as good as the first five, and then did five more without moving from his spot — they were superb — and then furled his muleta until it was the size of this page and he passed the bull five more times in the same way, the horns going around his left wrist. The man and the bull looked in love with each other. And then after these twenty naturales, Amado did five more with almost no muleta at all, five series of five naturales had he performed, twenty-five naturales — it is not much easier than making love twenty-five times in a row — and then he knelt and kissed the bull on the forehead he was so happy, and got up delicately, and went to the barrera for his sword, came back, profiled to get ready for the kill. Everyone was sitting on a collective fuse. If he managed to kill on the first estocada this could well be the best faena anyone had ever seen a novillero perform, who knew, it was all near to unbelievable, and then just as he profiled, the bull charged prematurely, and Amado, determined to get the kill, did not skip away but held ground, received the charge, stood there with the sword, turned the bull's head with the muleta, and the bull impaled himself on the point of the torero's blade which went right into the proper space between the shoulders, and the bull ran right up on it into his death, took several steps to the side, gave a toss of his head at heaven, and fell. Amado had killed *recibiendo*. He had killed standing still, receiving the bull while the bull charged. No one had seen that in years. So they gave him everything that day, ears, tail, *vueltas* without limit — they were ready to give him the bull.

He concluded the summer in a burst of honors. He had more great fights. Afterward they gave him a day where he fought six bulls all by himself, and he went on to take his *alternativa* and become a full fledged matador. But he was a Mexican down to the bones. The honors all turned damp for him. I was not there the day he fought six bulls, I had had to go back to America and never saw him fight again. I heard about him only in letters and in bullfighting newspapers. But the day he took on the six bulls I was told he did not have a single good fight, and the day he took his alternativa to become a matador, both his bulls went out alive, a disgrace too great even for Amado. He fought a seventh bull. Gypsy magic might save him again. But the bull was big and dull and El Loco had no luck and no magic and just succeeded in killing him in a bad difficult dull fight. It was obvious he was afraid of the big bulls. So he relinquished his alternativa and went back to the provinces to try to regain his reputation and his nerve. And no one ever heard much of him again. Or at least I never did, but then I have not been back to Mexico. Now I suspect I'm one of the very few who remember the happiness of seeing him fight. He was so bad when he was bad that he gave the impression you could fight a bull yourself and do no worse. So when he was good, you felt as if you were good too, and that was something no other torero ever gave me, for when they were good they looked impenetrable, they were like gods, but when Beloved Remington was good, the whole human race was good — he spoke of the great distance a man can go from the worst in himself to the best, and that finally is what the bullfight might be all about, for in dark bloody tropical lands possessed of poverty and desert and swamp, filth and treachery, slovenliness, and the fat lizards of all the worst lust, the excretory lust to shove one's own poison into others, the one thing which can keep the sweet nerve of life alive is the knowledge that a man cannot be judged by what he is every day, but only in his greatest moment, for that is the moment when he shows what he was intended to be. It is a romantic self-pitying impractical approach to the twentieth century's demand for predictable ethics, high production, dependability of function, and categorization of impulse, but it is the Latin approach. Their allegiance is to the genius of the blood. So they judge a man by what he is at his best.

By that logic, I will always have love for El Loco because he taught me how to love the bullfight, and how to penetrate some of its secrets. And finally he taught me something about the mystery of form. He gave me the clue that form is the record of a war. Because he never had the ability most bullfighters, like most artists, possess to be false with their art, tasty yet phony, he taught something about life with every move he made, including the paradox that courage can be found in men whose conflict is caught between their ambition and their cowardice. He even taught me how to look for form in other places. Do you see the curve of a beautiful breast? It is not necessarily a gift of God — it may be the record life left on a lady of the balance of forces between her desire, her modesty, her ambition, her timidity, her maternity, and her sense of an impulse which cannot be denied. If we were wise enough, bold enough, and scholars from head to motorcyclist's boot, we could extract the real history of Europe from the form elucidated between man and beast that we glimpse again in recall of the bullfight. Indeed where is a writer or a lover without a knowledge of what goes on behind that cloth where shapes are born? *Olé*, Amado!

Theatre

The Playwright as Critic

Not so very long ago the National Foundation on the Arts and Humanities had a symposium for an invited audience of newspaper critics. Conducted by Roger Stevens and Carolyn Kizer, the symposium was given the formal title of "What's Wrong with Criticism in the Performing Arts," and Session One took place in a conference room of the Whitney, with Arthur Schlesinger, Gerald Weales, Clive Barnes, William Phillips, Michael Smith of the *Village Voice,* and myself.

Now, it would be nice (and doubtless out of character) for me to describe which opinions were held by the others, and what shape was taken by colloquies between the speakers and the invited audience, but I cannot, for *The Deer Park* was already in rehearsal that day, and I rushed up to the Whitney for a half hour, said my piece somewhere toward the end of that three-hour conference, and was out again, on the way back to Christopher Street downtown in the Village and rehearsals at the DeLys. So I had only an inkling of what had gone before, but it was enough to improvise ten minutes of talk. Because what came through the echo of completed conversations was the old and essential antagonism of the artist in the theatre (the playwright, actor, director, yea, often the producer!) toward the cruel, rigorous, even unreasonable demand of the opening-night reviews, that cry of protest because all the years of writing, the months of preparation, and the repetitive soul-killing weeks of rehearsal must still come down to the electric hour when the drama reviewer sprints from the theatre, snatches his opening lead from the well-tuned bag of his wit, and is off to his desk, say, say, his guillotine. Three times out of four, nine times out of ten, the work is doomed. If it is an exciting, difficult play, imperfectly presented (as, for example, might be said of *Slow Dance on the Killing Ground*), then the odds are nineteen out of twenty that the critic, the two or three or four good men inhabiting those nerve-festooned portals between the theatre and the public, will do the job in, and the play does not live.

We are all familiar with this profound plaint. But the correctives and/or the preventatives lack salt. Invariably they suggest that the critic see the play after it opens, that he take his time, that he brood upon the nature of what he has seen. All this, while sensible, is nonetheless depressing. That, in fact, is what I began to say at the symposium in the Whitney. For it seemed to me that the opening-night review with all its inequities, yaws of judgment, its surrealistic surgeries upon aesthetic value, is nonetheless indispensable to the theatre, and I would not enjoy writing a play and seeing it produced if I could not have an opening night before a full posse of critics. For that is also a part of the play. That is its dramatic edge, its confrontation with the history it will or will not make. Those opening-night reviews, written to the demand of fever speed, are a ritual at the heart of the drama. A professional theatre without the sense of crisis provided by opening night is like a marriage in city hall.

Yet what a huge price is paid for the excitement of the opening-night review. The desire for success lucubrates secret prostitutions in the soul. Some are not so secret. A theatre whose economic foundations are built on the opinions of five or six men (now reduced to four men, or three men, or two, can it be even one man?) is a theatre whose aesthetics must be built on the most anomalous mechanical principles — the intake pipe is on the outlet valve: the theatre becomes geared to the taste of the newspaper critic, which is to say — not his taste, but his need. And his need — we can make no mistake here — is for simple plays.

A drama critic is a man of some integrity and discipline — he could not otherwise fulfill the professional rigors of his work. Like all men of integrity, he prefers to do a good job. A simple play offers just that opportunity. Its moral situations may be novel but they must be clearcut (go back to *The Moon is Blue*), its characters are happiest when amusing or worthy of our compassion, but they cannot be too contradictory or complex. In a play with five characters, four preferably must be comfortable to the mind so that the play may concentrate on the fifth — perhaps I am thinking of *Come Back, Little Sheba*. It does not matter. Fifty plays a season, good, bad, magnificent, or atrocious, fulfill this formula. The simple play enables the reviewer to make his assessment on the evidence before him. He can mark the play precisely on the scale of his accumulated experience. The simple play — all else equal — inspires the critic therefore with a benevolent sensation; he can feel like a good man doing a good work of appraisal.

The only difficulty is that the simple play alienates the theatre from life, for in life, moral situations are rarely novel, but invariably overloaded with counterpoint, and the people who surround you are not always comfortable to the concepts of the mind; indeed, they often prove most depressing just at the moment when they are presumably most worthy of compassion. In contrast, the simple play provides a wish fulfillment — it extracts a neat pattern from the flux of the unruly: it has, in consequence, as much to do with life, this simple play, as a hairpin has to do with jewelry, but the hairpin is what prospers, the hairpin becomes nine-tenths of the stock in the jewelry store. The theatre roots itself in the simple. Actors learn to look for precise results, directors look for moments — call them tricks — since a simple play depends for its success on offering, let us say, one hundred moments of pleasure rather than fifty, and playwrights develop an eye for linear mechanisms of plot which will lift them from the moral bogs of their theme.

It comes down to one thundering, if matter-of-fact difficulty: You cannot predict success for a play once it is sufficiently complex to need a night's sleep for comprehending it. Any dramatic theme which requires an audience to return to their unconscious later that night, in order to evaluate the depth of what is being said in the theatre, is carrying a most ambitious monkey on its back, for the drama reviewer does not have the time to put the play together in his sleep and write about it in the morning. He must take it as it is, all confusion to the fore, deal with it in the same partial terms of comprehension that we feel when we meet a gallery of dazzlers, freaks, heroes, and creeps at a party and can't begin to divine what is going on until the morning after, not until our sleep has done the work of assembling a little more of what we have seen into some conjunction with the stiff-necked patterns of our mind.

These were my remarks at the symposium — these, more or less. I ended with some vague notions paraded forward about the possibility of existential criticism — a hint that the drama reviewer recognize the impossibility of reviewing difficult plays immediately, that he write for the morning daily, "No review today — it's too early to tell. I'll write about it in a week, and maybe I'll even go to see it again. Maybe I won't. Let us see. In the meantime, I suggest this play might just possibly be worth keeping alive."

We are asking for miracles, yes? We request the authority to relinquish his infallibility. A faint dream. The moment is not near. No, I was obviously making my plea with a particular play in mind — no accident that beneath the hat of the symposiast was the steel helmet of the playwright. I was thinking of *The Deer Park,* and its particular strengths and weaknesses, delights and *longueurs,* after ten stunning maniacally depressive days of rehearsal, and I was thinking as well of the monumental impossibility that any drama reviewer born could review this play to his own satisfaction (or mine!) an hour after he had seen it, when I had lived with the events, crises, and themes before me for near to eighteen years, had worked on the play for ten, had rewritten it four times. It was by now perhaps the dearest work of all my work. There were times when I thought I even cared more for it than the novel from which it was delivered; it was certainly different from the novel, narrower, more harrowing, funnier I hoped, sadder, certainly more tragic. It was also more multilayered. If I were a novelist trying to write plays, I was also trying to put more into this play than I had into the novel. If the compass was obligatorily more narrow, the well was being dug to a deeper water — I realized at one point that I had a work with thirteen characters, and not one of these characters was unworthy of a play for himself. Indeed, it sometimes seemed to me that I had compressed ten plays into three hours.

There was an idiom in the theatre I could not bear. It was the one which brought all arms and aid to the lowest common denominator of the audience. I was tired of seeing plays which went along carefully, thoughtfully, and decently for two hours in order to arrive at a small but perfect dramatic explosion. Any audience which did not know all the steps from opening curtain to explosion was an audience not worth writing for, since the American public was by now finally saturated in plot, in genre, in situation, and the twenty stratagems of denouement. So why not write a play which went from explosion to explosion, or — since this is not the Fourth of July — from one moment of intensity or reality (which is to say a moment which feels more real than other moments) to the next — a play which went at full throttle all the way. Which is precisely what was done this summer when *The Deer Park*, a four-hour play, its third draft five years old, had an hour or more taken out of it, a transition which cut away all dramatic scaffolding, connective tissue, road signs, guides, and left the play stripped to its essential connections, the movement ideally from one real scene to the next, with the audience left to fill the spaces between.

I had my play then with thirteen wide-open characters and a set of one hundred blackouts or quick scenes I called changes, quick as the cuts in a movie, for it seemed right to capture the dislocation of life in Hollywood by a play which played like a movie — although not quite! Wait until you see! And I was pleased. For the play occupied a space which had been left uninhabited too long, that area between the explorations of the realistic play and that electric sense of transition which lives in the interruptions and symbols of the Theatre of the Absurd. *The Deer Park* was conceived to live in the land between. It was — could you term it so? — an existential play. A surrealistic comedy about the nature of tragedy I called it once in a fatuous moment. For I was trying to tell in this play something of what I knew about sex and love, and no theme — here comes our paradox — is more difficult to present in the theatre. None more difficult, because — dear reader — there is a no-man's-land between sex and love, and it alters in the night.

We go to sleep convinced we are in one state, we awaken in the other, and murderous emotions patrol the everchanging line of no-man's-land. You do not write a play about sex and love which is a simple play, a situation comedy, a switcheroo of slamming doors and lovers under beds, no, rather you try to induce an existence which is like an animal or a beast or a beautiful woman, a being which breathes and is mysterious and not altogether accessible and changes all the time. Ideally, it stays fascinating, then haunting, it is a play to which you go back, a play with which you fall in love, a bitch, tears of blood in her heart, the perfume of the Indies in her flanks.

We are at the core of the comic, are we not? A playwright in love with his play. It calls for Voltaire, Shaw, or our own Albee to delineate it. Stick in the needles. Bring forth the pots. Lay on the acid. This playwright is ready to burn for the love of his own dramatic work. There were too many years when he dreamed of *The Deer Park* on Broadway and the greatest first night of the decade, too many hours of rage when he declaimed to himself that his play was as good as *Death of a Salesman,* or even, and here he gulped hard, *A Streetcar Named Desire*. Yes, his play was there, so he felt. Then years went by, and experience was gained in the theatre and knowledge that a play like *Streetcar* was a miracle, and angels without dollars must also have helped it on its way. Finally the playwright learned that if he would see his play at all, and see it right, he would see it in that land below Broadway, in the terrain of a true turf, the Village, at a jewel box in red velvet (red velvet at least was there) called the Theatre DeLys, the theatre of the lily, yes, and there off-Broadway it would have a chance to live, perhaps there it could survive those opening-night reviews the playwright was certain could not be steeped in joy, and he studied the play in rehearsal and hoped *The Deer Park* was really as good as he believed, for then he could read any review, that would not be hard, for when you know the work is good there is a particular sweetness to the sad taste with which you imbibe negative opinions of yourself. But, dear readers, I let you in on a secret — there have also been moments in rehearsal when I have said to myself, "Dear Messieurs Chapman, Kerr, Nadel, and Watts — if you do not like my play, what horror if I am obliged to agree with you."

On the other hand, there have been moments of magic when the dialogue and the action and the set — but we have bragged enough about this theatrical baby. Here is a cigar to celebrate the birth. If you will look at the label, you will see it says: "Theatre DeLys, eight performances a week. Be advised the actors speak so clearly you need not miss a line."

II

Since it is obvious from the previous part of this introduction that the playwright was in love with his play long before opening night, the question for the second part may be: what does he think of *The Deer Park* now that it breathes on the live and all but bleeding boards, and the quickest answer, madam, is that he broods but a little about his own dear play and thinks often of the life of the theatre.

But, wait! *The Deer Park* opened to a curious set of reviews, mixed in the extreme: "Unearthly depravity," said my old friend, *Time* magazine, kicking us in the ear.

"A blast of fresh air," was the manly word from the *Wall Street Journal*. Others cried out we were "passionately comic," "shocking and funny," so forth. Nonetheless, nearly every review was condescending. While it was more or less agreed that for a flamboyant and somewhat overrated novelist, the apprentice playwright had a modest flair for the theatre, it was also generally regretted that our apprentice included long soliloquies whose sentiments were sophomoric, platitudinous, and presumptively philosophical. It was further considered in meatball taste for him to pop in a speech about the war in Vietnam. That, by consensus, was regarded as an obvious attempt to modernize a ten-year-old play. Since the speech about Vietnam was lifted, however, from the novel and had therefore been written originally in 1951 and 1952 (with the Korean war on the mind), such criticism contained its unwitting ingredient for tonic — besides, excitement in the company was general. We were a hit. Not a smash hit, but a hit. So went the word in New York. When you are a hit, you are a victor. At least, you are running. You do not mind the pricks and darts.

Still the playwright was considerably confused. His play had been helped to keep running by extracting crucial nuggets from in and out reviews, phrases like "sensational," "soars like a skyrocket," "dazzlingly wicked," "endearingly wicked," "scenes which palpitate like the hearts of a couple in the act of love." Properly weeded, we were a full neon garden of fireworks, searchlights, explosions, comedy. "Evil is a fun thing," said Mr. Kerr, putting us down. We nearly put it up.

The theatre is like a marriage — you hate to lose. A marriage which goes down is like a ship which sinks; so is a play. Principles are thrown overboard to keep the living alive. You do not say, "We will shut down *The Deer Park* because there is something disgraceful and deadening to the heart in advertising a play which is serious, as a play which is not." You seize the quotes —

ripped, often as not, all bloody from their context — you make do with what you've got. The theatre reserves her awards for those who win. It is liverish to be a loser in the theatre. The play may be a hit for the wrong reasons, but you even feel good. If the reviews have had next to nothing to do with your intent, the illusion of winning is nonetheless sweet, even as staying alive is sweet. Our apprentice, therefore, could afford to be intrigued by the reception of his play. He had a hit on the basis of quoting reviews he could not quite recognize as being related to his own work — they seemed to speak of another play. (Perhaps some work of collaboration by Céline and Saroyan.) Of course he had a production where virtues were mixed with flaws — he knew the values and vices of his actors' performances to a point, or thought he did. He had a large blessing and small curse for every actor in his company and it was a fine company which had shown courage on opening night, all thirteen actors. He had a bit of love for the director, and moments when he could strike him dead. Yet the playwright's soul was in its yaws again. He felt becalmed in a nasty double-edged murmur, as if the hint of a breeze tickled first one ear, then the other, then all sails fluttered. He was annoyed. He felt he had lost his own sure sense of value. He did not know how much he liked his play, nor whether it was really any good. Was it possible that it was only boring, comic, and sensational? And he had nothing by which to measure. He had not seen anything on Broadway in several years. So to keep his critical measure, he went on a tour of the theatrical season and saw more than a dozen plays in two weeks. He was then obviously anxious to learn a little of the nature of the invisible assignation between a drama critic and his favorite girl, a fat smash hit.

But first he had the good sense to contemplate in advance the differences between book reviewing and theatre reviewing. Doubleday, or Simon & Schuster, or any publishing house which goes by some such name, may spend half a million dollars for a book by Harold Robbins or Irving Wallace, but the novels of these writers will not be reviewed on Page One of the *New York Times Book Review*. The *New York Times Book Review* is guilty of many a crime, but it does not often commit gross hierarchical adulteration. Mr. Robbins may even be put on page fifty. He will certainly hit no better than page four. Odds-on he will get a bad or facetious review. And no one except the author will suffer too much. Not even the sales.

But on Broadway! Well, we know what happens to a $500,000 musical. It is a public event more important than the Royal Shakespeare Company doing Shakespeare — the big musical runs equal in glamour and category to the opening of a major new play by Williams or Miller or Albee. And is reviewed not only with the same solemnity, but the same hyperbole. Or more. The critics are often critical of Mr. Williams, but for the book and lyrics, we can write the quotes ourself. "An evening of magical wonder." "An occasion of musical splendor." "A heartwarming, life-giving two hours of uproarious fun." Quick! Give us the name of this musical so that we may see it. But the name, friends, is always *Our Newest Turd Has Just Moved In*. "Shit, señorita," says Broadway.

Full Stop! All speed astern! Dare the playwright speak thus of *Man of La Mancha* and *Fiddler on the Roof*? Can he include *The Apple Tree* without committing sacrilege? Yes, is the answer, he can. *Fiddler on the Roof* is declared a masterpiece when it is next door to a swindle; *Man of La Mancha* is a great creation, except — don't breathe it — there are pits of monotony in the core of its charm. *Apple Tree* is celebrated for introducing a new dimension to musical comedies; in fact it has shoved together a trio of one-act plays, two poor, one good, the total saved by the impressive talents of Barbara Harris.

Well, if our apprentice critic of the drama is not

merely on early foot, his thesis would seem to claim the professional reviewer has a double standard which is the reverse of the standard of the book reviewer: that the seriousness of your production — all rare exceptions admitted — is generally measured by the cost of your production. Be it understood the costly production is often a superb production with superb performances (usually by the dancers) but from the playwright's point of view, this is not so different from judging the literary merit of manuscripts by the excellence of the handwriting.

In the two weeks just past, the apprentice playwright saw a great deal of excellent handwriting. He saw *Hello, Dolly!*, and *Barefoot in the Park*, *Man of La Mancha*, *The Apple Tree*, *The Odd Couple*, *Don't Drink the Water*, *At the Drop of Another Hat*. He saw *Natural Look*, *The Homecoming*, and *Black Comedy*. He saw — he ran out of plays on Broadway. There was off-Broadway: *Mac-Bird*, *Eh?*, *America Hurrah*, *Hogan's Goat*, *The Mad Show*. He saw *The Deer Park* many times. He had evidence in plenty and some new thought to masticate in detail (for what is a critic without his teeth?). Finally, he even had a critical formula. It came from his own work. It explained the mystery of the schizophrenia in the drama reviewer's heart, for the answer was simple: there were two kinds of plays. That was the beginning of what it was all about.

Would you like a metaphor to ease your way? Let the playwright tell a story he heard last night. It is perhaps apocryphal, but not grievously so, for if the story is unfair, you could change the names of the artists until you had a proper fit. This, at any rate, is how the tale was told. Some years ago, Willem de Kooning gave a drawing to Robert Rauschenberg, who then promptly erased the drawing and signed his own name to the smudged page. Next, the erased drawing was sold. Children, we are not discussing the final absurdity of certain terminal positions in modern art right here, no, sir, we are in on a primitive rite, the writing of money. Primitive man took a stand on a stone. He said, "I am the leader of this tribe, and I stand on this stone, and so this stone has the value of all your tents and all your wives and all your herds and flocks." And since no one was strong enough to kill the leader, the rock on which he stood was money. Before money can be used for barter, it is first declared — it is made into money by an act of declaration. "I, Robert Rauschenberg, hereby make of this piece of paper a piece of money." An erased drawing is restored in value by a signature. Emptiness plus authority equals money.

It seems we are now ready to talk of certain plays, the ones which might put the signature on the erased drawing. They are authority stamped upon emptiness, they are money. The authority of such plays is that they are known as a hit. That is their value. That is how they give value to an audience.

Look at the nightly event. A horde of the hard-working pours in from the suburbs for a night of food and playgoing. If they are tired, it is not because they have toted that bale of cotton all day, no, they are tired because their nerves are stale, flat, bored, and unendurable from the stale, flat, unprofitable work they have done as a horde of the middle and professional class all day in offices which buy and sell commodities less interesting and less well-made than they used to be, and they have stifled in modern kitchens and driven children to school and gotten caught in suburban traffic and blinked their eyes against the glare of super shopping centers. They have rushed and they have waited every day of the week — they have lived lives devoted to controlling their environment — their umbilical relation to existence is now captured in the touch of a fingertip on the plastic button of some electrical machine. They are thus a class which is devoted utterly to control, and they have lost control of everything. If we are to dwell on the Broadway theatre audience and its relation to a hit, we can only talk first of the heart of the theatre — this liberal complacent materialistic greedy pill-ridden anxiety-laden bored miserable and powerless jumble of suburban couples who jam every Broadway smash for the first few months. Later, they are joined, and still later replaced, by tourists, conventioneers, small-towners about to drown in New York, and corporation label-men with the names of the hits to drop back into the office hopper at home. There are out-of-town philosophers buried among the culls of this audience, but out-of-towners in New York are usually using all their wit to dare the subway — they cannot arrive in their seat at their critical best, for they are in New York, Fun City, they want only to be reassured they will not be mugged in the next few hours. So their synapses blend in with all the fear-ridden reflexes of all the liberal couples from the suburbs, and what you get is the middle-class horror of America (and the hint of how Vietnam finally is possible), for our people are in their seats, sprawled out, nervous, vitiated, on the giggle, dying to be manipulated for external manipulation is authority, and they can need that. But only a hit will manipulate such an audience for they do not wish to contemplate ambiguity — ambiguity is the essence of their nausea and their fatigue. Listen carefully to such an audience laugh, and you can feel the undertow which attends the manipulation, you may even hear the silent machines which make the money. The Broadway audience being an over-manipulated apathetic flesh stirs only to the intense sound of such silent machines, for those who live in the suburbs are addicted to processes which make money as simply as juvenile delinquents are hipped on marijuana. Addiction, like faith, is focus from a point of reference.

Are we too abstract? Let us take the best of examples for the other side, and think of Zero Mostel, who is curator of a rich large talent. There are many who would say he is a great actor. Some might not agree altogether, but no matter, possessed of moments of grandeur, and moments not so grand, Mostel is nonetheless a major theatrical artist, for he glides like a shark through that medium of mood we might call prime attention in the theatre, his movements slice into the center of a laugh, a roll of his eyes turns a spill of amusement through the aisle. He is a comic wind.

But the evil is this. He does not need to act any more. He can come out on stage, and the audience will laugh. If he scratches his crotch, the house breaks down. If he looks at another actor and merely turns away, the ticket-payers are instantly in delight. Let me whisper the next. If some unknown actor made up to look like Mostel came out for a minute and stood still and scratched his crotch and looked at another actor and looked away, the house might break into equal combers of hysteria provided they did not know it was not Mostel. That collective Broadway flesh wishes only to be manipulated. Mostel rat-tat-tatting his fly is pressing a button to make them laugh. It does not matter whether he is scratching these jewels in *A Funny Thing Happened on the Way to the Forum,* or in *Fiddler on the Roof.* The act of scratching is more important than the play, which is why he is not always a great actor. Audiences laugh because Mostel is the signature on that piece of paper, he is switching on the machines which make the money.

Zero is, of course, an artist of the first rank. When one gets down to the real stuff, however, down to that stretch of hits on Broadway where one ten-dollar bill is the same as the next, when you get all the way down to *Cactus Flower* and talentless technicians of high skill like Barry Nelson, then you may be in the place where the Creation is denied.

There are those who will now suspect a thesis is coming. They may be confident. The thesis is soon to be made by discussing five plays which do not deserve to be discussed separately, for they are not five plays but one play, since their internal mechanisms of manipulation are not individual but collective, and came not out of artists but computers. So specific criticism would have no real bone to bite. Besides, these plays are traitors to the stage: their secret allegiance is to television. When we discuss these plays, we will not be so foolish as to talk of their separate plots, for that would assume the original impulse had been creative rather than computed. Good. These five plays are nominally called *The Odd Couple, Barefoot in the Park, Cactus Flower, Don't Drink the Water,* and *Natural Look.* In fact, by existential measure, they had the duration of only two-and-one-half plays to this reviewer, since he walked out of each one at the end of the first act (which is how first he discovered their common denominator). On such a commencement one might normally have to say no more than that the basic provender of these evenings was watered oatmeal, but months and years ago, the critics had all been in like Flynn, and so the audience responded on each of our nights with a particular barking of laughter which called to mind a human tissue in a Petri dish swaying to calculated shock. A revolutionary with a sawed-off shotgun might in a rage have sprayed the critics hard enough to keep them off their seats because no humanoid tissue could have liked these plays if he had been told they were not to be liked. Subsequently, however, by a work of fierce concentration, compassion for critics was generated by the mind. Drama reviewers, all said, must have been desperately miserable in infancy, and wretched little feeders, to so enjoy watered oatmeal TV. Five pieces of Show Biz — say, nay! — five pieces of Telev Biz — put five bowls of oatmeal down the New York drama critics' collective tummy. Five hits went up. Call it five minus one. Because *Natural Look,* a work as tasteless, empty, skillful, well acted, and well directed as the other four is a shade of a hair less satisfactory in hiding the fact that it possesses no fleshly meaning, and so it closes after opening night. Who knows where the styrene will crack? Plastic is a gas in solid form. It can only pretend to flesh.

Strike it like this: *Cactus Flower, Don't Drink the Water, The Odd Couple,* and *Barefoot in the Park* encourage underground spleen because they are the Theatre of Plastic, their content is TV, they are cooked of synthetics. Only danger is that the mode by which we perceive reality can indeed become our reality, a most elegant Marxian manner of saying that no medium is more of a message than TV — which may be why, despite the reek of the hot cigar butt, none of us can ignore McLuhan's total slogans. McLuhan has one great grip on the attention of this decade — we all know something in us slides off slowly and begins to die as we watch TV. So the medium is indubitably giving us a message. Feel the message. Salts wash out of your blood, hate and lust pass over to headache. Spook-show in the psyche, cramp in the groin. Love, tenderness, sympathy become vectors to anxious attention. Do not speak of what we see — what we see on TV can be anything — this is talk rather of lobotomizations which seep into the gray collective soul of the room after an evening of TV. Emotions are modulated (rather say: strangled, filtered, choked) while passing through the electronic valves of the transmitter and the set. Something leaves us each night we spend in attendance on the box. For the medium has one message — technological society will make certain you pass away on a bed into which national music is piped.

So these Cactus Flowers are not merely bad commercial plays called good by the bad taste of the critics, no, they are not even produced the way bad plays used to be, because back, way back then, in return for a definite waste of time, you could still get some raunchy funky little hint of theatre. But these Cactus Flowers offer preparation for nothing but the sick bed in the last ward. America has been watching television for twenty years and the style of television has transfused itself not only into the taste, but the demand, even the expectancy, of the suburban middle class — that precise compound of neurons and suet so capable of being smelted into money. Therefore, Broadway comedies now rush not only to be like television comedies, but actors are trained away from theatre in the process, and sometimes look like television sets come to life.

Television, after all, was the child of the Age of Conformity which came to America after the Second World War. Television produced a genre: moderate characters in modest situations. It offered endlessly recognizable detail, *surface* detail: supermarkets, highways, suburban streets, pastel-colored classrooms. However, the characters in such television dramas presented nothing which was biologically real. They bore the same relation to human beings which vinyl does to leather. And the reason was that the characters of these TV series were synthesized from incompatibles — the new documentary and the old soap opera.

Soap opera had a sentimentality which was surrealistic, but its characters — while altogether psychotic — were still real. Since they lived on your radio, their voices came out of a background much like a cave: there was no confusion in one's mind with the here and now of daily surface. The soap opera was material for your dreams. Whereas television puts forth the very latest surface of reality — it goes on hunts for real backgrounds, it is documentarily obsessed. The documentary is, it may hope, its honest buck. Since it then thrusts its own highly sophisticated mutants (hey, Ginger! hi, Flipper) of the old soap-opera characters into highly documentary situations, the dramatic product excites that same vivid sense of displacement from reality you can receive from a painted plaster hamburger by Claes Oldenburg five feet in diameter. You don't know immediately whether the object is comic, nauseating, or significant of some new reality, or even some new way of studying reality. Oldenburg's hamburger is, of course, a way to study a reality which is all before our fingers. But the housewife studying herself on a situation comedy in her electronic mirror does not know if the seemingly recognizable characters before her are in their bizarre situations because they have more wit than herself, or less; she pays for the human pleasure of recognizing some part of herself by a most indigestible psychic demand — she is plunged further into security and anxiety at the same point, and therefore further into obsession with herself. If the old radio soap opera encouraged schizophrenia by stimulating the housewife's buried secret plot (loyalty to the home vs. hots for the lover) television dulls her into nausea. Fundamental distinctions between the safe and the insecure, the reality and the dream, are marinated, dramatic oppositions are bypassed — powerful conflicts are first modulated, then mashed into one another. The side effect from such confusion is nausea.

Superb, you will say, now tell why television cannot offer stories and situations which are either frankly disturbing or honestly pacifying. Well, the medium is the message, yes, and a half-hour drama on television cannot be too pacifying or you will notice all too clearly the infernal sound of the set, feel its electronic harp, even — enter op art — see the very vibrations which erode your optic nerve. Yet one cannot go in the other direction: a story must not be too disturbing, for there is no actor's flesh and blood to warm you from a stage, nor, as in a movie, the bodies of the audience, no, you are all alone with your family and the emotional rigors of the tale, plus the psychic assault of the set. Television attacks the unconscious like a trip in a jet — you move from continent to continent or spectacle to spectacle without the accompaniment of a change in mood to prepare the flesh. (The unconscious thus becomes like that poor patient who is operated upon without warning.) So a work of deep drama on television would inspire anxiety, for one's own depths might open to what? — to the baleful electronics of which far-off God? what cold star? No, you keep it neat. The scene is recognizable to ward off any shriek, and the situations are odd and out of focus — just sufficiently unsettling to keep your mind off the flickering of the set. Estimate the difficult problems facing our Broadway Computers when they, loyal to the firm premise that all sound commercial theatre must be based on television tales (because audiences are now based on the narrative synapses of the television series), are next obliged to translate or computerize the technique from one medium to another. You now have real actors forced to imitate actors as they appear to us on a television set. You must have backgrounds which are recognizable, but situations which do not exist, you must reconstruct in the audience that hum of security and insecurity which is a television set. Since you have real actors who can be generally depended upon to give the audience a moment of true warmth at the end (since that is finally what the actors are for), the psychic payoff on all Cactus Flowers is huge — it is like watching television with a home-cooked meal at the end. The only one who can suffer in these plays is the actor, for he is thrust into a cancerous relation with his art — too much approbation too little deserved must flux his guilt, and skillful emotion skillfully applied to a situation which does not exist in the blood of his past experience must be as conducive to leukemia as kissing a plastic mask on the hour.

The medium is the message, and the message of television is electronic hum. The theatre will wash down from its old broken-down heights to the swamps of TV, the theatre — if it continues, as it will, to cohabit with TV — is close to an excruciating death by long wallowing, for the smelting operations will enlarge, and the big houses will continue to be filled with armies of pill-fed humanoids in for the night from television. The Theatre of Manipulation will swell in every joint. It will thrive like edema. And the critics will be the doctors who call this swelling, health. For it is true. To talk of Broadway is to talk not of amusement but disease.

Yes, it seems that no less a task is before us than to forgive all drama critics for invariably amputating the wrong organ — but then they are blind and ill themselves. Have pity on them. They are men who fell in love early with illusion and so cannot leave now that the lady has become an electronic ghost. Drama critics cannot see themselves as necrophiliacs. They must believe that TV's Theatre of Manipulation, watered surrealism and pistol shot gags, is still the butler to art, not its avenging ghost.

And is that all to be said for the season? These five plays which are one play and lead to no discussion of the stage, only polemics and existential analyses of the evils of television? No, the apprentice put in two weeks going to shows, and he is not likely to let anyone away without a capsule of comment for each evening. Besides, one would not wish the rest of Broadway to escape. Listen to more about *Man of La Mancha* and *Fiddler on the Roof*, stay close and you will pick up criticism — we whisper it — of *Black Comedy*, exactly where it crosses *At the Drop of Another Hat*. But first, a word from my own play. A director and a producer exchange dialogue:

MUNSHIN: Extraordinary.

EITEL: You really like it?

MUNSHIN: It's an epic study about the hole in eternity our country is preparing for itself. It's a poem. This can make the greatest picture in the last ten years.

EITEL: Collie, why don't you say what you really think?

MUNSHIN (*fingering his belly*): No audience would understand it.

EITEL: I think it would be amazing how much this would communicate to an audience.

MUNSHIN: You don't communicate with an audience, you manipulate an audience . . .

The producer is an old-fashioned producer. His type went out ten years ago. Producers are not so full of energy any more, and they study audiences with the aid of motivational research and statistics on consensus. Mr. Munshin had a simpler idea. To manipulate an audience you put on a rubber glove (although he did not need a rubber glove) and you put your finger up as far as it would go. Pop! That was the old-fashioned movie and the old-fashioned smash Broadway success. Well, history is composed of layers — one is not the first to suggest it. So talk of TV's Theatre of Manipulation must not be confused with good old Collie Munshin's plumber's snake of a finger. No, Collie was brought up on Zing, went the strings of my heart — emotional sap must be there to keep Collie happy. The old Collie Munshin Theatre of Manipulation depended not on thin emotionless mismarriages between surrealism and the documentary, but on *schmaltz, shtick,* and Collie's finger maneuvering up the seat of all critical opposition.

Well, it sours the face to say this, but one can get so pleased with the fact that this abysmal old theatre of corned manipulation is not dead, that the sins of *Fiddler on the Roof* and *Man of La Mancha* could kindly be forgiven, if lunar hyperbole had not been attached to them.

But, hear! *Fiddler on the Roof* may not be the greatest musical ever made. In fact, it may be never nearly so good as *Pal Joey.* If Sholom Aleichem was almost a great writer, his particular weakness was a determined inability to confront evil in intimate forms — he preferred to present evil as some external abstract force — a catastrophe, a pogrom, a drunken peasant. With such a view, one is always close to the danger of the over-sentimental. (Look! That good man got killed for nothing.) *Fiddler on the Roof* (adaptation from a book by Maurice Samuel, *The World of Sholom Aleichem*) has added Samuel's own pervading sentimentality to Aleichem's sweet wit, and the result — surprisingly tuneless — is a hard all-out Munshin-ish manipulation of Jewish audiences. *Fiddler* plays with no quarter on emotions of self-righteousness, self-pity, ignorance, and guilt. In fact, guilt should well be mentioned first — it is so obviously felt by the audiences for that past they have evaded (no, let us say they have jettisoned) in the race to the suburb, it is the blood guilt of all the prayers which have not been said, and all the stones which have not been laid on all the graves of all the grandparents. The audience is milked like a cow, but the loss of milk feels sweet to them, for these suburbanites know next to nothing of life in the *shtetl* — it is all revelation to them — they are pleased to discover their own past is nearly so colorful as the old country life of Sicilians and Bavarians and Ukrainians. Yes, indeed, *shtetl* life is indeed colorful as presented in *Fiddler on the Roof* — but not very much more accurate than a musical about peasants and gypsies by MGM.

Man of La Mancha is a more exciting play and so commits a greater sin, for it manipulates one of the deepest desires of us all — which is to be noble. It plays with the joy of fulfilling this dream, and the agony of losing it: so it moves audiences to tears. But it is only a good play, and work on such a theme begs to be great. *La Mancha*'s music is thin when arias might be near, and its language is undernourished. It does not inhabit the high desires nor fill the dungeons of the emotional architecture to which it pretends. It merely gives a hint of a spark and lets the audience blow it into fire with the gale of that most curious hunger — to be noble, to be true to one's dream. But the play is not true to the demand of the theme — rather it is clever enough to see that the time has come to send Jeanette MacDonald and Nelson Eddy to college. Survey of World Literature I — Don Quixote!

Let us rather make a terrible confession, for that is a way to arrive at the point with a minimum of ballast and all sails high — the brute liked *Hello, Dolly!* He liked it better than *Man of La Mancha* and *Fiddler on the Roof.* It was in fact likable because it was too crude to manipulate even a ten-year old. It had only its own gusto to offer, and the best music of all the shows, and the best dancing. So it was good the way a ball club is good. Therefore, it expressed one aspect of the theatre, only one half of the theatre, but that half it expressed altogether — that mindless half which speaks of physical health, sex, top bananas, and bazazz. Besides, it had Ginger Rogers giving what may have been the best performance she ever gave on the night the apprentice critic saw it, she did everything with a kind of stomp-it-out kick-it-up vitality, and the love of birthday cakes was in her eye, she had the rare beauty of the plump blond when the blond is concupiscent, and at the end she received bravos like a bullfighter and deserved them. And even gave a curtain speech with happy smiles and generous tears. A noisy evening ended in theatrical rainbows of love. The theatre can get away with anything when it makes a rainbow.

The theatre can also get away with anything when it is sufficiently surgical to make a brilliant incision into the nature of reality, or of desire, and do that in pure theatrical context. Witness the vast success respectively of *Black Comedy* and *At the Drop of Another Hat. Black Comedy* cuts right into the phenomenology of the real. It points out that if you encounter a hot hot-dog and roll in the dark, your hand will fly away as if it had encountered a turd, a dog's muzzle, or a hot set of tools. Now turn the light up for the audience, but let the actors pretend they are in the dark. Yes, we have sudden and brilliant incision into the nature of reality. Study those actors, ho! One laughs for the first twenty minutes and then waits for the moment when the play will step out to explore its premise. But *Black Comedy* has got the playwright's hand on the silent machine which makes the money and so it refuses resolutely to explore its own magic. Instead, it rushes to cash in its profits. Like a truly nasty upper-class London accent, it goes in for a witless repetitive obsessive strangling of the premise. It explores no more. Our audience having been exercised first to laugh, is then extorted to laugh, finally is tortured and at last debauched by laughs which are by now become no more than conditioned reflexes, and therefore leave the psyche as quiet and empty as the theatre ten minutes after final curtain. When the English loot a bank, they even get the pennies which roll under the carpet.

In line with this sort of robbery, absolute thoroughness is indispensable, and Flanders and Swann, our next protagonists, are thorough — they mine every aspect of the muted desire to share in theatre which characterizes their most special sort of audience. The brute could say that *At the Drop of Another Hat* is prime pigeon feed for Wasps, for they are the most underfed patrons of the theatre, and he would be right. *At the Drop of Another Hat* is resolutely non-nasty, and keen as calling cards. It suggests in its assortment of songs and anecdotes (funny little ditties about the need of others to be obscene, extracts from Tolkien, etc.) the buried and doubtless not altogether bona fide memory of the best and wittiest visits of a fine British clergyman and his sexton on Sunday afternoons in June in golden British gardens there in the quiet twilight of the empire — nothing can move the heart of a Yankee banker more. *At the Drop* is indeed so resolutely non-nasty that one senses the real ugliness of the proceedings is buried in the profoundly admiring complacency of audience and performers for each other as they swell their breasts back and forth, mourning secretly for the power of empire they think has been lost, when in fact, it is the same people ultimately who fly the planes and burn the babies.

Which brings us to psychosis. In addition to *Hello, Dolly!*, there were five plays for which the brute had good words, and four of them had to do with madness, and only one, *MacBird*, was, with that, content — the three others, *America Hurrah*, *The Mad Show*, and *The Homecoming* pushed on into the most modern movements and logics of madness, on to the most advanced field of psychosis. So these three plays explored the anxiety of living on a plane and looking for a void, and because they were deeply conceived, they had no impulse to manipulate, no, rather there was some depth of mood they wished to achieve by working up the details of an obscure magic between the audience and themselves. Therefore the plays roused a presence which was like a monster or a machine or a beast. (In *The Mad Show* it was a sad sweet humor about the eye of the wacky.) But in the two others the beast lived on the stage and shared your horror and so permitted laughter, and moments occurred in *The Homecoming* and *America Hurrah* where one was in the presence of that mysterious communion of mood which can be experienced nowhere but in the theatre.

This sense of a presence was achieved in *The Homecoming* through a quiet modest exhibition of the propinquity of the commonplace and the psychotic. Its glint of genius was to demonstrate the thesis by showing what exactly was equal to what. Each character recounting the dullest details of his day was equal to the casual attention of a family group as they watched a wife and brother-in-law roll on the floor in embrace. So it was perhaps a play which was talking about the end of any world we know or perhaps it was like a street one passes in a dream, and on this street a murder is committed. In your dream. In its turn, *America Hurrah* went through sometimes tedious, if always intelligent, insights into the maniacal surface of all programmed communications, and then exploded at the end with ten minutes that lived on the edge of the lip of the murder of all American life and the carnage of the psyche, and the death of the American vision.

Then, there was *MacBird*. *MacBird* had a truth for which the apprentice was not prepared. Beneath the parody was a wild sorrow, for suspicion flooded the heart that LBJ had more real life as MacBird than as Lyndon Johnson — one could conceive of him secretly watching MacBird with tears in his eyes: the role and the language gave him a stature life had denied.

This would be a fair quick summation of the plays one saw, and the lessons learned, and the coldest lesson came from the best plays — the future of the theatre seemed most rich where the material was most insane. A cold note. Therefore, *Hogan's Goat* was reserved for comment last, since it is out of category. A passionate and substantial work overwritten by a degree, it had another kind of sorrow, for it displayed the blood beneath the corruption and gave a feel of the muscle within the piety of the Irish in Brooklyn, New York, some generations back and that was no modest achievement.

Do you get the point? Good plays like *The Homecoming, MacBird, America Hurrah, The Mad Show, Hogan's Goat* (and you know the other) are plays which attempt to find a piece of that most mysterious and magical communion some call ceremony, some church, and some theatre. They are plays which attempt to reach a moment sufficiently magical to live in the deepest nerves and most buried caves of the memory of the people who have seen them, these plays speak of the fire at the edge of the wood and hair rising on the back of the neck when the wind becomes too intimate in its sound. The theatre lives (if it lives as anything more than a spinster aunt on allowance from movies, television, and the record business), the theatre lives on what it can do uniquely, on moods of depth and perfume and terror and exaltation and cascades of laughter which no other form can provide — it is a ceremony which takes place in a cave, and philosophers, priests, painters, tyrants, and athletes must collaborate, the bodies of some must harmonize with the minds of others. When it is really good, what it offers can be found in no other form of art, for then it is like religion for the irreligious and gives promise of something which may live forever. Its impermanence is the life of its power. But that is only true of those finest plays which never manipulate, and there are not so many. This year on Broadway the number is down to two or one, this real species of theatre has about given way to all the hybrid giants in the palaces on Broadway, those Cactus Flowers whose sins against the loving heart of the Lord are performed at the rate of a thousand a minute, for a thousand humanoid hearts are laughing at jokes which were conceived in the same place they used to package thalidomide and will package the actors tomorrow when the actors perform the benefits for themselves in the camps of concentration. "Shit, señorita," says Broadway.

Film

Some Dirt in the Talk

Wild 90 is the name of a full-length underground movie which a few of us, soon to be cited, filmed on four consecutive nights in March this year. It was done in 16-millimeter and recorded on magnetic sound tape, and since the raw stock costs of processing 16-millimeter sound and film run about thirty cents a foot or ten dollars a minute of shooting, we shot only two and a half hours in all, or $1,500 worth of film. Obviously we couldn't afford to shoot more.

Still, for reasons one may yet be able to elucidate, the two and a half hours were not so very bad, and from them was extracted a feature film which runs for ninety minutes. It is a very odd film, indeed I know no moving picture quite like it since there are times when *Wild 90* seems close to nothing so much as the Marx Brothers doing improvisations on *Little Caesar* with the addition of a free run of obscenity equal to *Naked Lunch* or *Why Are We in Vietnam?* It has the most repetitive pervasive obscenity of any film ever made for public or even underground consumption, and so half of the ladies are fascinated because it is the first time in their life they have had an opportunity to appreciate how soldiers might talk to each other in a barracks or what big-city cowboys might find to chat about at street corners. But then the ladies are not the only sex to be polarized by *Wild 90*. While the reactions of men in the audience are more unpredictable, a rough rule of thumb presents itself — bona fide tough guys, invited for nothing, usually laugh their heads off at the film; white-collar workers and intellectual technicians of the communications industries also invited for nothing tend to regard the picture in a vault of silence. All the while we were cutting *Wild 90*, we would try to have a preview once a week. Since the projection room was small, audiences were kept to ten, twelve, or fifteen people. That is an odd number to see a film. It is a few too many to watch with the freedom to move about and talk aloud that you get from watching television; it is on the other hand a painful number too small to feel the anonymity of a movie audience. Therefore, reactions from preview night to preview night were extreme. We had banquet filmings when an audience would start to laugh in the first minute and never stop — other nights not a sound of happiness could be heard for the first forty minutes — embarrassing to a producer who thought just yesterday that he had a comedy on his hands. Finally we had a formula: get the hard guys in, get the experts out.

That makes sense. There is hardly a guy alive who is not an actor to the hilt — for the simplest of reasons. He cannot be tough all the time. There are days when he is hung over, months when he is out of condition, weeks when he is in love and soft all over. Still, his rep is to be tough. So he acts to fill the gaps. A comedy of adopted manners surrounds the probing each tough guy is forever giving his brother. *Wild 90*, which is filled with nothing so much as these vanities, bluffs, ego-supports, and downright collapses of front is therefore hilarious to such people. They thought the picture was manna. You could cool riots with it, everybody was laughing so hard.

Whereas intellectual technicians had to hate it. Because the tip of the tablecloth was being tilted, the soup was encouraged to spill. There was a self-indulgence in the smashing of Hollywood icons which spoke not only of an aesthetic rebellion (which some of the media technicians would doubtless approve) but *Wild 90* hinted also of some barbarity back of it — the Goths had come to Hollywood. Based on the gangster movies of the thirties, the movie nonetheless had a quasi-Martian flavor, a primitive pleasure in itself, as if it had discovered the wheel which made all film go round.

Testing this brand-new little American product, cutting it, shaping it, serving it to samples of audiences, made for an interesting summer. *Wild 90* was not the greatest movie ever made, no sir, and the actors would receive no Academy Awards (because they swore too much) but the picture, taken even at its worst, was a phenomenon. There was something going on in it which did not quite go on in other movies, even movies vastly superior. It had an insane intimacy, agreeable to some, odious to others. The dialogue was sensational. Where was a scriptwriter who wrote dialogue like this?

BUZZ CAMEO: I ain't gonna get killed here.

THE PRINCE: Look. You're gonna get killed, or you're not gonna get killed. But you don't know shit. You don't know when you're gonna get killed or how you're gonna get killed, and you just shut. Shut.

BUZZ CAMEO: The Prince. The Prince tells me.

THE PRINCE: You're nothin' but a guinea with a hard-on in your arm. That's *your* hard-on. (*A sound of disgust.*) Unhh.

BUZZ CAMEO: How about my short arm? How many guys I put away for you, daddy-o?

THE PRINCE (*mimicking*): How many guys I put away for you, daddy-o. Unhh. Unhh. Unhh. (*Three derisive punches to his own biceps.*) I'll tell you how many guys you put away for me. One and a half! One and a half!

TWENTY YEARS: Right. The other half I had to take care of. That's how good *you* are.

THE PRINCE (*keeping up the tempo*): Punk. Unhh. (*The arm again.*) Punk.

TWENTY YEARS (*jeering*): What a mistake. What a mistake. Cameo, he says he can handle Thirty-fourth Street. (*Scream of derision.*) Hah! Thirty-fourth Street he can handle. He can't handle his own joint.

Yes, where was the scriptwriter? Who was he? And the answer — is that no hat could fit his head, for he did not exist. The dialogue had come out of the native wit of the actors: *Wild 90* was a full-length film for which not a line of dialogue was written.

Well, explanations must now be promised — we may even intimate that closet history is about to be disclosed, and of an underground film! Gather near! Listen to the subtle events which preceded the shooting.

Last winter, while the play of *The Deer Park* was having its run at the Theatre DeLys, some of the cast of *The*

Deer Park used to drink together at a restaurant named Charles IV in the Village. Actors like to fill the tank after a performance. It is not only their reward, and their sedative, but it is possibly a way of accommodating their soul back to the place from which it was vacated by the more meretricious lines of their script. Now, *The Deer Park* was not signally meretricious, it was after all well-written, but perfect it was not, entirely honorable, no, it was not, lacunae of intent had collected, and since devils and demons rush to inhabit every gap, there were lines in the script the playwright could not necessarily defend to the death. Those are the sort of lines which turn actors subtly, even unconsciously, to drink. Because they have to use the best of themselves to conceal the worst of an author.

Well, drink they did then, and on any given night it was better than even you could find much of the company in their more or less civilized cups, eating a little, drinking away. We were a nice company, relatively free of jealousy, intrigue, or liaison due mainly, it might be submitted, to the fact that *The Deer Park* was full of passion, jealousy, intrigue, conniving, etc., and so the actors could be relaxed of that by the time drinks had come. (Indeed it is exactly in those wholesome family comedies the critics love so very much that you will find the actors rife in the green room, and everybody banging everybody up the back door.)

After drinking sessions went on awhile, they took a particularly modest form. Hugh Marlowe, Rosemary Tory, and Rip Torn had the longest parts, very long parts they were, so they were naturally the ones most in need of regular hours. Usually, they would be the first to leave, and Buzz Farbar, Mickey Knox, and myself would go drinking into the closing, while my wife, Beverly Bentley, and her friend and colleague, Mara Lynn, would talk at the next table on whichever subjects blond sorceresses find of moment at three in the morning. Whereas

Knox, Farbar, Mailer (later to be known as Supreme Mix) slipped each night into a game. We used to play at being Mafiosos. We would try to talk like Dons. We would go on so much as twenty or forty minutes at a time talking about any subject at hand in the allusive use of metaphor you can catch a hint of now and again when one or another Italian in the rackets will lay it on the line. We even picked up names. Twenty Years, Buzz Cameo, the Prince.

Of the three of us, Knox was the only real actor. He had been acting for twenty years and more, and had been in two dozen movies, half of them gangster films, he had experience on the stage and television, was a member of Actors' Studio, had worked on the production of half a hundred Italian films in Rome in the last ten years, he spoke Italian fluently. Buzz Farbar, however, had never acted but for a stretch as Don Beda, the orgiast, in *The Deer Park*, a part which began as a stunt after work for him (and remained a stunt in the sense that the part of Don Beda is one of the theatre's most difficult small parts to play). Anyway, Buzz had done his best. He was a good team man, a former Golden Gloves boxer, a football star at Dartmouth, then publisher of Legacy Books at CBS — he had not been a great Don Beda, but there was probably not an actor in New York who could have been — the part requested Porfirio Rubirosa or some Castilian with Persian silk. At any rate, Buzz Farbar may have made no immortal Don Beda, but he certainly did wing a good shtarker as Buzz Cameo in each late-nightly round of the Maf Boys, and yr author who had never acted at all in any way (except every day of his life — a quip to be examined further, close readers) did his best to hold up his end as the Prince. We played the Maf Boys. It was our answer to the Chelsea Girls.

We even got good at it. How close we came to portraying any mobsters of certified class, I do not know, but we

had experiences. Drinking our booze and acting for ourselves in the restaurant, we would get good enough upon
occasion that the room would seem weightless, and the
air ready to spark. There was a tension afterward to
judge the value of the moment. We were either getting
up a mood which was more accurate and quintessentially witty than anything worked on by actors or game
players before about the subject of the Mafia, or we were
merely whacked up on booze and the mystery resided in
the supernatural properties of grain spirits, their ability
to fog all perception of creative value, and inflame the
positive judgments of misperception. Say! I conceived
the idea it would be fun to get a good cameraman and
film a half hour with sound of the three of us sitting
around a restaurant table. So we talked about that for a
time. And as the winter went by, as Supreme Mix, which
is to say, Farbar, Knox, and Mailer, did the Maf Boys on
the unphotographed wing a couple of times a week at
Charles IV, the picture got discussed with the savor of get-
rich-quick schemes worked on in a Brooklyn kitchen, and
so showed promise of becoming a project you talk about
with too much enjoyment ever to undertake. But we had
fun. Night after night. There is a dialogue in the movie
which captures a little of the style we had when metaphor was in flower.

BUZZ CAMEO: I'm goin' down to the Beach.

TWENTY YEARS (*to Cameo*): Ya know there's one thing
about singin' — it leaves ya hoarse.

THE PRINCE (*to Cameo*): If you leave, ya know what
you are? You're the prunes.

BUZZ CAMEO: Prunes? You're the dunes.

THE PRINCE: Yeh. You're the real prunes.

BUZZ CAMEO (*a reference to burial grounds*): Ponds 'n
dunes?

THE PRINCE: You're prunes. The cream's comin' out your ass.

TWENTY YEARS: You got no feels.

Farbar did not let the movie go. Calling me very early one morning, he pointed out that Mickey Knox was leaving for Rome in ten days. In the following week we had to make the movie if we were ever to make it at all. When he was reminded that we had no photographer, no lights, no set, no properties, nothing but my steadfast promise to immolate a thousand bucks (with five hundred more to burn in reserve), Farbar promised to bring together the rest of the ingredients. (That, gentlemen, presumably, was how the old two-reelers were made.) He arranged a meet with D. A. Pennebaker (of Leacock Pennebaker, inventors of portable sound-film cameras, makers of *Don't Look Back*). Pennebaker had four nights free, and he would film us for four nights. Since Knox was still playing Collie Munshin in *The Deer Park*, we could start only after his performance each evening, which meant acting must begin at midnight. No problem. Those were our drinking hours. Acting and drinking could get together like kissing cousins. There persisted, however, the problem of locating a set. For we had taken on one more ambition. We had decided to try for more than a short film about three hoods disporting in a restaurant, we would rather take off from a contemporary piece of local history in Brooklyn. A year or more ago, the Gallo gang had undertaken a war with Joseph Profaci, by repute a *don capo* of Cosa Nostra. For self-protection the Gallos finally holed up in a little building on President Street, while the police put the block under crash surveillance to keep them from getting killed. Well, Supreme Mix knew nothing about the Gallo gang, in fact had no desire to take a page from their material, no, Supreme Mix was looking to be another gang, the three characters created before anyone was reminded of the Gallos. Yes, we would be our own three characters holed up in a loft, down by the beginning of the film from a company of twenty-one men to three men, living alone. That would give us the situation on which we could improvise. But where could we find an empty loft, and over the weekend? No, we had to settle for a big and empty room in an office building.

Monday night, we moved into the set, sat drinking very carefully for an hour or two, looking to recapture the style of Charles IV, and finally began shooting. But we could not recover that mood. Charles IV was a drinking spa with agreeable food, it had an attractive hat-check girl, moderate lights, soft booze, you slipped into *ambiente*. Now we were in the empty office, in a square room, twenty-five by twenty, with packing crates, clothes hung on pipes, fluorescent lighting, and one light bulb supported from a cord. Mood oscillated in the illumination of prison. We weren't three hoods at a restaurant. We were holed up, riding each other's nerves. It was obvious we would never find an objective correlative to the question: did we do a good imitation of three topflight hoods having drinks? No, we were in a different game — the camera on us now, and the knowledge of ten dollars a minute clicking away in film and sound. Our first dialogue was wooden, aware of itself. Action lagged. As a reaction, we weren't out at sea two minutes before the picture prematurely began. After a statement by Knox that we had been holed up in this place for twenty-one days, Farbar suddenly came back, "Twenty-one days you been sucking my joint!"

It will be remembered we were working without a script. We were going to talk back and forth. In absolute freedom. Out of it, went our premise, would come the action. No one was necessarily ready, however, for this action. Knox is a hard self-centered man who likes to keep his dignity unruffled. People were in no hurry to go around calling him names in his daily life — suddenly he was getting it in a movie. It was wrong. Mafiosos rate themselves on their own brand of elegance. The director thought of stopping the camera, but something in the action had come alive. Next, the director reasoned — the film going on this while, of course — that if three Mafiosos were indeed holed up for twenty-one days in a loft, they might not have the use of metaphor available on happier evenings — no, they might be snarling on the bone, not kingpins of the rackets now, but rather back to adolescence, hoods on the corner. The feel of that was real. So obscenities continued — they took on love's own patina of wit. Verbal action between Mickey, Twenty Years, Buzz Cameo, and the Prince flourished. Insults winged like darts, dignities rose, vanities fell — a style came out of it. The actors had an action which carried out of that first insult and went from line to line without undue self-propulsion. This action was to carry the cast through the night and the next three nights, the visits of ten other actors, nine of whose performances were finally to be kept. "A motion picture grew out of it," as they say on Puffs Avenue, although in truth you could say a motion picture staggered out of it, while toe-dancing over the bottles, and then kept its balance — although the disconcerting angle at which it careened was yet to be seen.

But we have to depart from this sketch of a narrative. It does not tell the real history of what was going into *Wild 90*. That is private, personal, subterranean, and buried in the psyche of the actors and the director. Since this director is an intellectual of sorts he could not engage in a creative act without a set of major theses to support him. While he thought he was merely engaged in a $1,500 junket out to movieland for four nights in a row, he was actually delivering some old and close-to-forgotten experience which had been perhaps more obsessive than he realized, obsessive for years. He had thought he was making the movie as an exercise in a few nuances of a very special brand of Camp, gangster-movies-Camp — he was actually being more serious than he knew, although indeed he was not to discover this until he had spent months cutting the film and had begun to write about these matters. Then he realized that under the bed of the making of *Wild 90* were some dusty themes of singular complexity: themes such as Hollywood, acting, existentialism — no less — and the logic of the real disease of the film — no less. Not to mention old wounds of the ego.

BUZZ CAMEO: Twenty years. Twenty years of shit, that's what you are. You're twenty years of nothin'. You're the prince of what?

TWENTY YEARS: Listen, big mouth . . .

BUZZ CAMEO: The prince of my pickle, that's what you're the prince of.

THE PRINCE: That's what I'm the prince of, your pickle — your pickle with its dirty little warts. French tickle, Buzz Cam.

Item: Do you know that back in World War II, a few of us used to walk those Army legs with this thought: someday I'm going to write a book and expose the fugging Army. And yea and lo, that was done, thanks to James Jones.

Item: Then in the postwar, we used to see movies, and flushed with the confections of new ego status, used to say to ourselves, "Someday I'm going to make a movie and expose that fugging Hollywood." And you know what happened? Two of one's books were made into movies, The Naked and the Dead and An American Dream were the names of these movies, and the first was one of the worst movies ever seen, and the second was inferior to

*it, or so I hear, because I couldn't get myself up to go and
see it. And had nothing to do with these movies except
get paid for them, in fact both of those movies were made
without the author receiving a postcard from the producer, and so author could plead* mea non culpa, *but for
the additional fact that Hollywood paid very well for
those two books, and nobody forced the author to sell
them. So the author is helpless when some snaggle-
toothed goat-hair-bearded very late adolescent comes up
in a bar, clears his throat, and says, "Mr. Mailer, how
could you violate your ideals by allowing* An American
Dream *to be sold to the people who made the movie?"
Mr. Mailer must then button up and roll with the nausea
implicit in the rhythms of his interrogator's adenoids,
because there is no right reply left. You cannot say, "I
have become a little more corrupt than the last time you
saw me," to every adolescent around. Besides you have
to be over forty to appreciate the good Hemingway's remark that a man once past his own last point of terminal
honor, can from there on proceed only to lose more and
more of his soul, and the trick is thus to sell your soul
dear, to fight a tough rearguard battle and take as many
of the enemy as you can. (Which presumes a God back
of your soul, and devils to slay.) Well,* An American
Dream *was sold and I didn't take any of the enemy. They
took parts of me.*

*Now, what can you know, Under-Thirty, of these pas-
sions to write a book which will expose the Army, or make
a movie which will put a light to the gas in Hollywood's
leaky oven? These are unnatural passions when you,
young reader, have cut your reflexes on Bergman, Fellini, Antonioni, and everybody can see through the Army
by now. You don't want to reform Hollywood. It has its
thing, you have yours. Let Dick Van Dyke shake hands
with Debbie Reynolds any day.*

*But for those of us who grew up in another time, and
got to hate Hollywood intimately . . . do not despair*

of explanations. Hollywood was like a mother-in-law's mother-in-law. Locate your time historically. This was before Kerouac. Eisenhower was just beginning to hump the rhetoric to our respectful attention, Life magazine was still confident it could show people how to live, the CIA was then invisible but for a gleam in the secretary of state's eye, the corporations were still manufacturing products which were not wholly inadequate to their uses, and packaging was dull. Newspaper editorials reflected no quiver of doubt. Harlem was still a place to visit. And Hollywood was committing hara-kiri with a blunt knife. For those were the years when they got the communists out of Hollywood. All those poor writers and directors who had written all the patriotic movies in World War II — they had been the only ones who believed in Hollywood, they thought of her as a peasant queen with monumental capacities for reformation. Of course a character in a novel once said of Hollywood communists that they have the strength of big-breasted women, and these movie writers and directors were stuffniks. Which is to say they were stuffy with old platitudes which had rotted in old sentiments and they loved to try to stuff such stuff into everybody's head. Once they were exiled from Hollywood, or squeezed down into black-market work, the town lost its balance wheel. Under the pressure of television, it went all the way over to what it had promised to be at the beginning — an undifferentiated androgynous daisy chain, a victim of sexual entropy. Film power passed on to Europe. These communists had been the moral center of filmland, the bourgeois ever-living ever-loving family center, or at least in combine with the analysts they had been, and they had striven to make box-office pictures about social problems with middle-class answers. "Maturity" was the word they loved. Cigars used to glisten like wet turds when they intoned maturity.

That was the Hollywood one wanted to dynamite. That

silly monstrous cancerous country which ate at the best of oneself. It is just about gone now.

As a young man soon after the publication of The Naked and the Dead *I tried to work in Hollywood for a spell. I did my best, I wanted to amass experience for a novel, and so wished to succeed in the movie business in order to have the richest novelistic experience. But I wasn't very good at succeeding. There was something about the process of scriptwriting which did not fit with any reflex of mine. Like most young writers I was a hint phonier than I had to be, and borrowed influences at large (where would* The Naked and the Dead *have been without John Dos Passos and James T. Farrell?), and the upper reaches of my novelistic brain were mixed with the heavier greases of the lower academic literary apparatus, to wit, I thought in terms of symbols, forms, allegorical structures, classical myths — you know like many another touted young talent I could barely write a sentence if there was no way to convince myself it was not on five levels. Nonetheless, I still sensed that under all the Associated Merde and Dreck incorporated into my literary system, there was still a way to create, which was the only way to do it. And that was to keep the act of writing simple. If you wrote a thousand words on a morning and they proved later to be a good thousand words, and not a single formal thought entered your conscious mind while you were writing them, well, all the formal thought in you had gone then into the writing — none of it had been fed back into the ego-pool thinking box, there to be wasted.*

That was the good way to write, and presumably the good way to act and direct, and conceivably to box — it took even longer to learn that it might be the way to make love. Doubtless. The nature of anything life-giving, like a good movie or a good word, must remain secret for the simplest of reasons. For every lion of our human species there is, as we all know, a trough of pigs, and the pigs root up everything good so soon as the super-highway is laid out for them. So the best stays hidden. It must be that way.

And out there in Hollywood, I learned what pigs do when they want to appropriate a mystery. They approach in great fear and try to exercise great control. Fear + Control = Corporate Power. Corporate Power applied to art produces a product which is on balance equal to Liberace stripped of his virility.

Now, readers, we have not been treated to this much language for me merely to beat old Hollywood on the head with my stick. I want rather to underline and soon try to analyze the fact that the process of commercial film-making has a natural tendency to liquidate the collective human entity of the film, and so it is a living miracle, nothing less than a miracle, when a good big-budget movie is made, once you know, as few do, how absolutely deadening is the productive machinery of the cinematic full-length feature film.

Consider the movie script. A man or a team of men, who have the habit of regarding themselves as writers, begin by discussing a story. It is ninety-nine to one that the story originates not with them but with a book, magazine piece, play, former movie — we can skip these steps. Working on someone else's story is like raising another man's child. The moment a writer moves away from his basic connection to that unconscious which gives original words to the pencil in his fingers, art in its turn has given up a half-life. Witness, then, these Hollywood writers, singly or in team, who hobnob with producer, director, story editor, hordes of labially directed anxiety types who talk all the time. Large fear and large control — those are the protagonists who write the script. It bears the same relation to real writing, these endless discussions about form, plot, twist, and rooting interest, that a medical examination in the Army bears to the act of love.

Then comes the director and the producer, an ugly

jealous passionate fecal marriage of bitch and stud. That overworked scenario is ignited into its first roar and flame when producer and director set out to bugger one another. Indeed that's how agreeable bad movies sometimes get made. It's art by act of war, however, and the actors get ground between them.

Then we have the actors who deal with existential situations like love, sex, disaster, and death, all those ultimates whose ends are by their nature indeterminable: you are in an existential situation when something important and/or unfamiliar is taking place, and you do not know how it is going to turn out. Whereas professional acting consists of getting into situations where the actor knows precisely just how everything in the plot is going to turn out. The script is there, and from it he cannot escape very far. Acting and existentialism are therefore at the poles. If existentialism is ultimately concerned with the attractions of the unknown, acting is one of the surviving rituals of invocation, repetition, and ceremony — of propitiation to the gods. Talk of ultimates, maybe the actor lays ceremonial robes on his back in order to allay our fear of the wrath which lives in the pits of metaphysics. Ceremony is designed, you can say, to mollify the gods, to safeguard us from existential situations precisely because ceremony is repetition. There is some quality primitive, powerful, and weight-free about the act of acting once you get into it, something so close to a real existential situation, yet not by real measure dangerous at all, that actors often know the delight of children, whose inner landscape you may remember is always existential, for the denouement of a situation is to a child unknown and dangerous until that moment when the outcome is perceived.

Actors have it well made then if they can enjoy the act of acting, for they may at once propitiate the gods of dread, feel the power of full men, and have the sensuous empyrean awareness of a child, not to mention his tact.

Great popular actors are not called idols for nothing. They are revered as God, lover, and child all at once.

Now, of course, the model presented is too attractive. There is always for the stage actor the tension, horror, and most existential moment of the opening night, and there is besides, once the actor is not on the stage, the unspeakable insecurity of his life, the uncertainty of work, bread, love of his fellow actors, the existential (which is to say: dangerous) privations of poverty, the manic uprooting yaws of success which can propel him into a profound alienation away from the most rudimentary clues to his identity. It is not so easy to walk through life uncertain if you are god, fool, hero, or clown, or eventually some new species of man. Rich or poor, the likelihood is great that the actor has the most existential private life of any artist — if nothing else, he is obliged to live closer than other artists to the mystery of personality itself, which is — if you consider it — related directly to the mystery of choosing one style of personality in preference to another, provided of course one possesses the power to exercise more than a single style well.

But we must follow this through. If I, living with a woman, choose a style for my personality which, crudely, we may say is not quite me, I am nonetheless in a real relationship, certainly I am if my adopted personality is sufficiently imaginative, cohesive, and convincing, that is to say, well enough acted, to make the lady think it is — forgive this — the real me. Because then the real emotions of my sweet mate with their real concomitants, her very gifts and blows, begin to rain on me, and I prosper or falter on the basis of my adopted personality. Yet if I had adopted a different style of personality for the same woman, the gifts and blows would have been different. Now think of the actor who commands a choice of adopted personalities. The particular style he takes on for any role becomes as much an existential choice as the pose of the lover — the actor is subtly rewarded and/or punished by the real reactions he arouses and disappoints in his audience, which audience becomes for practical purposes the next thing to his real mate. How disagreeable then, even brutal, is the situation of the actor when his role is not adequate to him, when he cannot act with some subtle variations of his personal style. But, indeed the actor, living uncomfortably in that psychic ground between the real and the unreal, consummate creature of modern anxiety, can find his reality only in a role worthy of his complex and alienated heart. What chance then has he in that abominable industry script we have already described or in that bucket of fecal passions swilled in by director and producer? Not to mention our patriotic apparatus of bullies, censors, and banks which hangs like insect repellent over the making of films.

No, the actor, if he is a good talented sensitive actor, is shoveled between the maw and the mangle. For if his personality now consists of a hundred personalities, they are nonetheless like a hundred fine tools. Even if he can find some relationship to the script, and be not contradicted fatally in his work by the other actors or the director, and be not betrayed by the producer, not cheated by the cameraman, nor the film editor, nor sickened too profoundly by his publicity, he, the actor, must run nonetheless into the most unendurable trap of them all which is that the magic of the relationship he and the other actors have breathed into one another despite the script is a magic which must soon falter before the tyrannical insistence of the script that all characters and events be funneled through the narrow orifice of committee solutions to aesthetic problems. So the exceptional tools of the exceptional actor, his ten hundred antennae, his blades and springs, fine nerves and subtle heart, go all shuddering through the anesthetized fields of a com-

mercial script: he must violate all he has learned about relationship and its thousand-footed sensitivity.

Taken even at its best in the occasional script which is first-rate, noble, fine, and good — you may look long for such a script — with a director and producer who are wise, sensible in the art of interruption, illumined with those proper fires which can light a fire in the actor, and with a budget not so enormous that every scene must groan with the pomposities and platitudes of money pressing its weight upon itself, in this ideal situation, even here, with the best of honest lines to speak, the actor must still warp his art and devour his liver and/or his soul to make his exquisite sense of relationship submit to the form. At its worst, the making of films for popular consumption is a liquidation center for talent — at its best it is still a rabidly unnatural act, and everyone connected to it is, soon or late, miserable.

Well, it is hardly our aim to give comprehensive listing of the efforts directors have made to break such tyranny; so it is not our intention to talk of Rossellini and De Sica, of Ingmar Bergman, Fellini, Antonioni, of Truffaut. Nor is it part of the agenda to try for a quick run through the underground film and artists so diverse as Warhol, Brakhage, Kenneth Anger, the late Ron Rice, a dozen others — their variety is extraordinary, their research into techniques, orgies, optical extravaganzas, animation, surrealism, exquisite photography and claustrophobically inept photography have slashed out a hundred indications of new trail. Nor pertinent to talk of documentaries: no discussion will be found here of the work of Ricky Leacock, Shirley Clarke, Helen Levitt, Emile de Antonio, the Maysles brothers.

No, the point rather to be made is that with every rare exception admitted, with all honor to the five or ten good commercial films a year and the fifty other such films which will seem better in twenty-five years than they do now, and with all homage to the wit of the Camp, its triumph in 007, with all credit to the technical innovations of the underground, and the occasional epic or quiet piece of genre from the documentary, the fact remains that the contemporary film does not do enough, it does not give enough of a mirror to the complexity of our century. The production of the high-budget film is too massive to be sensitive. Of course, there are rebels in revolt upon this operation and they have explored their innovations out to insanity, but they have tended to avoid the center of the problem which remains: how to get a little of the real life — always complex — of a good actor into a film. That still remains the accident rather than the rule. The good professional actor succeeds occasionally against all odds — his eight or ten or twenty years of apprenticeship, his dedicated training, enable him to breathe a simulation of real life into the mechanical resolution of the commercial script. But at a predictable price: dead liver, soul a bit more in hock. Whereas, the greater liberty of the low-budget underground film is of necessity given to an unpaid actor who is therefore invariably an amateur, and so tends to project an agreeable, innocent, usually bizarre self-consciousness (much like the square and crazy flavor in the postures of a home movie). The underground movie tends for this among other reasons to become an inside joke, and looks for playful situations or nightmares which members of the club can appreciate out of the focus of their own games. But the average underground film is not rushing to give a mirror of the time, just an amusement-park mirror.

Now, the documentary, in contrast, is, of course, founded on our century, nowhere else, but since it substitutes legally real people for actors, the merit of the documentary still depends upon the importance of the situation, and not its subtlety or nuance. If we can conceive of putting the camera on a man in a witness box up on real trial for his real life, the possibility, although not the certainty, is present that the man may not try to act the way he thinks he ought to act before a camera. But Heisenberg's Principle of Uncertainty probably applies. Do you remember? The particle of the atom being observed by the recording apparatus is directly (unhappily for science) affected in its movements by the presence of the apparatus. So with the documentary. There is its flaw — right in the germ plasm of the documentary. The camera, recording a real man, creates a relative unreality. If I know the camera is recording me, the real Norman Mailer, playing Norman Mailer, then I am in the unhappy position of working directly for my own product, me. Consider this for a moment: it is almost impossible not to be false at some low level, false the way the president of a small business will be unctuous when he is interviewed about an item his company is making. Is the real-life manufacturer going to say the item is sleazy? Never. In fact, he may not admit even to himself that his new commodity is anything but good; nonetheless, the knowledge that he can only say it is good, that he has no option to do otherwise, infects everyone surrounding him, interviewer, cameraman, sound man, future audience. The fact that everybody knows what he will say, before he says it, produces that characteristic woodenness which besets the documentary, the television interview, and any photographic situation where the protagonist is there in his real name. The consequences are too numerous, the traps too consequential for the man who bears his own name to reveal a real theme to the camera.

We have then exhausted all the alternatives but the one which went into the making of Wild 90. The assumption must now arise that the director has been saying all along that Wild 90 is his secret solution to all these ills. But it is not true. The director would swear it. He would even be forced to admit that it is worth a fight to pretend *it is even a good movie. If it has its defenders, it has also its detractors and some of them would say that the first virtue of* Wild 90 *is that we get a good leisurely opportunity to see Mailer make an ass of himself.*

Nonetheless, one will pretend that Wild 90 *is good. In fact, the director, prejudiced, blown up with every imperative of self-interest, actually believes that his film contributes to no less than the general weal. So he will proceed to talk about its powers for uplift.*

TWENTY YEARS: There was once a guy an' he saw a little bird who was half dyin'. He was wounded. Hey, Prince, listen.

BUZZ CAMEO: Go ahead.

TWENTY YEARS: So he picked up this bird an' he said, "This bird gotta be warm." He looked in the field and there was a lotta cow flop — steamin' — it was warm. So he put the bird in the cow flop an' he figured that's gonna make it right. And he left — left the bird there. And the bird kinda warmed up — felt good. Started to tweet. Went tweet, tweet, tweet, tweet, tweet. . . . And . . .

BUZZ CAMEO: What a long story.

TWENTY YEARS: There was a fox an' he looked over the cow flop an' said, "Geez, never heard cow shit tweet before." And he walked over — he trotted over — an' he saw the bird an' he gobbled it up. Now the moral is — listen — it may not always be an enemy that puts you in shit, and it may not always be a friend who's gonna take you out of shit, but if you find yourself in cow shit, never sing. Got it? Never sing. If you ever find yourself in shit, don't sing.

What did we end up with? A picture about gangsters? Not quite. It is hardly certain there were ever three Italian gangsters like this, or three Irish gangsters, or even two and a half Jewish gangsters. Farbar, Knox, and Mailer had all grown up in Brooklyn, but they were not Italian. Still, nobody grows up in Brooklyn without learning something about Sicily. And that is what comes through in the movie — our idea of the Mob, and that partakes of the noblest spirit of comedy, because twentieth-century reality suddenly appears on the screen. It is not social reality, nor documentary reality, certainly not historical reality, nor even the reality of the Hollywood myth, no, it is a kind of psychological reality — it is our obviously not altogether perfect idea of what this movie should be like — and that proves to be very real, for it is at least evidence on the road to reality. Whereas most movies give indications only of the road to the void.

That is the nerve which illumines the picture. To everybody's surprise, Twenty Years, Cameo, and the Prince became more complex than characters usually become in a film. The picture took on that intricacy of detail and personality which is reserved usually to the novel or the extraordinary foreign film. It did not happen because the prime players were necessarily so talented, so improvisational, nor so deep, but because they were engaged in a way of making a movie which — considerably more than the average movie — had something to do with the way people acted in life. Yet the way people act in life is so general a notion for purposes of discussion that it may provide a superior means of focus to consider instead how people live in their dream.

It seems we have come back to the making of the film only to desert the subject immediately. A further expedition remains to us: the director's most revolutionary notion about the meaning of the dream and — its country cousin — the art of the novel. Without it, he could not truly describe the critical difference between conventional professional acting and the existential variety presented in *Wild 90*, nor could he prove his case that the conceivable reason his actors are so good is that they do not have lines to remember.

THE PRINCE: You listen. How'd you get that cleft in your chin? Old lang syne, that's how you got that cleft in your chin.

BUZZ CAMEO: Ya know, I realize you guys resent me 'cause I'm the best-lookin' one here.

THE PRINCE: You're the best-lookin' guy in the what? In this filthy hole? I'd hate to be the best-lookin' guy in this filthy hole. Wha' do you got to say to yourself? I'm the best-lookin' guy in a filthy hole.

Freud saw the dream as a wish fulfillment. It is a grand theory, but it hints of the sweets and sours of middle-class life and bouts of nocturnal enuresis. For if you are in the middle class, you do not have to make out well on a given day, you can brood about a loss, indulge a fantasy on the conversion of failure to success — yes, if you are middle class, the dream is a wish fulfillment. Art comes to the middle class on that bypass called sublimation.

But to the saint and the psychopath, the criminal, the hipster, the activist, the athlete, the stud, the gentleman sword, the supple stick, the dream is something else — a theatrical revue which dramatizes the dangers of the day — a production in which the world of the day is dissected, exaggerated, put together again in dramatic or even surrealist intensity in order to test the power of the nervous system to pass through shocks, ambushes, tests, crises, and pleasures — future impacts of which the unconscious has received warning the day before. In the quick blink of a friend's eyes, in the psychic plumbing of an odd laugh was disclosed to the unconscious a hint of treachery. So that night the scene is replayed in its complex condensation with other scenes, and the

Navigator in the mind of the hipster delineates for himself a better map, figures a little more precisely how to chart a course through the possible rapids soon to be encountered in his life.

The metaphor is shifting. It now seems that everyone has not only a private theatre for dreams but is possessed of a helmsman, or scout, or Navigator, who uses charts drawn from the experience of the past, maps drafted out of the emotions, education, and miseducation of childhood, the nuances, surprises, and predictable patterns of social life. These charts — submits our proposition — are altered every day of our life on the basis of what the day's experience has brought. They are kept up-to-date in order to transport us from the present into the unexpected contingencies of the future.

What am I saying really? Nothing more or less astounding than that every mortal (but for an occasional monster or vegetable) is elaborating somewhere in his mind the conception of a huge and great social novel. That unwritten unvoiced but nonetheless psychically real and detailed novel is precisely the map and/or chart from which the Navigator plots his course and selects his range of acts for tomorrow. (Indeed the dream may be the creative process which adds new refinements to the novel every night.) Yes, we not only possess that great novel in the map rooms of the self, but we are forever improving it, or at least altering it.

Let us ruminate upon this magnificent news. In the unconscious of each of us is then a detailed conception of a vast social novel greater than most of the vast social novels which have been written. In every last one of us just about lives a great novelist. Better than that. The Navigator not only dips into his fantasy or his dream for inspiration and information to serve up to the ever-evolving unwritten pages of his book, but he employs the goods he finds. He goes out the next day and walks the stage of his life as an actor. For we are not only novelists all, but we are actors all. Having a detailed conception of the world, accurate here, inaccurate there, we attempt not only to deal with the world on the basis of this conception or novel, but we push and press ourselves into styles of personality (like elegance or humility or graciousness or candor) which are not quite ourselves but will provide, or so believes our Navigator, a more effective mode for handling the events of our day. In short, we pretend to be what we are not. We are Actors. We are at least Actors a good deal of the time. Some of us are better than others, some more precise than others, or more passionate in our display of all-but-true emotion, but we are all vastly better actors than we suspect. At the least we are all more or less successful in seeming a little more or less sweet or powerful than we really are. Yet, and this is the horror of bad art, that social novel in the vaults of the unconscious, no matter how great, is nonetheless flawed in each of us by the misleading portraits of people and institutions we are fed via television and Hollywood. If the maps in this chart room of the unconscious are elaborate, they are also anchored on systematically induced misconceptions of society, and so are often as profoundly inaccurate as the maps with which Columbus set sail for Cathay. Of course a chart room with inaccurate maps is inviting its Navigator to courses of action which can plow a reef, and the actor who is serving as helmsman in the actions of the day may be psychotic in his lack of attachment to the reality of the wheel directly before him. Meretricious commercial art does not lead merely to bad taste, it pipes the nation toward psychosis. If you would look for an answer on why America — a conservative property-loving nation — is obsessed with destroying other nations' property, the answer can be found as quickly in bad movies as in bad politics. Which returns us to our quest: how does one get to the grail which blesses the making of a movie not entirely without honor?

Knock on door.

THE PRINCE: Who're you? Wait. Wait. Wait. (*Picks up gun, goes to door.*) Carmela. How are ya? Carmela. Hey Mickey. Mickey, look who's here. Your wife.

Carmela enters with a carton of milk.

TWENTY YEARS: Carmela. Ahhhhh. How are ya, Carmela? Why you come tonight? I mean, we need the milk, but you shouldn'ta come tonight. Carmela, you look great. Ahhh. How're the kids?

CARMELA: They ask for their father.

TWENTY YEARS: Yehhh. (*Looks her over, frowns.*) Listen, I see you went to the hairdresser. What do you go to the hairdresser for when I'm here? I mean, I don't like you to go to the hairdresser when I'm here. What do you got to get the nice hair for?

CARMELA: For you.

TWENTY YEARS: For me? I haven't seen you in a week. What is that crap? What's happening out there?

Follow it, now. Farber, Knox, and Mailer had a datum — three hoods in trouble holed up in a joint for twenty-one days. For that much, they were in accord. For the rest, they had each their own idea of what was going on, just as in everyday working life, if three businessmen meet, for example, at lunch, their datum could be that they are meeting to discuss some particular business. Yet each man remains his own protagonist. Since there is no written script, each of the three businessmen tends to see his own problems and feel his own personality in the foreground. Each of these businessmen has his own idea of how he wants the lunch to go, what he desires for a result. To the extent that the lunch drifts away from him, he tries to maneuver conversation back to where he thinks it should be. While he is working at this, he is also bluffing a bit, pretending to be friendly one moment, disinterested another, and all the while he is up to his ears in the lively act of shaping and trying to improve his existence by employing adopted, or at least slightly adapted, personalities. He is therefore acting. For — it is worth repetition — acting is not only the preserve and torture rack of the professional actor, but is also what we do when we enter into new relations with man, mate, associate, or child — we start with an idea of the situation before us and a project in our mind (or on occasion a vision) of how this situation can or should end. Then we work to fulfill our project. At the same time, the other man or woman is working to satisfy his plan. He is also acting. Acting in some degree at least. The result is not often geared to obey either project, but turns out willy-nilly to be the collective product, good or bad. That is about what happens at every business lunch, football game, fornication, prizefight, dinner party, and improvised performance. The product is the result, the result of the efforts, hang-ups, cooperations, and collisions of exactly as many protagonists as there are people involved. In life — let us underline the fell simplicity of this — every man is his own protagonist, he is out there acting away on his own continuing project, himself. Whereas in scripts, in written scripts, the natural tendency of any writer who might be dealing with three gangsters in a room would be to present, for purposes of clarity, no more than one protagonist and one project: the other characters would be subtly or not so subtly bent to serve the hero and his grip on the plot. So the other characters would become abstracts, stock characters. So movies remain just movies, simpler in their surface than life. That is why they are enjoyable, that is why they are also unsatisfying to our sense of existence.

In *Wild 90*, however, we had no script to reduce us — we were able to play through a situation with our own wit rather than with someone else's. Therefore we had an enormous advantage over an actor who has rehearsed his lines. For he has to pretend he is thinking of the line as he speaks, when in fact he is trying to remember it. That is indeed why most amateur actors are wooden — in their need to remember their lines, they can do nothing else for they are made uncomfortably aware by the bind of another man's words in their mouth that they are up there acting, and therefore exposing themselves. In contrast, we were forced, as in life, to speak where the moment led us. We were, consequently, forced to use only our own idea of how and where we wanted the picture to go, and this made for considerable intensity and concentration — which is exactly what actors look for. Moreover, the three of us shared, as shooting progressed, in the direct recollection of what we had already put into the film. So, we were forced to draw upon that instinctively, build upon it, naturally, just as people collect their varieties of mutual or gang experience in any new operation. So we also developed an unspoken but not often dissimilar idea of how the movie should move ahead, and this idea was always in danger of being disturbed and in fact sometimes was dislocated by the new actors who paid us visits — wives, girlfriends, prizefighters, brothers, police — because they knew less about our life in that room than we did. Again we moved on some parallel to what the situation might be in life. If the three of us were constantly needling each other, fighting, setting up reconciliations, forming alliances of two against one only to shift again, forever assaulting one another's egos, or putting them back together, it was different when the Outside arrived, when the police came, or our girlfriends came, for then our three separate little visions of the film tended to become one family project, we were metaphorically now more equal to a crew, we worked with the new actors to slip them, even force them, into our idea of what and where the picture should be, and the new actors worked to slide or yank the picture back over toward their idea. Conflicts, therefore, did not show via plot, or by the camera angles of hero vs. villain, rather from that more complex opposition which is natural to every social breath of manner, that primary if subtle conflict which comes from trying to sell your idea in company when others are trying to deny you. And, note this, with the same ambiguity attached to the moment, the same comic or oppressive ambiguity. For as a scene goes its way in life, we do not always know if our plans are working, or our scheme is about to be shot down, whether we are winning in our purpose or others think us a fool, we merely work to get our way and usually have to let it go at that.

That was about how our work went. We shot for four or five hours every night for four nights, never doing retakes, *never doing retakes* — for that would have gummed the experience on which we were building. Besides, we did not have the time or money. We rocked along for four nights, and finished with something like three hours of film, much in debt to the considerable skill of the lone cameraman. Pennebaker moved his twenty-four-pound rig through our scenes like an athlete, anticipating our moves, giving us fine footage to cut into ninety minutes of comedy, ambiguity, ease, candor, vitality, barbarity. Buy a ticket! But you may never get to see it. The instincts as a director are confessed to be deep and salving; the eye for editing, novelistically acute; the talents as an actor, swell, then monumental swell; financial courage as a producer, enormous; but common sense — no, I am void of that. For the last thing I said to the actors was: use any words you wish. They bathed their tongues in the liberty: obscenity pops from every pore of *Wild 90*. It evolved into the foulest-mouthed movie ever made, and is thus vastly contemporary and profoundly underground. If you live in a small town, you will not get to see it. Not if it's like the next small town. Which is a pity. For without a sound track this film is so chaste you could invite the bishop to a screening. Of course, he would be bored. Without a sound track, there's not much film to follow. Where was common sense?

But we invoke common sense with no great respect. It is obvious most of the merit of *Wild 90* is in or right next to the obscenity itself. The obscenity loosened stores of improvisation, gave a beat to the sound, opened the actors to figures of speech — creativity is always next to the verboten — and opens all of us now to the opportunity of puzzling the subject a dangerous step further.

THE PRINCE: Ya know he's the only guy I know, does a push-up, it hurts him in the ass.

TWENTY YEARS: He's got a big ass.

THE PRINCE: I wonder how he got the big ass. How'd you get the big ass?

TWENTY YEARS: Sittin'.

THE PRINCE: No, that ass is too big to get sittin'.

BUZZ CAMEO: That's a nice suit ya got there.

THE PRINCE: Ya know how he got that big ass? He got that big 'cause he has his radar in his ass.

Obscenity is, of course, a picayune topic for those not offended by it, but it does violence to the composure of those who are. It shatters a subtle and enjoyable balance — their sense of good taste. Yet the right to use obscene language in a movie (if there will come a day when the courts so decide it is a right) has at bottom nothing to do with questions of taste. One could show a man and woman naked in the sexual act, and yet done well, the filming could still be said to be in good taste — the film images might slip by as abstractly as the wash of waves against a piling. Yet I do not have the wish to film such a scene, good taste or poor. It is of course a problem no film director can decide in advance, for the twentieth century, our century of technology, the bomb, the concentration camp, the mass media, and the mass drug addiction, may yet be the century where the orgy and the collective replace the family. It is not necessarily a speculation to steep you in joy — in the depths of an orgy with the air full of smog, hard-beat fornications to the sound of air conditioners, nose colds, who indeed would want to film copulation in such a bag? Still, the century rushes toward this kind of investigation. One can easily foresee a movie which will depend for its motivation, nay, for its story itself, on the unveiling of the act. Still I would not wish to be the man who directed such a scene. These days, these years, we prong into the mystery from every angle, with scalpels, seminars, electronic probes, we cannot bear the thought any of this mystery might escape us; yet the nearer we come on our surreal journey toward the germ of the creation, the further we seem removed from a life which is collectively supportable — repeat: Vietnam, race riots, traffic, frozen food, and smog — all these certified brats of science — they are by-products of the technological race into the center of the mystery. So here there is no great desire to film the sexual act even if the camera work could be superb, the actors delighted in themselves, and taste all secure. You could almost say that the heart of the sexual act might be finally none of technology's business. And work in the world of the film is work in the fluorescent light of technology.

Yet here we have a director who makes a movie with more obscene language than any film ever made. How allay the contradiction?

The director would reply there is no contradiction because obscene language has nothing to do any longer with revelations of the sexual act, it is not even much of a sweetmeat anymore for the prurient, no, obscenity is rather become a style of speech, a code of manners, a transmission belt for humor and violence — it can shatter taste because it speaks of violence, it is probably the most ineradicable measure of the potential violence of social class upon class, for no one swears so much as the men of the proletariat when alone — that has not changed since Marx's time. Today obscene language bears about the same relation to good society that the realistic portraits of the naturalistic novel of Zola's time brought to the hypocrisies and niceties of the social world of France — the naturalistic novel came like high forceps to a difficult birth. Zola was tasteless, Zola outraged, Zola's work was raw as bile, but in its time it was essential, it gave sanity to the society of its time, it gave accuracy and deliverance for it helped to reduce the collective hypocrisy of the epoch, and so served to deliver the Victorian world from the worst of its Victorianism, and thus gave the world over to the twentieth century in slightly improved condition.

Well, one would not claim the shade of Zola's talents or merits for *Wild 90*. It is in the end a most modest pioneer work. It is indeed not even a naturalistic production, not nearly so much as it is one of the first existential movies ever made. Suffice the question in this way: we live in an American society which can remind you of nothing so much as two lobes of a brain, two hemispheres of communication themselves intact but surgically severed from one another. Between the finer nuances of High Camp and the shooting of firemen in race riots is, however, a nihilistic gulf which may never be negotiated again by living Americans. But this we may swear on: the Establishment will not begin to come its half of the distance through the national gap until its knowledge of the real social life of that other isolated and — what Washington will insist on calling — deprived world is accurate, rather than liberal, condescending, and over-programmatic. Yet for that to happen, every real and subterranean language must first have its hearing, even if taste will be in the process as outraged as a vegetarian forced to watch the flushing of the entrails in the stockyards. You can ask: what point to this? The vegetarian became a vegetarian precisely because he could not bear the slaughter of animals. Yes, your director will say, but let him see how it is really done, let him know it in detail. Then perhaps he will be twice the vegetarian he was before. Or maybe by picking up a gun to defend animals, he will kill humans and end as a cannibal.

Capital, you will say, your strategy for ambushing yourself is superb. You have just done in your argument.

No, rather something may have insisted on taking us further into the argument. The vegetarian, once become a cannibal, knows at least what he has become: if the world is thus turned a shift more barbarous, it is also a click less insane. Each year, civilization gives its delineated promise of being further coterminous with schizophrenia. Good taste, we would submit, may be ultimately the jailer who keeps all good ladies and angels of civilization firmly installed in the innocence of their dungeon, that Stygian incarceration whose walls are adorned with the elegant draperies of the very best and blindest taste. All kneel! Homage to my metaphor! The aim of a robust art still remains: that it be hearty, that it be savage, that it serve to feed audiences with the marrow of its honest presence. In the end, robust art pays cash, because in return for roiling the delicacies of more than one fine and valuable nervous system, it gives in return light and definition and blasts of fresh air to the corners of the world, it is a firm presence in the world, and so helps to protect the world from its dissolution in compromise, lack of focus, and entropy, entropy, that disease of progressive formlessness, that smog, last and most poisonous exhaust of the devil's foul mouth. Yeah, and yes! Ob-

scenity is where God and Devil meet, and so is another of
the avatars in which art ferments and man distills.

A Course in Film-Making

I. On the Theory

The company, jaded and exhausted, happily or unhappily sexed-out after five days and nights of movie-making
and balling in midnight beds and pools, had been converted to a bunch of enforced existentialists by the making of the film. There is no other philosophical word
which will apply to the condition of being an actor who
has never acted before, finding himself in a strange place
with a thoroughgoing swap of strangers and familiars
for bedfellows, no script, and a story which suggests that
the leading man is a fit and appropriate target for assassination. Since many of the actors were not without their
freaks, their kinks, or old clarion calls to violence, and
since the word of the Collective Rumor was that more
than one of the men was packing a piece, a real piece
with bullets, these five days and nights had been the advanced course in existentialism. Nobody knew what was
going to happen, but for one hundred and twenty hours
the conviction had been growing that if the warning system of one's senses had been worth anything in the past,
something was most certainly going to happen before the
film was out. Indeed on several separate occasions, it
seemed nearly to happen. A dwarf almost drowned in a
pool, a fight had taken place, then a bad fight, and on the
night before at a climactic party two hours of the most
intense potential for violence had been filmed, yet nothing commensurate had happened. The company was

now in that state of hangover, breath foul with swallowed curses and congestions of the instincts, which comes to prize-fight fans when a big night, long awaited, ends as a lackluster and lumbering waltz. Not that the party had been a failure while it was being filmed. The tension of the party was memorable in the experience of many. But, finally, nothing happened.

So, at this point next day in the filming of *Maidstone*, on the lazy afternoon which followed the night of the party, the director had come to the erroneous conclusion his movie was done — even though the film was still continuing in the collective mind of some working photographers before whom the director was yet to get hit on the head by a hammer wielded by his best actor, and would respond by biting the best actor on the ear, a fight to give him a whole new conception of his movie. What a pity to remind ourselves of these violent facts, for they encourage interest in a narrative which will not be presented in a hurry and then only a little, and that after an inquiry into the director's real interest which is (less bloody and more philosophical) the possible real nature of film — not an easy discussion since the director has already found a most special way of making movies. When he begins to discourse on the subject, he feels as if he is not so much a director as an Argument. He can literally think of himself as The Argument, some medieval wind — a Player who is there for harangue. Certainly in that precise hour of the afternoon when he took off his actor's cape and moved from Norman T. Kingsley back to Norman Mailer again, and gave an orientation on the grass of Gardiners Island, it could hardly be said that he failed to talk about his movie to the company. No, he made every effort, even went so far as to explain that his way of making films was analogous to a military operation, to a commando raid on the nature of reality — they would discover where reality was located by the attack itself, just as a company of Rangers might learn that the enemy was located not in the first town they invaded but another. Of course, even as he spoke, he felt the resumption of tension. There was still something wrong in the air. The picture, he could swear, but for some fill-in, was finished, yet the presence it created had not left.

He could, however, hardly complain if the film itself was still a *presence*. A condition of dread had been generated over the last five days which had put subtle terror and tension into the faces of people who had never acted before, lines of such delicate intent and fine signification as to draw the envy of professionals. That had been precisely the presence he wished to elicit. It was the fundament of his method, the heart of his confidence, to put untried actors into situations without a script and film them with simple or available lighting, work in the limitations of these means and unforeseen ends and exits to get the best available sound (which was not always near to superb), and yet, all limitations granted, he could by this method give a sense of the bewildering surface of his cinematic reality which was finer by far than the work of all but the very best film artists.

It was in other words, a Leviathan of a thesis, and he, with characteristic modesty, ignorant until a few years ago of nearly all to do with film-making, and still technically more ignorant than the good majority of mediocre directors, was still convinced he had wandered by easy progressions into a most complex and devilish way of working up a film. And now had the confidence he was a film maker. And the unique experience to convince himself that he was a pioneer, for he believed he had come upon a way to smash the machine which crushed every surface of cinematic reality, that organization of plot, dialogue, sets, professionals, schedules, and thundering union impedimenta which beat every effort to take a good story or a book and flesh it into movie film. No, something was wrong with that, something was dreadfully wrong with a process which wasted time, talent, and millions of dollars at a crack to produce cinematic works of the most predictable encapsulation. One could sit through such works and on rare occasion even enjoy a world of good taste and nice insight without ever a moment of sensuous discomfort, which was exactly equal to saying without a moment of aesthetic revelation.

Still it is something to skip at a leap over thirty years of movie-making apprenticeship he has not served, to propose that, all ignorance and limitations granted, he has found a novel technique, and is on the consequence ready to issue a claim that his way of putting a film together, cut by cut, is important, and conceivably closer to the nature of film than the work of other, more talented directors.

2

Of course, he makes no second claim that technically, gymnastically, pyrotechnically, or by any complex measure of craft does he begin to know the secrets of the more virtuoso of the directors and the cutters, no, he would only say that the material he has filmed lends itself happily, even innocently, to whole new ways of making cuts. That is because it has captured the life it was supposed to photograph. He is unfolding no blueprint. So there tends to be less monotony to his composition, less of a necessity to have over-illumined and too simplified frames, less of a push to give a single emphasis to each scene. His lines of dramatic force are not always converging toward the same point — nobody in his frame has yet learned to look for the reaction of the hero after the villain insults him, no, his film is not diminished by supporting actors who are forever obliged to indicate what the point of the scene is supposed to be (and are thereby reminiscent of dutiful relatives at a family dinner). So, his movie is not reminiscent of other films where the scene — no matter how superb — has a hollow, not so pervasive perhaps as the cheerful hollow in the voices of visitors who have come to be cheerful to a patient in a hospital, but there, even in the best of films always there. In the worst of films it is like the cordiality at the reception desk in a mortician's manor. So it could even be said that professional movie-acting consists of the ability to reduce the hollow to an all but invisible hole, and one can measure such actors by their ability to transcend the hollow. Marlon Brando could go "Wow" in *Waterfront* and Dustin Hoffman would limp to the kitchen sink in *Midnight Cowboy* and the lack of life in the conventional movie frame was replaced by magical life. One could speak with justice of great actors. Perhaps a thousand actors and two thousand films can be cited where the movie frame comes alive and there is no dip at the foot of consciousness because something is false at the root.

Nonetheless any such appearance of talent was close to magic. The conventional way of making most films usually guaranteed its absence. For there was an element which interfered with motion pictures as much as the blurring of print would hinder the reading of a book, and this flaw derived from the peculiar misapprehension with which the silent film gave way to sound, the supposition that sound-and-film was but an extension of the theatre, even as the theatre was but an extension of literature. It was assumed that movies were there to tell a story. The story might derive from the stage, or from the pages of a book, or even from an idea for a story, but the film was asked to issue from a detailed plan which would have lines of dialogue. The making of the movie would be a fulfillment of that script, that literary plan; so, each scene would be shaped like a construction unit to build the architecture of the story. It was one of those profoundly false assumptions which seem at the time absolute common sense, yet it was no more natural than to have insisted that a movie was a river and one should always experience, while watching a film, emotions analogous to an afternoon spent on the banks of a stream. That might have been seen instantly as confining, a most confining notion; but to consider the carry-over of the story from literature to the film as equally constricting — no, that was not very evident.

For few people wished to contemplate the size of the job in transporting a novelist's vision of life over to a film; indeed, who in the movie business was going to admit that once literary characters had been converted over to actors, they could not possibly produce the same relation to other actors that the characters once had to each other? Interpretations had to collide. If each actor had his own idea of the dialogue he committed to memory, be certain the director had a better idea. And the producer! Lifetimes of professional craft go into halving such conceptual differences. The director gives up a little of his interpretation, then a little more, then almost all of it. The actor is directed away from his favorite misconceptions (and conceptions). Both parties suffer the rigor mortis of the technical conditions — which are not so close to a brightly lit operating theatre as to a brightly lit morgue. Then the scriptwriter has dependably delivered the scenario with his own private — and sometimes willful — idea buried in it (and if the work is an adaptation, odd lines of the novelist are still turning over). The coherence of the original novel has been cremated and strewn. Now the film is being made with conflicting notions of those scattered ashes. Of course the director is forced back willy-nilly to his script. It is all he can finally depend upon. Given the fundamental, nay, even organic, confusion on a movie set over what everybody is really doing, the company has to pool all differences and be faithful to the script even when the script has lost any relation to the original conception, and has probably begun to constrict the real life which is beginning to emerge on the set. No wonder great novels invariably make the most disappointing movies, and modest novels (like *The Asphalt Jungle*) sometimes make very good movies. It is because the original conception in modest novels is less special and so more capable of being worked upon by any number of other writers, directors, and actors.

Still, the discussion has been too narrow. The film, after all, is fed not only by literature but by the theatre, and the theatre is a conspicuous example of how attractively a blueprint can be unfolded. In fact, the theatre is reduced to very little whenever the collaboration between actors and script is not excellent. Yet the theatre has had to put up with many a similar difficulty. Can it be said that something works in the theatre which only pretends to work in the film? If the first error perpetrated upon movies has been to see them as an adjunct of literature, perhaps the second is the rush to make film an auxiliary of the theatrical arts, until even movies considered classics are hardly more than pieces of filmed theatre.

Of course a film lover could counter by saying that he was not necessarily thinking only of such monuments as *Gone with the Wind* when he used the term classic. In fact, he would inquire about *A Night at the Opera* or *The Maltese Falcon*.

The difficulties had obviously begun. The Argument would be never so simple again. The Marx Brothers, for example, stampeded over every line of a script and tore off in enough directions to leave concepts fluttering like ticker tape on the mysterious nature of the movie art. Certainly, any attempt to declare *The Maltese Falcon* a piece of filmed theatre would have to confess that *The Maltese Falcon* was more, a mysterious ineffable possession of "more" and that was precisely what one looked for in a film. It was a hint to indicate some answer to the secrets of film might begin to be found in the curious and never quite explained phenomenon of the movie star. For Humphrey Bogart was certainly an element of natural film, yes, even *the* element which made *The Maltese Falcon* more than a excellent piece of filmed theatre. Thinking of the evocative aesthetic mists of that movie, how could the question not present itself: why did every piece of good dramatic theatre have to be the enemy of the film? It was unhappily evident to The Argument that any quick and invigorating theses on the character of movie stars and the hidden nature of the movie might have to wait for a little exposition on the special qualities of theatre.

3

A complex matter. You might, for instance, have to take into account why people who think it comfortable to be nicely drunk at the beginning of a play would find it no pleasure to go to a movie in the same condition. Pot was more congenial for a film. If the difference for most hardworking actors between movies and theatre seemed hardly more than a trip across a crack, the split to any philosopher of the film was an abyss, just that same existential abyss which lies between booze and the beginnings of the psychedelic.

Existentially, theatre and film were in different dominions (and literature was probably nearer to each of them than they were to each other). The theatre was a ceremony with live priests who had learned by rote to pool their aesthetic instincts for a larger purpose. So theatre partook of a near obscene ceremony: it imitated life in a living place, and it had real people as the imitators. Such imitation was either sacrilege to the roots of life, or a reinforcement of them. Certainly, sentiments called religious appeared ready to arise whenever a group of people attended a ceremony in a large and dimly lit place. But in fact anyone who has ever experienced a moment of unmistakable balance between the audience, the cast, the theatre and the *manifest* of the play, an awe usually remarked by a silence palpable as the theatrical velvet of an unvoiced echo, knows that the foundation of the theatre is in the church and in the power of kings, or at least knows (if theatre goes back to blood sacrifices performed in a cave — which is about where the most advanced theatre seems ready to go) that the more recent foundations were ecclesiastical and royal. Theatre, at all of its massive best, can be seen as equal to a ceremony, performed by noblemen who have power to chastise an audience, savage them, dignify them, warm them, marry their humors, even create a magical forest where each human on his seat is a tree and every sense is vibrating to the rustle of other leaves. One's roots return then to some lost majesty of pomp and power. Of course, theatre is seldom so good. None of us have had a night like that recently. Still, theatre has its minutes: a scene whose original concept was lost in the mixing of too many talents is recovered by the power of the actor to open relations with his audience. While he is engaged in an emotional transaction which is false by its nature (because he knows by heart the lines of apparently spontaneous passion he will say next), still he has to be true to the honest difficulty of not knowing whether the audience will believe him or not. His position on stage is existential — he cannot know in advance if his effort will succeed or not. In turn, the audience must respect him. For he is at the least brave enough to dare their displeasure. And if he is bad enough . . . well, how can he forget old nightmares where audiences kill actors? So the actor on stage is at once a fraud (because he pretends to emotion he cannot by any Method feel absolutely — *or he would be mad*) and yet is a true man engaged in a tricky venture, dangerous in its potentialities for humiliation. That is the strength of the theatre. A vision of life somewhat different each night comes into existence between the actors and the audience, and what has been lost in the playwright's vision is sometimes transcended by the mood of a high theatrical hearth.

We are speaking of course only of the best and freshest plays. Even in a good play something dies about the time an actor recognizes that he can be mediocre in his performance and survive. The reputation of the play has become so useful that the audience has become a touch mediocre as well; at this point in the season the actor inevitably becomes as interesting as a whore in a house after her favorite client has gone for the night.

Nonetheless, it is still reminiscent of orgy to have relations with two worlds of sentience at once, and when fresh, theatre is orgy. On stage, the actor is in communion with the audience and up to his neck in relations with other actors (if they are all still working together). A world of technique supports them. There are ways and means to live and act with half-thought-out lines of dialogue and errors of placement by the director, ways to deal with sentiments which have no ring and situations one knows by heart and still must enter with a pretense of theatrical surprise. An actor's culture exists, after all, for the working up of the false into the all-but-true; actors know the audience will carry the all-but-true over into the real and emotionally stirring if given a chance. So actors develop a full organ of emotional manifests. Large vibrant voices, significant moves. It all works because the actor is literally alive on a stage and therefore can never be false altogether. His presence is the real truth: he is at once the royal center of all eyes, and a Christian up before lions. So his theatrical emotion (which bears the same relation to real emotion which veneer of walnut bears to walnut) is moved by the risk of his position into a technique which offers truth. A skillful actor with false gestures and false emotions elicits our admiration because he tries to establish a vault under which we can seize on the truth since, after all, he has told the lie so well. Why, then, must that be an emotional transaction light years of the psyche away from the same transaction carried over to film?

4

It is because the risk in film is of other varieties. No audience is present unless the actor plays his scene for the cameramen and the union grips. And that is a specific audience with the prejudices and tastes of policemen. Indeed they usually dress like cops off duty and are built like cops (with the same heavy meat in the shoulders, same bellies oiled on beer), which is not surprising for they are also in surveillance upon a criminal activity: people are forging emotions under bright lights.

But it is no longer false emotion brought by technique to a point where it can be breathed upon and given life by audiences who do not know the next line. No, now the crew is a set of skills and intelligences. They are as sophisticated to the lines of the scene as the actors themselves. Like cops they see through every fake move and hardly care. The camera must move on cue and the sound boom, the lights be shifted and the walls slid apart — the action is easily as complex as a professional football team running through the intricacies of a new play or preparing a defense against it.

In fact, the actor does not usually play for the technicians. It is the director whose intelligence he will feel first, a charged critical intelligence knowing more of the scene than himself, a center of authority altogether different from a theatrical audience's authority (which is ready to relax with every good sound the actor makes). The movie director, however, does not relax then. The good sound of the actor can turn the plot inside out. No, here, the actor must work into a focus of will. The real face he speaks to, whether a step or ten steps to the side of the director, is a circle of glass as empty of love as an empty glass. That lens is his final audience. It takes precedence over the director and even over the actors he plays with. In the moment of his profoundest passion, as he reaches forward to kiss the heroine with every tenderness, his lips to be famous for their quiver, he is of course slowly and proficiently bringing his mouth up to the erogenous zone of the lens.

On stage, an actor, after twenty years of apprenticeship, can learn to reach the depths of an audience at the moment he is employing the maximum of his technique. A film actor with equivalent technique will have developed superb skills for revealing his reaction to the circle of glass. He can fail every other way, disobey the director or appear incapable of reacting to his direction, leave the other actors isolated from him and with nothing to react to, he can even get his lines wrong, but if he has film technique he will look sensational in the rushes, he will bring life to the scene even if he was death on the set. It is not surprising. There is something sinister about film. *Film is a phenomenon whose resemblance to death has been ignored for too long.* An emotion produced from the churn of the flesh is delivered to a machine, and that machine and its connections manage to produce a flow of images which will arouse some related sentiment in those who watch. The living emotion has passed through a burial ground — and has been resurrected. The living emotion survives as a psychological reality; it continues to exist as a set of images in one's memory which are not too different, as the years go by, from the images we keep of a relative who is dead. Think of a favorite uncle who is gone. Does the apparatus of the mind which flashes his picture before us act in another fashion if we ask for a flash of Humphrey Bogart next? Perhaps it does not. Film seems part of the mechanism of memory, or at the least, a most peculiar annex to memory. For in film we remember events as if they had taken place and we were there. But we were not. The psyche has taken into itself a whole country of fantasy and made it psychologically real, made it a part of memory. We are obviously dealing with a phenomenon whose roots are less defined than the power and glory of king and church. Yes, movies are more mysterious than theatre; even a clue to the undefinable attraction of the movie star is that he remains a point of light in that measureless dark of memory where other scenes have given up their light. He has obviously become a center of meaning to millions, possessed of more meaning than the actor next to him who may be actually more attractive, more interesting — definition of the phenomenon frays as we try to touch it. But has the heart of the discussion been sounded? Does it suggest that movie stars partake of the mysterious psychic properties of film more than other actors? that something in them lends itself to the need of memory for images of the past one can refer to when the mind has need to comprehend something new before it? We have to be careful. It is perhaps not so simple as that. The movie star may also suggest obsession, that negative condition of memory, that painful place to which we return over and over because a fundamental question is still unresolved: something happened to us years ago which was important, yet we hardly know if an angel kissed us then or a witch, whether we were brave or timid. We return to the ambiguity with pain. The obsession hurts because we cannot resolve it and so are losing confidence in our ability to estimate the present.

Obsession is a wasteful fix. Memory, when it can be free of obsession, is a storehouse to offer up essences of the past capable of digesting most of the problems of the present, memory is even the libido of the ego, sweetening harsh demands of the will when memory is, yes, good. But the movie star seems to serve some double function: the star feeds memory *and* obsession — one need only think back to one's feelings about Marilyn Monroe! The movie star is welcoming but mysterious, unavailable yet intimate, the movie star is the embodiment of a love which could leave us abject, yet we believe we are the only soul the movie star can love. Quintessence of the elusive nature of film, the movie star is like a guide to bring us through the adventures of a half-conscious dream. It is even possible the movie star gives focus to themes of the imagination so large, romantic, and daring that they might not encounter reality: how can an adolescent have any real idea whether he will ever have sex with a beautiful woman or fight for his life? Nonetheless, events so grand might need years of psychic preparation. It was therefore also possible that the dream life of the film existed not only to provide escape but to prepare the psyche for apocalyptic moments which would likely never come.

Some differences of film from theatre may then have been noted. Theatre works on our ideas of social life and our understanding of manners. At its most generous, theatre creates a communion of bodies and a savory of the emotions — it becomes a feast and a fuck. But film speaks to the lost islands of the mind. Film lives somewhere in that underground river of the psyche which travels from the domain of sex through the deeps of memory and the dream, on out into the possible montages of death — we need only think of any man who was rescued from drowning after he thought he was on the last trip down. Does he ever relate the experience without speaking of the sensation that his life became a film running backward? *It is as if film has an existence within the brain which may be comparable to memory and the dream,* be indeed as real as memory and the dream, be even to some degree as functional. It was as if the levels of that existential river which runs into ultimate psychic states would no longer read as perhaps once it did: sex — memory — dream — death; but now flows through a technological age and so has to be described by way of sex — memory — *film* — dream — death. Theatre has to be in the world of manners, but film is in the physiology of the psyche. For that reason, perhaps, film comes nearest to a religion as the movie houses are empty, it speaks across all the lonely traverses of the mind, it is at its most beautiful in precisely those places it is least concrete, least theatrical, most other-worldly, most ghostly, most lingering unto death — then the true experience of the film as some Atlantis of the psyche will manifest itself, and directors like Antonioni and Bergman will show us that the film inhabits a secret place where the past tense of memory and the future intimations of the dream are interchangeable, are partners in the film: there is an unmistakable quality to any film which is not made as filmed theatre but rather appears as some existence we call film. That existence runs through Chaplin and *Sunset Boulevard* and *Persona* — it runs through home movies. It was Warhol's talent to perceive that in every home movie there is a sense of Time trying to express itself as a new kind of creation, a palpability which breathes in the *being* of the film. The best of works and some of the worst of film works have this quality. One can even find it for flashes in cranky old battered films of the purest mediocrity late at night on TV, B-films without an instant of talent, yet the years have added magic to what was once moronic — Time is winking her eye as we look at the film. Time suddenly appears to us as a wit.

Of course, there are movies which have delivered huge pleasures to millions and never were film at all, just celluloid theatre convertible to cash. Some were good, some very good, some awful, but the majority of motion pictures, particularly the majority of expensive ones, have always labored against the umbilical antipathy of film for theatre. They were, no matter how good as filmed theatre, never equal to theatre at its best — rather, scaled-down repasts for the eye and ear. They had a kind of phlegmatic tempo and all-too-well-lit color which rarely hindered them from reaching lists for the Ten

Best Pictures of the year. They were pictures like *Okla-homa!*, *South Pacific*, *The Sound of Music*, *Mary Pop-pins*, and *The Best Years of Our Lives*. They were even such critical favorites as *Marty*, *Born Yesterday*, *Brief Encounter*, and *The Seven Year Itch*, or *Anne of the Thousand Days*, add *Lust for Life*, *All About Eve*, *Around the World in Eighty Days*, *West Side Story*. All that celluloid was super-technique for audiences who had not necessarily ever seen a play but were constantly nourished in the great cafeteria of the American Aes-thetic where the media meals were served up as binder for the shattered nervous system of the masses. To the owners of that cafeteria there was something obscene in the idea that one should not be able to translate a book into a play, film, or TV series — something arrogant, for it would say the difference between the movies just named and films like *Zabriskie Point, M.A.S.H., Naked Summer, Belle de Jour, Limelight, Diabolique, 8½, The Bicycle Thief, The Four Hundred Blows, High Noon, Easy Rider,* and *Weekend* were as the difference between crud and sustenance for that ghostly part of the psyche the film was supposed to enrich.

5

Very well. He had his point at least. There was film and filmed theatre; there were relatively pure movies, and there were money-making motion pictures which had al-most nothing to do with movies or memory or dream, but were filmed circus for the suckers who proceeded to en-joy them enormously (when they did — for some cost canyons of cash and brought back trickles), suckers who loved them for their binding glue, and the status of seeing them, and the easy massage such pictures gave to emotions real theatre might have satisfied more. These motion pictures, made for no motive more in focus than the desire for money, were derived from plays, or were written and directed as filmed plays, they composed three-quarters to nine-tenths of the motion pictures which were made, and they might yet be the terminal death of Hollywood for they were color television on enormous screens and so failed more often than they succeeded; the media were mixed so the messages were mixed — audiences tended to regard them with apathy.

Of course the films he loved were just as often watched in empty theatres, but if he would call upon the difference it was that they were not regarded in apathy but in subtle fear or mixed pleasure or with gloom or dread or the kind of fascination which hinted uncomfortably at future obsession. There was a quality he could almost lay his hands on in movies he admired and so would raise to the superior eminence of Film: they were experiences which were later as pure in recollection as splendid or tragic days in one's life, they were not unlike the memory of some modest love which did not survive but was tender in retrospect for now it lived with the dignity of old love. Such films changed as one remembered them since they had become part of one's psychological life. Like love, they partook a little of some miracle, they had emerged from the abominable limitations of the script, yes, they had emerged out of some mysterious but wholly agreeable lack of focus toward that script in the intent of the director and/or the actor, they were subtly attached to a creative mist, they had the ambiguity of film. For if filmed theatre could sometimes be effective, sometimes be even as perfect and deserving of admiration as *Midnight Cowboy* or *On the Waterfront*, such pictures still had their aesthetic fired by the simpler communication of the theatre where relations between actors usually produced a dramatic outcome as capable of definition as the last line of a family fight. "Go to an analyst" turned out to be the message, or "Lover, we'll get along," or "God bless us, we're unhappy, but we'll stick for the kids." If it is theatre so rich as *The Little Foxes*, it will say, "I am prepared to kill you, and I will." Since the need of a stage actor is to draw an audience together, his instinct is to simplify the play and concentrate it, give it a single crisp flavor. So theatre speaks. Powerfully or with banality, comically, or in the botch of hysteria, it speaks, secretly it almost always speaks vulgarly, for almost always it says, "We're here to tell you something about life. We've got a piece of the meat for you." Of course if it is bad theatre, conceived in advance as a television series or any other form of Cafeteria, then it is only there to tell you something about public opinion and how that works at the lowest common denominator. But good or bad, theatre functions at its simple best when every resonance of the evening can collect about a single point — that place where the actors seduced the audience to meet the play.

Film, however, is shown to audiences who do not often react together. Some laugh, while others are silent, some are bored. Few share the same time. They have come in on the movie at different places. For film always speaks of death. Theatre rouses desires between the living audience and the living actors; film stirs suicide pacts where each individual in the audience goes over the horizon alone with the star; film speaks of the ambiguity of death — is it nothingness we go to, or eternal life? Is it to peace we travel or the migrations of the soul? So the ambiguity of the movie star is essential, and it helps to understand that subtle emptiness which is usually present in the colors of their acting, that pause in the certainty of what they would say, that note of distraction and sorrows on the other side of the hill, that hint they are thinking of a late date they will meet after this guy is gone. Movie stars are caught in the complexity of the plot but they do not belong to it altogether, as stage actors do. It does not matter of whom we speak: whether it is Garbo or Harlow or Marilyn Monroe, Carole Lombard or Myrna Loy, even Dottie Lamour or Grable, the star is still one misty wink of the eye away from total absorption. Even Cagney, phallic as a column of rock, had the hint of bells ringing in his head from blows some big brother gave him in years gone by, and Gable's growling voice always seemed to hint at one big hunk of *other* business he would have to take care of in a little while. The charisma of the movie star spoke of associations with tangential thoughts, with dissipations of the story-point into ripples which went out wider and wider, out to the shores of some land only the waves of the movies could wash.

Now, much of that was gone. There were still stars, even in color film there were bona fide stars. There was Catherine Deneuve and Robert Redford and huge box-office familiars predictable as the neighbor next door and twice as vivid — Bob Hope and Lucille Ball for two. If film spoke of death, motion-pictures-for-money spoke of everything which was boring, unkillable, and bouncy, and could be stopped with a switch quick as TV, and was by couples necking in drive-in theatres. The film had also become brands of sex marked R, X, and Hard-Core, the film was epic documentaries like *Woodstock* and *Gimme Shelter*, the film was *Pound* and *Trash* and *Performance*, which some called great and some would not, the film was in transition, the film was in a place no one could name, and he was there with *Maidstone,* caught in the position of talking about a film made near to three years before. Three years was a decade in the recent history of the film. Half of the shock in his sexual scenes was nearly as comfortable by now as the lingerie ads in a fashion magazine, and his emphasis on film without script was evident in small uses everywhere, it had begun for that matter as long ago as Cassavetes' *Shadows*, a film of the fifties he did not particularly remember, but then for that matter, film without script had begun with the two-reeler and the sequence of action worked out on the director's white starched cuff. It was finally not to the point. He had had a conception of film which was more or less his own, and he did not feel the desire to argue about it, or install himself modestly in a scholar's catalogue of predecessors and contemporaries, it seemed to him naturally and without great heat that *Maidstone* was a film made more by the method by which it had been made than any film he knew, and if there were others of which it could be said that they were even more, he would cheer them for the pleasure of seeing what was done. But his film was his own, and he knew it, and he supposed he could write about it well enough to point out from time to time what was special and mysterious in the work, and therefore full of relation to that argument about cinema which has brought us this far, cinema — that river enema of the sins. Wasn't there whole appropriation of meaning in every corner of the mogul business?

II. In the Practice

He had, of course, embarked on the making of *Maidstone* with his own money, had in fact sold a piece of his shares of *The Village Voice*, a prosperous and sentimental holding. Not wishing to undergo the neurotic bends of trying to raise funds for a film he would begin shooting in a few weeks without a line of script or the desire to put anything on paper — he looked with horror on such a move! — he had small choice. Who would give him funds on past performance? In his first picture the sound was near to muffled; the second, while ready to be shown in the fall at the New York Film Festival, was nonetheless not yet evidence at a box office, and in fact had been sold to a distributor for fifteen thousand dollars, a small sale even for a movie which had cost no more than sixty.

It was of course possible he could have raised the money. The market was full of profit that year. Risk capital ready for tax loss could have been found. He did not try. There was some marrow of satisfaction in paying for it himself. So he sold a portion of *The Voice* and did not look back. The film was calling to him with every stimulus and every fear. He had, after all, conceived the heart of his movie in the days right after the assassination of Robert Kennedy, a time when it seemed the country was getting ready to blow its separate conventions apart (and indeed he was the man least surprised when the Democratic convention in Chicago had responsible politicians talking of the Reichstag fire). Besides, he was a guilty American, guilty with the others — he felt implicated in the death of Bobby, although he could never name how (short of fornicating with a witch on the afternoon of the deed) he must therefore be so responsible; nonetheless he was, he felt, along with ten million others — perhaps a backlash from years of living with Kennedy jibes and making some of them himself, perhaps from some unconscious delinquency which amounted to more.

In any case, a film he had contemplated for a year, a modest little film to take place in a bar with pimps waiting for their whores and then dealing with them, now turned inside out. He would use that original idea for the core of a larger story, as the sketch of a film to be made by a famous film director within a larger film. This film director would be one of fifty men whom America in her bewilderment and profound demoralization might be contemplating as a possible President, a film director famous for near pornographic films would be, yes, in range of the Presidency — what a time for the country! Now the last of his elements of plot came into place: there would be an elite group of secret police debating the director's assassination. What an impulse to put this into a script! But writing such a script and managing to direct it would take three years, and call for working with executives in a studio. Others would devour his story and make it something else. He preferred to make it himself, preferred to lose the story himself.

He knew from his experience with *Beyond the Law* (a film of the greatest simplicity next to this!) that when actors were without lines and the end of a scene was undetermined, one did not control the picture. Even if he would be in the middle of the film, would play in it as he had in the two others, would in fact play the leading role of the director (indeed find another actor on earth to even believe in such a role!), that did not mean the film would proceed as he had planned. At best, making movies by his method was like being the hostess at a party with a prearranged theme — at a party, let us say, where everybody was supposed to come dressed in black or white with the understanding that those in black should pretend to be somber in mood and those in white be gay. The guests would of course rebel, first by tricks, then by open stands. A beauty would arrive in red. The party would get away from the hostess constantly — as constantly would she work to restore it to the conception with which she began, yes, she would strive until the point where the party was a success and she could put up with her rules being broken. There would be art in the relinquishing of her strength. If the party turned out to be superb it would be the product not only of her theme, nor of the attack of her guests upon it, but her compensatory efforts to bring the party back to its theme. The history of what happened at her party was bound to prove more interesting than her original plan. Indeed, something parallel to that had occurred with *Beyond the Law*. He had started with an idea of putting together police, a police station, and the interrogation of suspects. But his actors had been as rich in ideas. In trying to keep them within his conception, the picture had taken on a ferocious life.

Yet with *Maidstone* he decided to gamble by a bolder step. Given his plot, he would be obliged to separate his

functions as director and actor. It would help his performance if the actor passed through situations he could
not dominate because he had also as director had the
privilege of laying his eyes on every scene. It was important, for example, that the secret police who would look
to assassinate him be able to have their plots filmed
without his knowledge. On that account he had assigned
directorial powers to several of the actors. They could
pick photographers to do their scenes, scenes he would
not see until filming was done. So too had he assigned
autonomy to Rip Torn who would play Raoul Rey O'Houlihan, his fictional half-brother, an obvious potential assassin in the film — whether Rey would actually strike
was tacitly understood to be open to the pressures within
the making of the movie. Since Rey would also have the
Cashbox, a Praetorian Guard loyal either to Rey or to
Kingsley, that must prove still another undetermined element in the film. Of necessity, therefore, would Rey have
photographers he could call on. So the company as a
whole had five cameras for use — four Arriflex and one
Eclair — five teams composed of a cameraman and
sound man who were sometimes interchangeable, each
team independent, each able to work under available
light conditions which might vary from splendid to ab-
surdly difficult, five teams to be spread out on certain
days as much as five miles apart, for he had managed to
capture the use of four fine houses for the week of shooting the film, an exercise in diplomacy he had not been
capable of on any other weekend in his life, he had the
estates, and kept them by a further exercise of diplomacy
through the weeks before the picture and into the shooting. There were crises every day and he was on the edge
of losing more than one set of grounds on more than one
day, but the torrent of preparations was on, his energy
was carried with the rush — in a few weeks they began
with a cast of fifty or sixty (new actors coming and leaving all the time), a capital of seventy thousand dollars,

an availability of forty or fifty hours of sound and film, an average of eight to ten hours for each cameraman in a week of shooting which would begin on a light day of work for Wednesday, would pass through the heaviest of schedules on Thursday, Friday, Saturday, Sunday, and finish with light work on Monday and Tuesday, an impossible speed for anyone fixed to the script of a movie as ambitious as this, but he had cards to play. They were his cameramen.

2

They had almost all taken part in the making of *Monterey Pop*, which had some of the best cinematography he had ever seen. They had many other credits. That was hardly the point. It was more to the issue that the stodgy unhappy catatonia of the old documentary, where people bearing real names sat in chairs and explained in self-conscious voices what they were up to, had been liberated by the invention of a *wireless* synchronizer between camera and tape recorder. A cameraman free of the caution that he must always move in ways the sound man could follow (since they had once been connected by a leash to one another) was now able to get around as he wished; he could stand on a ladder or slide on his belly, he could walk while filming and turn (years of technique had gone into acquiring a flat-footed walk which might approximate the old camera move on a dolly) but since he was not on tracks or connected to anyone else, so the path could be free in its curve. The eye of the lens could inquire into the scene. The cameraman could even shoot up from the floor between the bodies of men in a dispute or listen to a social conversation from a worm's-eye view beneath a glass coffee table — what play of light on the ashtrays and the highballs! Such shots went back of course to *Citizen Kane* — the issue was that documentary could now be open to subjects which were formerly closed. Since a camera on a man's shoulder was not as intimidating as the old huge camera on a tripod, the subject felt less like a prisoner booked into the stocks of documentary record-taking. Indeed a man who actually reacted to his voice and movements was photographing him. Animation could begin to appear in the face and voice of the subject. So the subject became more interesting. The documentary moved from the photographing of executives, engineers, and inventors to the faces of slum children playing in the street, or to the study of married couples on an evening at home (and in bed). A world of subjects too fragile in mood for the entrance of heavy equipment, high-power lights, and crews of technicians became available, and people who had formerly been as interesting in front of the camera as slabs of stone began to show a gleam in their façade. But *cinéma vérité* still had technical limits which awaited the development of high-speed film with very little grain and better portable sound equipment.

Cinéma vérité suffered even further from the basic flaw that people were playing themselves in real situations, and were therefore the opposite of actors. Instead of offering a well-put-together lie which had all the feel of dramatic truth, they gave off a species of fact which came out flat and wooden and like a lie. It was as if there was a law that a person could not be himself in front of a camera unless he pretended to be someone other than himself. By that logic, *cinéma vérité* would work if it photographed a performer in the midst of his performance, since a musician in the reverberating cave of his work was hardly himself, he had moved out of daily dimensions, he was a creature in a kingdom of sound. So films like *Monterey Pop* were able to explore the existence of a performer on stage as no fixed camera had been able to do. The crew was small enough to be lost in the lights and the audience. Their lens could move in, retreat, turn away and react, even swing to the beat. Film came back of Janis Joplin and Otis Redding, of

Jimi Hendrix and Ravi Shankar, which went beyond any film seen before of musicians giving a performance. It was precisely because the cameramen had worked free of the stipulations of a director. They knew more of what a camera could do than any director who had not spent years as a cameraman himself, they had lived in their conscious mind and in all the aesthetic ponderings of the unconscious with the problems of composition in a fast-changing scene, their eye for the potentialities of camera expression was their own. So far as a man could take a thirty- or forty-pound camera on his shoulder and still see with the freedom of an unimpeded eye they were ready, they could interpret: critical to the matter — they could *react*. It meant musicians could play without a thought of being photographed, and so were never inhibited by the restrictions directors and cameramen working on massive tripods were obliged to impose on a performer's movement.

It had been his own idea, however, that *cinéma vérité* might also be used to photograph feature-length movies which told imaginary stories. He had come to the thought by way of his first film. Even if that had ended as a disaster (because the just-tolerable sound he heard on magnetic tape was not tolerable with an optical track), there had been a period in editing when he saw something he had never seen in other films. The actors (he was one of them) were more real, seemed more — it had to be said — more vivid than in other films. He supposed it was because people in fictional situations had never been photographed with such sensitivity before. The camera moved with the delicacy and uncertainty, the wariness before possible shock, that the human eye would feel in a strange situation. The camera had the animal awareness of a fifteen-year-old entering a room rather than a Mafia overlord promenading down a corridor. It made him realize that the movement of camera in conventional film (in filmed theatre) had none of the real movement of the eye, just the horizontal movement of vehicles, the vertical movement of elevators, and the turning movement of a door on a hinge. The eye of such cameras moved in relation to the human eye as a steam shovel moves in relation to the human body. The professional camera, however, was smooth, as indubitably smooth as the closing of a coffin lid. If it passed through space with the rigidity of a steam shovel, it did not clank. That, unhappily, was left for the *cinéma vérite* camera. The price of greater sensitivity to the unpremeditated action of actors was a set of vibrations, shudders, clunks, plus a host of missed anticipations when the camera zoomed in on the expectation of an interesting response, and the actor, whom the photographer had picked, was dull. Yet even that was cinematically curious once one recovered from the shock that not every instant on screen was shaped into significance. For now the cinematic point became the fact that the photographer could never know precisely what was coming — he was *obliged* to anticipate and he could be wrong: a story began to be told of the uncertain investigation of the eye onto each scene before us. It expanded one's notion of cinematic possibilities, and it intensified one's awareness of the moment. When significant movement was captured, it was now doubly significant because one could not take it for granted. Watching film became an act of interpretation and restoration for what was missed — much as one might look to fill the empty unpainted spaces in old canvases of Larry Rivers — it was also kin to that sense of excitement which is felt at a party when insights are arriving more quickly than one's ability to put them away neatly.

By whatever point of view, he had then a corps of cameramen, and they were equipped to photograph scenes which might veer off in any one of a dozen directions — they were ready to be surprised. It stimulated that coordination between hand, eye, and camera balance which was the dynamic of their art, surprises gave style to the rhythm and angle by which they would move in or zoom away. Once, after an impromptu free-for-all had developed in the filming of *Beyond the Law* with actors' bodies finally locked on the floor like a heap of twist-roll dough shaped for the oven, the cameraman had said, "You know I'd like to cover the camera with a case of foam rubber." And added wistfully, "Then I could just get in the middle of the fight next time." Such ideas carried to their conclusion might slip nonstop miniaturized cameras with built-in lights up the cervix to a baby's fist so the trip through the canal could be photographed, but that was years away from its unhappy debate — for the present he had cameramen who were nimble enough to work in close to a scene and get away (most of the time) without bumping the action or photographing the sound man. Or each other, if two cameras were working different angles.

Later, comparing two men's work on the same scene, he would come to observe that each man had a mode as characteristic as a literary style. The work of one was invariably well-composed, austere, tasteful; another would be alert to the play of forces between two actors — he would have talent for capturing that body language which would most accentuate what the actors unconsciously were doing. Another had little interest in the turn of a scene, but was fascinated with visual minutiae — occasionally his minutiae were more interesting than the scene. Some were best at photographing men, others at studying women or the mood of a landscape. Some were workhorses, some were delicate. Some were delicate and still worked like horses. He came to applaud his cameramen during the week of shooting the film, for there were days when they worked for sixteen hours, bodies quivering from fatigue, yet rallying to steadiness when they worked — the love affair was to go through a turn or two when he sat in a screening room for two weeks and studied the forty-five hours they had brought back, saw the unexpected mistakes, the loss of focus on sudden shifts of action, the edge of the microphone in the frame when the unforeseen move of an actor had flushed the sound man. And wistful disappointments when scenes on which he had counted mightily had lost their emphasis because the cameraman had not seen what he, the director, had seen, had not been in the same state of psychic awareness. And there were miles of footage, filmed in his absence, where the actors had gone wandering and the cameramen had let them, idiocies piled on idiocies, wooden muddy characterless footage, the depression of the cameraman visible in his lack of desire to give visual shape to a tiresome duet. Loss was everywhere in the forty-five hours.

But there were bonuses and benefits where he had never looked. Scenes he had thought uninspired as he played them were given life by the art of the photographer, and scenes he knew were good were made even better by choices of angle he would not have had the foresight to pick himself. If he lost what he desired in one scene, he found himself compensated in another. As the months of editing went on, he would feel at times like a sculptor discovering his statue. The chisel could not go where it wished, but there was a statue to be disclosed if one would follow the veins of the stone. So *Maidstone* began to emerge, not the idea for a picture with which he had begun, but another which had come out of it, a metamorphosis for which he was prepared, since in parallel to the flaws and bonuses of his *cinéma vérité* photography the *Maidstone* emerging was as much better than the conception with which he had started, as it was inferior. If it was a movie of another sort than he had first conceived, it seemed to him finally that there were not too many movies like it, for *Maidstone* was a film which had been made out of the materials of its making, a movie which had had almost no existence in plans or on drawing boards or detailed budgets before it was begun, a movie delivered out of film material which had come to life in the heat chamber of seven days of intense improvised and scriptless film-making, so a movie which had a curious first existence in itself not easy to describe and then a later existence which did not come from the stone but the shape of the film maker's hand. If he had arrived at six or seven hours of footage he considered suitable or agreeable or useful or tasty or splendid or fine or essential, if the smelting had reduced forty-five hours of film to a seventh of itself, there was still, he knew, a length to which the material must shrink by way of brooding, rubbing, and polishing, by elucidation then de-infatuation with pieces of film or conceits of story he had loved too much at first to relinquish. It would be a work of months, and then finally of a year (and a second year to follow) of mistakes and losses, blunders and mislaid gems of film strip, but when done, it would be his conception, he would by then have *written* a movie using strips of film rather than words, a movie different from the film anyone else would have made out of the same six or seven hours of usable film, would have written it as uniquely and differently as any one writer would have been from another writer if both were working on the same topic and had the same dictionary. It was his film. He had framed some of the language, and others had framed the rest of it for him, but by the time he began his editing, it was all part of the same dictionary; he had created *Maidstone* out of the given; so it was entirely different from films which had devoted their effort to creating the given from a script, then nailing it up according to plan.

In the act of this most particular film-writing, his pencil become the size of an editing machine,* he dis-

* With the advent of electronic editing from video tapes the notion of *writing* one's movie out of the film at one's disposal —

covered where he thought the nature of the film might lie, and so tried to end with a film which would be in itself the nature of film, a metaphysical dumpling of a remark which is close to indigestible. Does it make it easier to suggest that even as an angel may be the nature of goodness and beauty, so to look at an angel is to obtain a picture of humans from heaven? By analogy he wanted a film which would live in the mind like a movie star, that is he wanted the film itself to be the movie star, some evocative, ambiguous presence which was always suggesting the ghostly but most real intrusion of the *special* existence of cinema.

3

But he anticipates. He has come to the peroration before he has reached the middle. It is a natural mistake for a film maker. A novelist learns early in his career that beginning, middle, and end are a part of literary time, and cause direct notice when shifted, but in film no time exists but the order of progression. A film is made by one piece of film being stuck onto the next and that is the only scheme of time which prevails. Afloat on the full tide of a film we see an actor who looks twenty years old. In the next cut he looks sixty — we do not jump immediately to the conclusion that it is forty years later, no, we may have to recognize it is his idea of himself forty years later, or his recollection of a previous life when he was sixty. Indeed it may be a shot of his grandfather — we wait for the next cut. If it explains nothing, merely goes off to further adventures of the twenty-year-old, the isolated cut has its peculiar existence — it is a warning or a symbol or an omen, something — it sticks with its incomprehensible flash even as we have flashes in life of people we know well who are seen for an instant doing

since it promises to be quicker and easier — becomes next to inevitable.

something we cannot comprehend — the town patriot sticks his tongue out at the flag: next moment he is, as always, smiling on his cigar. Did we see the tongue go out or did one crazy cell in our own head imagine it? That is a fair preparation for film. One can put anything next to anything in film — there is a correlative in some psychic state of memory, in the dream, the *déjà vu*, or the death mask, in some blink of the eye or jump of the nerve. So one can work whole stretches of film free of any thought of the story. A piece of film can be put next to another piece of film regardless of plot — it will work or it will not work. Of course, this is exactly the place where the mystique of film begins and one starts to talk of its nature. Every beginner of a film cutter becomes willy-nilly an amateur philosopher about the time he recognizes that you cannot attach one piece of film to another simply because it makes sense for your story. If the cut is poor, the screen will jump. A virtuoso can make it jump to one side, then to the other — that, too, is a psychic state the film can offer, but it is like the dying spasms of a broken tooth — can the average film afford such pain?

No, there was a syntax to film movement. The slow sweep of a man walking to the left and out of the frame could be followed by the sweep of another man walking to the right. If the tempos were similar, the movement was restful. If the second man walked faster than the first the logical expectation was for a faster and more intense scene on the third cut. Some action would obviously be getting ready. What it was would hardly matter. A fight could follow between two men or two dogs, an airplane could dive, a train go by, or a woman could scream, then turn immobile and the freezing of her movement would go into the strictures of the scream. You could do anything in film if you could do it. Of course, some cuts were vastly better than others but led you to more exquisite troubles since several beautiful cuts in a row awakened expectations which oncoming material would have to satisfy. If there was nothing that good to follow, it was like stopping in the middle of the act.

On the other hand, mediocre cuts could follow one another, each cut more or less endurable, until suddenly a cut would go dead. The cut had seemed reasonable for the plot but it left a feeling in the lungs analogous to breathing the exhaust of a bus. Cuts were like words. You could put many an ordinary word next to another word but you could not put them all. If your last name was Klotz, you might call your son Chris, but you would not call your girl Emerald, not unless your ear and the ear of fashion were in a special little race that year. Godard made jump cuts in *Breathless* which no one had been able to endure before, did it out of all his experience as a cutter, and from his artistic insight that the verboten had moved to the edge of the virtuoso. Yet, you may be certain the twenty precise cuts before the jump cut fed subtly into it, if indeed the jump cut had not become the particular metaphysic of that film.

Still, some cuts work, some do not. Some cuts work in extraordinary fashion. One cannot understand why two pieces of film otherwise unrelated seem agreeable next to one another, even appear on screen with that same unfolding of mood the sun suggests as it works at last through a cloud. Poetry is working. A few words which had little to do with one another are now enriching each other. Peerless grapefruit peel! In color film the effect is twice to be noticed. For the syntax of good movement can be reduced by the color, or, since color film is easily as malleable to editing as black and white, an otherwise indifferent movement will be given resonance by the shift of color. It does not matter what is used. A good cutter with enough film can cut a run of images which will give pleasure to an audience. If there is no story present, no other exposition or logic than the aesthetic of color, composition, and movement, then there is a length to such a film, and it is not usually more than a quarter of an hour. Give a hint of story, however, and the interest of the audience might ride for twice as long. The good cutter is like a very good skier. He does not study the trail ahead, he sets out down the mountain, makes his turns as they come, does his checks, his drops into the fall line, his traverses into the hill, then tips around and down again. It is beauty to watch. If we add the knowledge that he is in a *race*, the beauty is hardly diminished and our tension is certainly increased. It is not unlike what happens when a hint of story is added to film montage.

Now, however, create a complexity for which film is uniquely suited. Offer a situation where the film seems to tell the audience the skier is in a race, then a minute later seems to indicate he is not in a race. All the while we are following his descent — now the race seems to be on again. To the attention and irritation of not knowing which situation is real, and to the beauty of the photography, have been added ambiguities of context. A fine slippery shiver of meaning comes over us because the situation has altered a little faster than our comprehension of it. Film can offer such sensations as no other art.

If, then, he was ready to start with a conventional, even supercharged movie plot (which he knew would be quickly warped, intensified, dissipated, and altered) and if he was equally ready to throw a Colosseum fodder of actors almost totally untrained into such maximum circus, it was because he had learned that improvised scenes with *cinéma vérité* photographers gave many more opportunities to the cutter than the choices open to a film editor who was working on a movie whose rushes came off a script. For, whether trained or untrained, actors in any improvised scene had hardly any more idea of what the final relation of their scene would be to the eventual movie than a man in a love affair may know if his woman will be with him for the rest of his life. So there was an indispensably intense air of the provisional and the real to the actors' work. They were not present to send off signals, as actors with a script must unconsciously do, that the end of the scene was near. Therefore, any improvised scenes which worked in whole or in part, which is to say had vitality or flashes of vitality, always gave some interesting ensemble of movement that could be used as the springboard for a quick or curious cut to the tempo of other actors in other improvised scenes which were also working well. Indeed, one could cut away from a continuing scene at any point — for the script was still to be put together. That was a choice which film with a script would rarely offer. With script, each scene was staged and thereby necessarily acted with its little unconscious beginning, little middle, and little end. Options for interesting cuts were on the consequence blocked. A scene which ended with a book being laid with measured finality on a table tended all too often to require an ensuing movement equally full of the slow and the stately. That was legitimate if the flow of the movie called up such a tone, but it was deadening if the next scene in the script wished to get off to a quick start. That next cut could no more ignore the last pause than a conversation could glide over the remark that a friend had passed away.

Improvisation obviously gave more freedom to the cutter, so much in fact that the logic by which one began to connect pieces of film to each other seemed at times to arise out of the very logic of film — even if the logic of film was a concept as deeply buried as the logic of language and so might have to wait for its first tentative elucidation by a semantics of film. What appeared as the immediate difference was that with improvisation and free cutting the story was not obliged to be present as the walls and foundation of a movie, but rather became a house afloat on some curious stream, a melody perhaps on which many an improvisation was winging — it was as if story now had the same rare relation to film which images bear to language. The influence of story now was partial, not whole. For even as language consists of both the concrete and the abstract, of particular images and also of concepts which have no image, so any logic of film could contain elements of natural story and elements of movement which were opposed to story or simply indifferent to story. The *resonance* of film, the *experience* of film — words were of diminishing use here — seemed to derive from some necessary tension between the two, even as language seems to require that we pass from image to concept and back.

But if *Maidstone* (as a prime example of the logic of film) is already once removed from words, it is twice dangerous to keep speaking of it without offering a little more of the particular experience which produced it. If the obvious suggestion arises that the experience resides in the nature of improvisation, one may be forgiven the excessive symmetry of next suggesting that the concealed properties of film and improvisation are parallel (which is why they may belong together). We look at film, any film, and chaos is to a degree ordered. (We can, for example, photograph a wastebasket and it has become more an object of order than it was before.) We know we are looking at a life which is not quite life although it will certainly shift the way we live. So improvisation also orders chaos — gives its focus to random emotions — also becomes a life which is not quite life, and yet, even more than film, improvisation suggests it is indeed ready to become life. Ready to become life? Are we speaking of the moment when a fantasy, which is to say a psychological reality in the mind, transcends itself and becomes a fact? We are probably back to the last afternoon in the filming of *Maidstone*.

4

Given his theories on improvisation, there was a problem to filming *Maidstone*, and it was fundamental. While he took it for granted that any man or woman who could talk under stress was usually ready to burst forth with an improvised characterization (almost as if the ability to act, like the ability to make love, had been waiting for its opportunity), still one could never forget that art is art and self-expression is all too often therapy. The need therefore was to have a scheme which would keep the improvisation from flowing over into a purge. Some constraint had to be found for each scene; ideally, an overlying constraint had to be found for the entire film. In *Beyond the Law*, the problem seemed to solve itself. Being a policeman or a suspect arrested for the night was apparently one of the formal, even primeval scenes of the unconscious. None of his actors had trouble believing they were either policemen or under arrest, indeed his actors were richer in the conception of their role than the author would have been if he had written it for them. Nor had his presence as a director even been necessary in every scene. He had filmed most of *Beyond the Law* on an unrented floor in a seedy office building. It was perfect for giving the sensation that one was upstairs at a police station. Since he had set up interrogations between his detectives and suspects in separate rooms, three camera teams worked apart from one another in the different interrogation chambers. As in a police station, detectives came in and out, questioned a man, took off. Other detectives came in. After a period of filming, the floor of the office building might as well have become a police station. There was a babble of sound throughout, prisoners were arguing, weeping, protesting, going silent, detectives were bellowing or intoning charges, sounds of a beating in one room were agitating an unstable prisoner in another. Half the movie had been

4

4

filmed in two nights, filmed on a sea of sound and cinematic sensations.

Now, however, he was ready to make a film of no simple premise and much complexity. Ideally, many of his scenes would be subtle. Any demonstration of the value of making a movie by this method would depend consequently on how elusive, light, and sinister, were the effects obtained. The proof that his method had resources could only be demonstrated by capturing delicate qualities which none but the most carefully prepared films had hitherto provided. Since he also wished his picture to be nothing less than comic, farcical, sexy, on the edge of horror, and with more than a hint of the ghostly, the concoction would not be automatic to obtain.

Still, he believed he could get it if he could only provide an atmosphere, some pervasive atmosphere, in which his untried actors would arrive at a working mood. For *Beyond the Law,* his police station had provided that atmosphere, provided it as forcefully as a movie being made in a coal mine. But *Maidstone* would be filmed half in open air; the other half would take place in living rooms and sitting rooms which were models of the exotic or the established. Any prevailing atmosphere could not be simply created by an ideal set — rather it would have to come from the presence of the film-making itself descended as some sort of spirit-resident upon East Hampton, a somewhat frightening film, to be certain, for its central figure was a man living in danger of assassination. Since improvisation was never dependable, far from it! the theme was uneasy to all. Murder is another of the primeval scenes of the unconscious. The impulse, however, is guarded by bulldogs in fifty restraining collars — murder was not likely to occur this week on the cheap. Nonetheless, it was only a month and a little more since Bobby Kennedy was dead. That was a thought which lay heavy. Another was the instability of fifty or sixty actors, some white, some black, all congregating and soon fornicating in two small hotels. Nor were the scenes to be played likely to reduce any tension.

He was not so paranoid as to see the venture daring more than a most risk-diminished form of Russian roulette. Surely, not more than one chance in a hundred, say at the most unlucky, one chance in ten of a real assassination attempt, but whatever the percentage, the practical working movie point was that one percent of real risk introduced a paranoid atmosphere of risk which might be put at twenty percent. And that was a percentage to work with, a percentage to keep the cast in a state of diabolical inclinations, some sensuousness, and much dread. How could legitimate fear not arise that some innocent bystander, some bit actor, would catch a maladroit effort at assassination intended for another? So a presence for the film had been created. The fear of assassination hung over the cinematic shooting like the faintest luminous evanescent arch of the ineluctable beyond, yes, some pale shade was there, some representative of the ghost-world of film there along with everything else, along with chaos, cries of love in the grass, and the physical grind of the work, the rush of scenes, the military madness of schedule. Actor and quartermaster, general, production engineer, and the only substitute for a script girl, he had himself more roles than ever before in his life, and staggered through *Maidstone* with the brain of an exhausted infantryman, his mind obliged to work as it had never before, work constantly and without respect for its age, vices, and sedentary habits. Since he also had not slept more than four hours a night for the last two weeks of preparation, keyed to a pitch which if struck could have given off a note, he was speaking slowly for the first time in his life, his brain too used-up to talk fast — the picture was later to prosper as a result since people for once could hear him! — he had nonetheless to wonder at the oddest moments (for there was an unmistakable rainbow of fear and elation in the breath of his chest and it did not leave until the film was done), had to wonder why he was taking such a peculiar chance, which if small was still unnecessary, and knew it had some murky soil of congested roots in the irrational equation that Bobby Kennedy had taken a large chance for a large goal, and he must — in some equilibration of all the underground pressure systems of guilt — now find a way to take a smaller chance for his own private goal, suspected he would never have made this movie or even conceived of it if he had not sat in a room with Bobby Kennedy a month before his death and failed to realize danger: that the man was in mortal danger. So he had a motive not far from obsession: one could return to it over many a year.

Of course his other motive was professional, even elegant in its professionalism. For the fact that he not only made a movie about a possible assassination but gave it structure as a game, even offered the fierce privilege of autonomy to actors who were scheming up plots for his possible cinematic assassination, must also mean that the presence was now being fortified. So he played his part, acting for at least half of his working day rather than directing, his own role certainly helped by that delicate baleful edge of presence which might lead to artwork, a debacle, or outright disaster. He had no idea what was being hatched about him. He knew only that a variety of large and little plots gave every indication of generating some focus, some steam, some point of a gun, and went through days with staggering schedules, his best reason for speed the instability of the situation. His actors were in for a long weekend. Any longer and the presence would explode or worse, appear absurd, dissipate. Each day in fact he was losing actors, some from frustration, some from fear, some of them good, some promising. Potentialities of story which hung on their presence would have to take a turn. He was not worried at that, not worried by any item of plot or arrival or departure. They would, as he told the company, take B if they could not take A.

So he lived on the fine fever of making the film, hardly aware of any hullabaloo but his own; he was become a powerless instrument of his own will, pleased at bottom to be out of touch with two whole sides of his film — the assassination activities of the secret police, and the possibly murderous ones of the Praetorian Guard — stayed like some animal in a zone of hunters knowing the great fatigue of a high alert, his senses an adrenalin of warnings whenever Raoul Rey O'Houlihan–Rip Torn was near, for he knew as if Torn were his true brother that the web of intriguings had Torn at the center, that if psychic biddings and curses were flying like bats through the ranks of the company, then Torn was the hole in the roof where they all came in. What pressure! What logic and what torture! What impulse! For Torn was more than an actor, he had in addition to debate his attempt to be the assassin. The vanity of a proud actor, not nearly recognized sufficiently for his talent, for the remarkable force of unholy smolderings he could always present, now had to become a vanity pushing him to take the center, to move from that secondary position of acolyte to the leading part, and preempt the part, be the killer who invaded the hill. Yet he was also first centurion of the guard to protect Kingsley from the point of the threat, and took his mission seriously, yes, with all the seriousness of a profound actor steeped in his improvisation. Ready to die in order to save Kingsley, he was also ready to kill him — anything but to have the quiet insistent pressure of the picture pass into nowhere, all threats stilled, his own role stilled.

So the night before the afternoon on the grass, the night of the assassination ball became O'Houlihan's high agony. Raoul Rey–Rip Torn had become the center of the film, the focus of every loyalty to the director, yet the wild card in every plot, since it had become an unspoken convention that the attempt of assassination would be on the night of the ball (as if actors in a sustained improvisation ganged naturally to the idea of a focus of plot), so in the hours of the night as the party went by, plots arose and were shattered or missed, or evaded, the director never feeling more real in the role. Uncertain of the size of the attempt, or whether the attempt was even yet to come, not knowing if he played in a game which was a real drama, or worked for a drama just so absurd as a game, he did not accept the more obvious gambits of plot which were offered him. If obvious, they seemed ridiculous, as though one gave assent to pressing a button which would release a boxing glove in one's face. No, he took up posts, or promenaded for two hours — impromptu bodyguard always about him — hung in the situation for two hours, and the time done and the party over, spoke now not to Rey but to Rip as if the movie were finished, as indeed he thought it was, for nothing but a few elements of the dream called "The Death of the Director" would be filmed on Gardiners Island with the company next day, a day in fact for picnic and celebration that the film was over. His own danger had been as one part in one hundred or less, but he was glad it was done, and so said to his fictional brother, "I don't know if we got anything tonight, but it's still all right," thinking to himself of the dozen different ways he could cut the film (his security residing in a documentary on the making of an unsuccessful film since there was always footage of his own voluminous directions to the cast) and so saying, went to bed and finally to sleep, and the next day found to his horror that on Gardiners Island after the lecture of orientation was over that the presence of the dread was returned, but now shorn of elation, shorn of a rainbow. There was something heavy, then awful in the air, he knew he was in more physical danger than at any time before, and as Torn came walking toward him across the green, hammer dangling from his hand, he remembered taking off his black leather vest and holding it like a short folded cape in lieu of a better weapon, and after the fight, too furious to speak to Torn for many a month, outraged that Torn had broken the unspoken convention of their film — that violence cease with the end of the filming of the ball — was yet obliged to discover in the months of studying his forty-five hours of reels that his own blunder had been enormous in giving so much autonomy to Torn and the other assistant directors. The work they had done was by sections good, but not finally good enough. The buried half of the film he had been waiting to see would remain for the most part buried. He had been left with the most embarrassing work of all, an ego trip, for he had been the hardest-working actor in the film, and so the film was his, it was all too unhappily his, and all too much of him, since that was the part which unfortunately worked the best. Torn had therefore been right to make his attack. The hole in the film had called for that. Without it, there was not enough. And with it — he glimpsed as he worked each day with his editors that a film was emerging which he would yet be pleased to call his own for it was a mysterious film and became more mysterious as he thought on it. It was reminiscent first of the image he had held of the ski race which was on, then declared off, then put on again — the film shifted from context to context in modes as obsessive and haunting and *attached* to memory as those recollections of indefinable moments between sleep and a dream where context shifts, only to shift back again — we are in the dream . . . no, it is the edge of day. So Proust had floated his reader on a hundred-page procession of state from sleep to wakefulness into sleep.

In *Maidstone* the context moved into some other place. It was a film about the surface of reality and the less visible surface of psychological reality. For if everyday reality was a surface, or a crust, or a skin, psychological reality was a balloon which lived as a surface so long as the air of belief was within it. And since he had come to write his *Maidstone* after all the film was in, he chose the mysterious shifting character of its surface as the subject, and looked to show just how many of its realities were psychological realities which could suddenly be exploded and then where had they gone? What was left of such reality? It was a project he could never have commenced with words, nor even with the fiction of a story, but *Maidstone* had been filmed not only as an imaginary event but as a real event, and so was both a fiction and a documentary at once and then become impossible to locate so precisely, for what came nearest to the hard hide of the real? Was it Norman Mailer, the self-satisfied director, instructing his cast for the last time, or was it the suddenly real head of Norman T. Kingsley that Torn as suddenly attacked. (Yet his hammer had been held carefully on the flat to reduce the damage.) For if the attack was real, the actor upon whom it was wreaked should not be, and would not be unless the attack became fiercer still, fierce enough to kill him indeed. Then Kingsley would have become undeniably more real than Mailer.

It was a species of realization — that the hide of the real remains real only so long as the psychologically real fails to cut into its existence by an act which makes psychology real — the tongue would twist in its turnings on such a philosophical attempt faster than the film. For it was possible *Maidstone* inhabited that place where the film was supposed to live — that halfway station between the psychological and the real which helped to explain the real. As time went on, he saw that the cutting he did by newly acquired instinct was with purpose, and had a logic to reveal the topography of that halfway station. For *Maidstone* kept promising developments of plot which never quite took place, even as we travel through our lives forever anticipating the formation of plots around us which do not quite form. We are always looking for real stories to ensue which never exactly enact themselves as we expect, yet we still work at such times as actors in the real story of our life, pursuing roles which can become our life at any instant the psychological can become the real — as occasionally it will. For out of fifty stories in which we are at any instant enmeshed (fifty sets of expectations that next week we fall in love or to-night we go out and get drunk and have a terrible fight), not three times out of fifty, not two, nor one does the expected event occur. And then it does, it happens, it takes place out of the stored force of all the denouements which did not take place. So Torn attacked out of all the plots of other actors, Torn became the presence of the film, the psychological reality that became a literal reality out of the pressure of all the ones which did not. So that film about a director who would run for President became instead a photographed event of simulated plots and threats kept under high pressure by the curious curse of playing with photography of the female in the act of love, of playing with the curse of love which is gone, of playing with the curses of matrimony, yes, that film of an event which was a thousand events (of which nine hundred and ninety had small issue, or none, or were never photographed) became at last a film of the ineffable shimmer of reality, even became, as its director had wished, the star itself. Then it was that the presence of the film crystallized into the *geist* of *Maidstone*, Rip Torn. A superb actor at a pitch of intensity was there finally to reveal the premise on which a film had been built, even offer the essence of a method which might yet become the future of the film. For is it not a common premise to many a lover of movies that the hidden wealth in every strongbox of the cinematographic are those sequences of footage where the event has been in-nocent of script and yet resonant with life? Of course! We are talking of nothing other than movie stars in frames where the mood has been pure. Mood is our only acquaintance with the sensuous properties of time. And film is the only art which can search, cut by cut, into the mystery of moods which follow and accommodate one another; film is the only art which can study sudden shifts of mood which sever the ongoing river of time a fine film has set in flow. So we search for the pure in film as we search for the first real tear of love. We are a Faustian age determined to meet the Lord or the Devil before we are done, and the ineluctable ore of the authentic is our only key to the lock.

PART
TWO

HINTS
TO
THE
AESTHETIC
OF
THE
STUDY

One
Literary
Critique

Up the Family Tree

The book was the event of the season. Not, of course, as a huge best seller, or inspirative of awe or celebration — no suggestion in publishing ranks that Princess Margaret was doing her memoirs — this was more like the fraternity initiation of the year. A medium plump, very rich, and very late Freshman, bastard son of a founding family, was actually going to submit himself to an all-out hazing, and against all the advice of his furious family, furious to the point of biting their white icy lips (accustomed for years to no kisses but the most perverted!). One kissed the devil indeed, but no member of the family submitted to a hazing conducted by yahoos and muckers with names like Richler, Fuller, Bermel, Puso, Beam, or

Predictable Hicks — what a squalid yard of humpty-beaters and hard-ons. No fate could prove undeserved for Norman said the family in thin quivering late-night hisses. (For like every family which had kissed the tail of Satan's cat — say it on! — the hole! they spoke after midnight in voices like snakes and beetles and rats, hiss and titter, prick and sip.)

Yet the hazing, while brutal — coarse, intimate, snide, grasping, groping, slavering, slippery of reference, crude and naturally tasteless — was still on the side of charity if one compared the collective hooligan verdict to the earlier fulminations of the Inner Clan, yes, even if one had to face up in the reviews to such models of pig-sweat in aspic as the following: "a career expressed as a matchless 360-page ejaculation" — Bermel, *New Leader;* "The Egghead (I use the slightly dated term to lock Podhoretz in the persona he is so much at pains to discard)" — Raphael, *Sunday Times;* or Richler in the *Nation* — "deplorably inbred . . . intolerable show-biz characteristics . . . grubby details . . . careerist adventures . . ." Yes, if pig-sweat, envy, anaemic sniper-hots, and spite stand out in many a review as obviously as a Watusi shaking his feathers, the fact remains that the public reception of *Making It* with all its suffocating air, since no review was ready to call the book evil, or label it great, was nonetheless — all horrors of hazing in evidence — was nonetheless kinder to Podhoretz than the first kiss of the clan.

If *Time* and *Newsweek* (career men naked in their own homeland) hated *Making It,* why the *Times* was there on daily and Sunday to give it a good respectful word, so was *Life* — grace of the guest reviewer, John Aldridge. The *Nation,* the *New Republic,* and the *New Leader* spit (no doubt to show the very balls of integrity in daring to attack the editor of *Commentary* — who was there to say they were a veritable gang of unde-scended testes?). The *Wall Street Journal* was mild and

Waspy, avuncular in its gentle sting — so was *Sat Review*. The *Progressive* came in swell. *Book World* was bitchy and bright, the *National Observer* offered objective notes of praise, the *Washington Post* was vitriolic: "egregiously phony," it said. The *Plain Dealer* called *Making It* fine reading. *Women's Wear* picked up its skirts and wooed with both feet in the air — "fascinating and appalling" her verdict. If the *Los Angeles Times* was whipping the heads off flowers, "sophomoric, humorless . . . constricted, shallow, contrived," the *St. Louis Post-Dispatch* called *Making It* "a book, and a good one at that." Even the *New York Review* was left at the end of its long tether in bemusement: "We may surely hope that successive volumes will permit us to follow the career of this remarkable, still young man. And they may be more mellow; sometimes as we age, memory softens our perceptions of reality. In *Podhoretz Returns* and *Son of Podhoretz*, the monster may turn out to have a heart of gold." That was about the way it went. No, then it went worse! All the reviews were surpassed at the end by a draft horse of a review in *Esquire*, ten thousand words and more by the fiction editor of the *Saturday Evening Post*, America's own Rust Hills, a prodigious many-nostriled neigh of a report, here fair, there foul, often full of hay, designed to prove that Podhoretz was an enemy of the novel and Hills its first defender, the whole dominated by a series of nine caricatures of Podhoretz by David Levine so connotative of old nightmares in the pages of *Der Stürmer* that one was finally obliged to wonder what occult species was Levine and how ammonia-odored was the hand which held the drawing pen of such a crotch — did the fingers stink of crap or bat or pigeon's piss?

Well, no vast joy to be found in such reviews for the writer of a book, particularly when it is his first full-length book, and was written with high ambition and in the teeth of the shaking ague of confronting the highest

literary standards all packed like blood oaths and cove-
nants in himself — one does not acquire love for literature at the feet of the Trillings and pay no price in outsize awe. Nor does one practice as an honorable literary
critic for years, doing one's best by one's lights to cut the
morbid anomalous tissues of ill-conceived work without
starting in terror out of sleep at night at the thought of
what groans and revenge are buried in the tombs of expired books — now shakes the hand of the critic-surgeon
as he lifts his scalpel to — all ghouls awake — to
sharpen his own creative pen for the expression of his
own creative urge. Predictably, there will be New Leader
Bermel to macerate the urge into "a matchless 360-page
ejaculation." Yes, the bad breath of the future assassins
can be smelled already in the wood.

Besides, the presumptive book writer is an editor, and
of a magazine which if not universally well liked, is per-
force everywhere respected. (Which is to say five hundred writers and spokesmen will never forgive the editor
of *Commentary* for his tastes, choice, correspondence
with them, exercise upon their manuscripts, or just general rejection of work, ideas, unholy passions.) The editor is a man known for the solidity of his culture, the
centrality of his position in the Liberal Establishment,
the depth of his sanity, sense of proportion, and independence equal to no less than the feat of resurrecting a
half-dead magazine; known as well for the power of his
friends, the warmth of his own personality, the charm
and brilliance of his wife, the lusty wit of his children,
the modesty of his own self-effacing humor — the man
is endowed; wisdom and worldliness are his; he has one
foot in the stirrup of all good spirit, and the other is on
the kneadables of the sweet ass of success. Who but a
very brave or foolhardy man would in such a fine condition sit down to write any kind of book at all, who but a
demented scribbler would choose to dive through the
plate-glass window of his own splendid showcase in

order to allow an outside mob of hungry assassins, literary gung-hos, and assorted rhinoceri to come roaring in to examine the goods with knives, feet, and teeth. Who but a quivering whip-full of masochism would dare to end such a book with the following two paragraphs, one wretched for all of its moderate length, the other as indigestible in its brevity as a plastic peanut?

> For several years I toyed with the idea of doing a book about Mailer that would focus on the problem of success, but in the end I decided that if I ever did work up the nerve to write about this problem, I would have to do it without hiding behind him or anyone else. Such a book, I thought, ought properly to be written in the first person, and it ought in itself to constitute a frank Mailer-like bid for literary distinction, fame, and money all in one package: otherwise it would be unable to extricate itself from the locks of the dirty little secret. Writing a book like that would be a very dangerous thing to do, but someday, I told myself, I would like to try doing it.

> I just have.

Yes, who could commit such a blunder of self-assertion, self-exposure, and self-denigration but my old dear great and good friend Norman Podhoretz who brings the mind of a major engineer to elucidating the character of complex literary structures but would seek — for such is the innocence of his good heart — to climb the Matterhorn on ice skates.

Now, of course, if Podhoretz's great and good friend Norman Mailer is to say this now, it is with wisdom which comes after the fact. For *Making It*, taken on its own terms, while never possessing a chance for real fame and real literary distinction (because of flaws to be yet discussed) is, seen by a dispassionate eye in manuscript or galleys (and no eye so dispassionate as the look of an old friend) is, *Making It* is, yes, a perfectly decent and honorable book very well written for much of its length, and respectably written for the rest except for ten or twelve isolated phrases, sentences, and paragraphs so unhappy, ill-chosen, and aggressively flatulent that no reviewer with an eye to the cruel could fail to notice, and not even the kindest of critics would be ready to defend them. Small wonder that these miserable phrases crop up again and again in every review, thereby giving the impression of a graceless, malodorous, repulsive, offensive, self-aggrandizing work when in fact the overall style is — but for these scattered criminal lapses — a style restrained, cool, self-observant, modest, dispassionate, analytical and gifted with an agreeable variety of aperçus on matters such as status, class, privilege, and clan. It is an interesting book, very interesting in its way, and offensive not at all except for its precise lack of offensive threat, which irritates in about the way of any defenseless presentation. In summation its only thundering demerit is that it is not a great or major book, and it may be that nothing less was required for a literary venture by an Establishmentarian critic and editor in Podhoretz's position than to produce just such an overpowering work. Probably nothing less would have done. Instead, Podhoretz by a major effort of will against what must have been the rock-quaking tremors of his own heart, produced a minor work of much excellence, seriously flawed. It was doubtless an expensive book for the author — so much energy spent, so little fame; so much talk, so little good will; but great authors like great generals can be tempered by disastrous campaigns as well as victories; it is — wipe the old metaphor — exactly when an author begins to think not of the blow he will take to his own liver, but the shot he will deliver to the target, that he is ready for real literary game. Podhoretz is sufficiently sturdy, honorable, clear-eyed and talented to deserve the most thorough going-over, provided the attack is clean and offers the dignity of a dispassionate critique, which of course is exactly what he did not get. So, let us go to look at *Making It.* Mysteries will confront us there, not the least being the exceptional hostility it aroused in the Establishment while the book was still in manuscript.

The Establishment has properties, not the first of which we might suggest, is its absolute detestation of any effort to classify or examine it. (Anyone doubting this last assertion is invited to recollect the outsize wrath of Jackie Kennedy at the modest inside anecdote or two of her life as told by William Manchester, a wrath whose overflow was to cost Bobby Kennedy ten points of national popularity in a year of great decision.) No, any sociologist who would attempt to analyze the Establishment would do well to begin with the assumption that it is a temple, and its members are priests and priestesses, its center of worship is a hole, a Holy of Holies, its altar undescribed. Power which is not material must dwell in mystery, its most refined codes are best left uncodified — indeed a scholar might hope to demonstrate that the Talmud could not be committed to writing until hope for the restoration of the Second Temple was lost; the intimations of such power are rarely verbal — they exist in the curve of an inhibiting eyebrow, the form of a line.

2

Podhoretz, schooled as a critic at Columbia, then Cambridge, was to arrive in the pages of *Partisan Review* with a full set of preoccupations provided by Trilling, but his critical stance — solid, doughty, authoritative, and hugely egalitarian (this last to be explained in an instant) — owed much to Leavis. Leavis was, of course, a veritable monster of taste, a rabid hanging judge of the smallest literary pretense — he derived from a line who would behead the king if the king did not meet measure — but Leavis was nonetheless egalitarian: he obviously believed that the critic performing a thorough total work of scholarship, steeped in the traditions, lore, style, moral filaments, and spiritual saps of the work he considered, alert in every quiver of his senses to the nuances and defections in the fabrication of beauty or power within the poem or prose before him was, if ready to make that total effort, a work of art in himself, a living critical creation face to face on equal terms with the work; so, hugely egalitarian.

Such total commitment can come only to an Englishman or a Bolshevik, come to them, that is, and remain. A young American can be steeped in such a discipline for a time, but there is no ballast in America for joining ideological priesthoods which offer no uniform. The only invisible American priesthood with ballast is the Establishment, and that is never ideological.

But Podhoretz was ideological, ideological three times over, by Jewish Theological Seminary, Columbia, and Cambridge; any well-equipped mind passing through three such separate disciplines could hardly be expected to encounter future experience free of any set, liberated from preconceived stance.

To the contrary, Podhoretz like many an intellectual before him could use as his *cogito, ergo sum:* I cerebrate, therefore I see. No matter how sensuous the nature, sense experience in such men tends to become the raw material for the processing mills of new hypotheses. That is a superb way to do a kind of literary criticism, perhaps the best kind of literary criticism for which we can ask, since a work confronted by no critical hypothesis can merely be admired or despised, and thereby open questions of taste, but it cannot improve our mind by allowing us to consider simultaneously the work in question and the critical approach. We may enjoy the style of a critic who eschews hypotheses or we may reject it, but we cannot imbibe that deepening of context (that awareness of the work, the critic, and the world containing them both) which is the marrow, indeed the very satisfaction, of reading a critic who lays siege to a work with his hypothesis. The value of a hypothesis is that it can be tested, tested by the evidence of the work, tested by how much it fails to explain, tested indeed by the fact that it will remain as the best working hypothesis until a better one comes along to replace it. That is the most energetic kind of criticism, probably the most creative, and when done well, certainly the most stimulating to any reader who like Podhoretz lives in large part for the joy of cerebration. And Podhoretz is probably as good as any critic in America at this kind of writing. Indeed his only serious competitors might be Steven Marcus, John Aldridge, and Irving Howe.

Emphasis has been put upon this kind of criticism because it is so quintessentially part of Podhoretz's way of writing, even his way of life (since *Commentary* more than any other comparable magazine attracts articles with hypotheses) that when he came to do a book it was natural for him to begin with a hypothesis. The only difficulty was that he was now dealing not with an aesthetic artifact but with himself, not with literary criticism but a species of narrative fiction which is much too quickly thought of as autobiography. That word is appropriate to use if we are considering what a man writes about himself after his career is more or less done — he is at that point less than he used to be, his possibilities are generally consumed, his externals are known, and he is probably in fair shape to see himself as others do, since his old age itself testifies to the fact that he could live with his legend much in the same manner others responded to it. By this logic, autobiography is obviously biography done by oneself, auto-biography — someone else could presumably have been as intimate with the material. But when a man writes a book about himself in the beginning or middle of his career, then his work if at all penetrating is not a biography so much as a special category of fiction, precisely because his choices for future career are still open, his possibilities remain numerous, his conflicts are as alive as his enemies, his feelings as tender as his friends, and his sense of himself is as confused, complex, even bewildered as his sense of others. So he must make that same creative abstraction from life that a novelist makes when he cooks up or conceives a character out of one or more people he partially comprehends. The character if successful comes to life, the character engages a series of events which he shapes, and fails to affect, and from his strivings the reader may draw some comprehension, even a hypothesis. If the reader is a critic he will measure the character by this hypothesis, and we as other readers will be aided in comprehending the character (let us say it is Leopold Bloom) by the critic's hypothesis, that is until a better or more fashionable hypothesis comes along.

Yet the character must first be created. If a man is writing an accurate narrative about himself with real people and their real names, and this narrative arises because some imbalance or pressure or obsession or theme persists in dogging the man through all his aesthetic or moral nature until he sets to work, then he is willy-nilly caught in the act of writing into the unexplored depths of himself, into those regions which are as mysterious to him as other people. So he can comprehend, no, rather he can deal with himself as a literary object, as the name of that man who goes through his pages, only by creating himself as a *literary* character, fully so much as any literary character in a work of undisputed fiction. That is the only way a man in mid-career can begin to approach the mysterious forces which push him to write about these matters in the first place. He is off on a search. Like Theseus he will encounter his experience on the point of his walking stick; here, his pencil. To the extent that he succeeds in making a viable character who will attract literary experience metaphorically equal to the ambiguous experience in his life which impelled him to write in the first place, so will he be able to set out on that reconnaissance into the potentialities of an overpowering work. But it is no easy job! To the complications and hazards of creating an interesting imaginary character are now added all the real dangers of mentioning real names and real events, with all the uncharted — since works of this sort are rare — all the uncharted and spooky perils of uprooting a hundred established complacencies in a hundred real places. The perils may be no worse in reality than offending a few thousand readers by a novel, but one doesn't know, there is a point of no return implicit in such an endeavor. Moreover, one is presenting a personality which will be better or worse than one's own, and people will react to it with the same love or hate they reserve for characters in a novel. One is advancing and endangering one's career by writing the book, the book is now a protagonist in the progress of one's success. Self-interest naturally slants a word here, literary honesty bends it back there. One does not know whether to tell the little lie or shrive oneself. An overload of choices descends on the brain of any ambitious man engaged in giving a contentious portrait of himself. Yet that is not even the worst of the difficulty. The real woe is that one is forced to examine oneself existentially, perceive oneself in the act of perceiving (but worse, far worse — through the act of perceiving, perceive a Self who may manage to represent the separate warring selves by a Style). It is necessary to voyage through the fluorescent underground of the mind, that arena of self-consciousness where Sartre grappled with the *pour-soi* and the *en-soi;* intellections consuming flesh, consciousness the negation, yes, the very consumption of being. One is digesting one's own gut in such an endeavor.

This ulcerous claim check now stamped, let us take up
an existential hypothesis: *the* Norman Podhoretz in the
book called *Making It* is, we will assume, a fictional
character, an editor of a well-established magazine, well
regarded, etc., etc. He is not yet forty, not by several
years, but is tormented out of the sum of all vectors of
ambition, caution, desire, fear, honesty, horror, honor,
courage, and personal dissatisfaction to write a book
about himself. Why? He thinks (that is, the character
thinks) it is because he has a major thesis, something
new to say about success and the ambiguities of its state,
the relation of others to his success. He has even a thesis
in his mind as he begins his book. We can quote from
it:

> For taking my career as seriously as I do in this book, I
> will no doubt be accused of self-inflation and therefore
> of tastelessness. So be it. There was a time when to
> talk candidly about sex was similarly regarded as taste-
> less — a betrayal of what D. H. Lawrence once called
> "the dirty little secret." For many of us, of course, this
> is no longer the case. But judging by the embarrassment
> that a frank discussion of one's feelings about one's own
> success, or lack of it, invariably causes in polite com-
> pany today, ambition (itself a species of lustful hunger)
> seems to be replacing erotic lust as the prime dirty little
> secret of the well-educated American soul. And since the
> natural accompaniments of a dirty little secret are
> superstition, hypocrisy, and cant, it is no cause for won-
> der that the theme of success rarely appears in our
> discourse unattended by at least one of these three
> dismal Furies inherited from Victorian sex.

The thesis stated in the first pages, *Making It* then
goes on to describe the adventures of the protagonist. If
they are in the main intellectual, they are nonetheless
novelistically interesting, because they partake of the

most basic American tale of them all — the young man from the provinces who moves to the city and succeeds. If the trip is here only from Brooklyn to Manhattan, the character, quite aware of his universality, remarks, "One of the longest journeys in the world is . . . from certain neighborhoods in Brooklyn to certain parts of Manhattan. I have made that journey. . . ." Since the real, as opposed to the fictional Norman Podhoretz, is a man with a firm sense of neighborhood, he is doubtless quite aware that he has in life moved from Brownsville to West End Avenue — which is not quite up to the claims of his fictional journey; a look at his neighbors would remind him that the literal physical move is not an empire superior to jumping from Brownsville to Eastern Parkway. But this is the trouble with the book from its root. As a fictional character, Podhoretz would already be absurd — a pompous man, full of snobbery, but so blind to any true version of snobbery that he would palm off his address as superior. In life, as the real Norman Pod, he is of course speaking metaphorically. Those "certain parts of Manhattan" are not where he lives, but rather are enclaves of society where he, unlike his West End Avenue neighbors, has entrée. But he has already, unwittingly, like a novice novelist driven a separation between the real life of the detail and its inadequate fictional manifest. His book is thus from the beginning of its first chapter two books, one for readers who know him, another for readers who don't. And the reason is simple. The art of the novel begins with a primary demand: the novel must be in its fashion literal. Since it is not life, its life depends on the scrupulous accumulation of its details. In order to make a fine phrase, Podhoretz took a shortcut with the novelistic facts. That need not be fatal in criticism, but such shortcuts, particularly at the onset, distort the magnetic field of the novel. Already, to readers who do not know him, he is living in a fancier neighborhood than in fact he inhabits; to readers who do, there is a gap between the literal Norman Podhoretz and the less conscientious fictional presence in *Making It*. That is perhaps the last and most difficult demand of this special category of fiction — that one must succeed in creating a character who is not fatally separate to those who know the author and those who don't.

Nonetheless, after this opening flaw, the character Norman Podhoretz in this special-category-of-fiction continues well. We move through early chapters which have the quiet authority of good art, engaging near-tender accounts of his relation with a snobbish teacher exacerbated into "depths of loving despair" by the contrast between his intellectual promise and his red satin Cherokees Social Athletic Club jacket. We continue, through glimpses of his family, the implicit psychic mechanics — *tastefully* delineated — of his separation from family and neighborhood, his immersion, or partial immersion, in the subtle intoxications of life at Columbia (which is to say, the life of the spirit with most intuitions plucked from the grinds of the subway wheel) and good analysis follows of the play between open and concealed scholastic ambition.

I can see now, of course, that I must have caused the "snobs" as much pain as they caused me. If I envied them their social composure and their apparent self-assurance, they must have envied me my freedom from the scruples which governed them and the consequent torrent of unhindered energy on which I was able to call. These scruples had nothing to do with morality; they had to do only with the code of manners governing ambitiousness which seemed to bind everyone at Columbia but me. It was a code which forbade one to work too hard or to make any effort to impress a professor or to display the slightest concern over grades. Since most of the "snobs" in question were serious students, however, the code hemmed them in, and since most of them were also ridden with ambition — quite as much, I think, as

I — it forced them into secret transgressions, made them feel guilty, hypocritical, and ashamed. Yet I, a flagrantly open violator, instead of being punished, was being rewarded; I would probably even wind up, a "snob" once bitterly remarked to one of my friends, with Columbia's choicest prize, a Kellett Fellowship: "Can you imagine *him* at Oxford or Cambridge? Sammy Glick in the *Agora!*"

Which is, in fact, exactly where he succeeds in making it, to Clare College at Cambridge. Descriptions follow — spare, comprehensive, artfully discerning of the differences in education, ambitions, class, and country. Much good analysis, modest but pertinent, so convincing in the modesty that even such large remarks as the following

I became a Leavisian — not, perhaps, the most ardent of his young epigoni at Cambridge, but, in all truth, the others being a singularly dreary and humorless lot, the most adept . . .

are acceptable precisely because one has come to trust this detachment through the quiet severity of observation which accompanies less agreeable insights.

The novel continues well. It is an odd novel up to here, dry, almost ascetic in its details, so sparse indeed in its sensuous descriptions and so leisurely in its analyses of the protagonist's changing intellectual and social stances that one admires the courage of the novelist — he dares to push his novel in the direction of the informed sociological essay where in order to nail analysis one may even smuggle in a piece or two of carefully protected personal material. The difference, and it keens our interest, is that the tone here while close to abstract in its impersonality is never self-protective. On the contrary, it reveals, then reveals more, never guards the subject.

This tone continues for more than half the book. Podhoretz returns to America, has his first entrée into circles which are written about as if they were the equivalent to him of Versailles for Saint-Simon. There is here a gulf he does not sight completely to the bottom: there is probably a hint too little irony now in his portrait of the young literary man, extraordinarily self-made, who is feeling such vast admiration for purlieus like *Commentary* and *Partisan Review*. There was indeed a time when *Partisan Review* was the kind of duchess who could cut off more than one literary head with a stroke — it inspired fear in young authors which must have been equal to the terror of French courtiers when they first beheld the palace, but there are still differences to recognize — Philip Rahv with his mouth around a hot pastrami was not quite the novelistic equal of Louis XIV showing his knee (and if William Phillips looked like Richelieu, Richelieu was indubitably wearing his tweed jacket).

It is at about this point that the novel begins, most subtly, to falter. It has been economical, provocative, near to austere, and all readable as a narrative up to this point. If we still know little about the hero, what we do know has that tone of authority which suggests hope of a small classic in the making — we accept the hero, believe him, want to know more of him, and of his adventures. In fact, the novel continues thus good for a while — fine chapters in much the same tone carry Podhoretz through five months in New York while waiting to go into the Army, then a stretch of two years in uniform. We have at this point traversed more than half the book, and there has been but one false note — a faint hint of the stricken in describing that literary establishment of New York which Podhoretz calls The Family. There is despite all criticisms well-taken, all ongoing analyses of The Family's desires and prejudices, obsessiveness, cannibalism (of reputations, not flesh — so far as we know) there is still a hint of the one weakness which is fatal to the young novelist: flattery. The mouthful of pastrami in Rahv's mouth persists in being too small. So do all the other mouthfuls. Wherever there is a personal or professional reference to Dwight MacDonald, Mary McCarthy, F. W. Dupee, John Thompson, Lionel Trilling, Diana Trilling, Paul Goodman, Robert Warshow, Elliot Cohen, Hannah Arendt, Daniel Bell, Nathan Glazer, Irving Kristol, Steven Marcus, Rahv, Phillips, Jason Epstein, Plimpton, Mailer, Bob Silvers, Lillian Hellman, Sherry Abel, W. H. Auden, Leslie Fiedler, Alfred Kazin, Dan Moynihan, Richard Goodwin, Harold Rosenberg, Isaac Rosenfeld, Arthur Schlesinger, Delmore Schwartz, Susan Sontag, Murray Kempton, Mike Harrington, and a number of others (the index to the book suggests we are reading Main Currents of New York Thought) you may be certain the reference is invariably as attractive as the sort of remark one makes when giving a reference to a Foundation for a friend. The kindness palls. It is the one mark of timorousness in the book. Only Saul Bellow and Jimmy Baldwin are shown in any kind of unattractive light and then with care and preparation of context in order to strike no undue foul blow.

It is deadening. It saps the book, downs it not because we have been expecting an exposé of everything low, dirty, and vulpine in the New York literary establishment, nothing in the tone of the book has offered such an expectation, no, the disappointment is organic to the needs of the undeclared novel. We are being offered a restrained muted limited account of a young provincial, a local example when all is said of a Julien Sorel who is making his way up in the world. Not, of course, through a judicious mixture of sexual and social audacity, but by an uncomfortable sometimes self-torturing accommodation between the power of his ambition versus his irrepressible demands for an integrity to his expression. What more fascinating event, after half a book's worth of the best preparation, to see our latter-day Sorel make it and lose it and make it again with The Family, that peculiar colony, aviary, and zoo of the most ferocious, idealistic, egotistic, narcissistic, cultivated, constipated, brilliant, sensitive, brutally insensitive, half-productive, and near-sterile gang of the best and worst literary court ever to rise right out of the immigrant ranks of a nation. The comic and tragic aspects of that gang take one's novelistic breath away — the satiric possibilities put it back.

Well, of course one may say this is merely Mailer's view of The Family, not Podhoretz's — the author of *Making It* is entitled to his own view. No argument. It is just that his view cannot be developed in any direction. What is one to make of an Establishment which is so kind and splendid in its personnel? The sum of the individual portraits Podhoretz offers of this Quality Lucifer Lit Biz Clan is so full of sugar that one cannot begin to comprehend his abstract portrait which in contrast presents The Family (in general terms so vague one cannot perceive a single figure in the fog) as no better than any other Establishment. Truth, if The Family adds up to the kind sum of the specific charitable parts Podhoretz gives them, then the demand on him is to write a novel of insuperable difficulty (or even a sociological analysis of the same difficulty) which is to say — an Establishment composed only of the kindest folk: into their ranks enters an ambitious Provincial — what a novel!

No, one does not recognize Plimpton, and Silvers, and Rahv, and Epstein, and Phillips, no, nor Mailer, and Trilling, and Sontag, and Kristol. It is not that they are despicable all, nor mean, nor even full of rapine — it is that they are complex, as unendurably complex as our century is complex, and so *Making It* ceases to be a novel just so soon as its protagonist enters the climax of his narrative; we are projected right out of that rare aesthetic vineyard where autobiography dares to become that special and most daring category of fiction which is its inner necessity, and instead we are now forced to jog along on the washboard road of a memoir. Characters come in and out, observations are made, names file through, Podhoretz suffers, becomes an editor, thrives, we do not care — the novel has disappeared — the interplay between ambitious perception and society which has been the source of its value now gives ground to the aesthetic perplexity of the author who must flounder in the now novelistically alienated remains of his hypothesis — that success is the dirty little secret. Now he has no novel on which to work it, only sketchy anecdotes, abortive essays, isolated insights, and note of the drone — repetitions. A fine even potentially marvelous book gets lost in a muddle, finally finishes itself and is done. No joy in closing the back cover.

One must wonder. How does a man who has the simple guts to begin such a work in the first place lack the nerve to hump it through to the end? And the answer, if one is to ignore such natural motives as impatience, overwork, or general anxiety, is that the instinctive fear of a sophisticated writer at attempting to explore an Establishment is even greater than the well-established fear of the ridicule he will know at presenting himself as a character. A writer as forceful and well geared for exposition as Podhoretz reveals personal anxiety in his work not through deterioration of style so much as through deterioration of intellectual connection. By the time the book is done, the hypothesis of the "dirty little secret" and the dwindled novel have disengaged from one another, separated, we assume, by dread of invading the theme, dread of exploring the intimate play of hero and Establishment. It is no mean matter to put oneself in a real novel, but it is a nightmare to take on a true Establishment, such a nightmare that we need not wonder why Podhoretz deserted his possibilities as thoroughly as if Stendhal had presented the family of Mademoiselle de la Mole as charming.

All right, then. Let us make a quick pass at the little mystery of why Establishments provoke such vitiating fear in writers as seasoned and dedicated as Podhoretz.

4

The clue is to be found in the reception of *Making It* when the work was still in manuscript. The author's anticipatory dread was not ill-founded. Despite a $25,000 contract, the first publisher, Roger Straus, rejected the book. Publishers do not reject books in such cases because they dislike them, but because they find the long-term consequences disagreeable; the verdict of just about everyone in the Establishment who then read the manuscript was negative. Which is to say scandalized, shocked, livid, revolted, appalled, disheartened, and enraged — an excessive reaction for a book which is finally at worst a not altogether compelling memoir. What could cause so intense a reaction, so intense an overreaction?

Establishments are like banks — they release value only if it will return with interest. Podhoretz was obviously giving something away. But what was it? This is the question which remains unanswered, and has in fact attached itself to the book so closely that the reviews which followed publication were more a function of the Establishment's initial antipathy than a pristine reaction to the book itself — indeed, many reviewers expecting a work where names would be named and reputations outraged were therefore splenetic with disappointment; others, feeling the book had been killed before it saw print, were solicitous of its merits.

One could of course give the author credit for having unearthed a thesis (that success had replaced sex as the dirty little secret), a thesis sufficiently explosive to dynamite many buried Establishment furies, but the thesis while meandering in and out of the book was not organically attached to the work; rather it appeared now and again like an added starter. One could dislike the thesis and still not mind the book. Besides the thesis itself, if novel, did not seem quite accurate. It was the sort of illumination which could apply for particular Establishmentarians, but was utterly inapplicable for others: indeed, The Family as a whole gave off the aura of all Establishments — they were obviously as interested in success as any other bank. While they did not talk a great deal about it, and were reasonably dialectical about money — resenting Mary McCarthy's modest haul, while not at all unimpressed with the size of Capote's — it would have been not impossible to defend the opposite thesis that the need for success in one's métier was so taken for granted in these salons that there was no necessity any longer to talk about it.

It is better to chase our little mystery by remembering that Establishmentarians please their peers when they write works of symbolic intensity like Trilling's *The Middle of the Journey* or memoirs of unsurpassed sweetness like Kazin's *A Walker in the City*. They charm when they write trivia about New York with agreeable tone — as in Jason Epstein's fillip for the *New York Review*, they impress when their theses are rich in reference, comprehensive, original, and assertive, as are Harold Rosenberg's on New York art. Indeed, Establishment writers displease The Family only when they fail to present themselves as critical, intelligent, superior, and *in their cool*. The only piece remotely comparable in its innocent assault on the total temper of The Family was Diana Trilling's account of going to hear Allen Ginsberg read his poetry at Columbia. That is writing with such simplicity of affect and directness of response that it may live longer in literature than anything else by the lady — it has the tone of enduring literature — yet it was loathed in its time, loathed one may suspect for the defenselessness of its approach since Diana presented herself not as a distinguished critic (which had hitherto been implicit in her style) but as a bewildered faculty wife: the Establishment reacted as if they were being thereby sucked down into a mucker's muck.

So we may as well assume that the lightnings Podhoretz aroused came not because he was revealing the dirty little secret of others, but because he was exposing himself, and this act of self-exposure was received by The Family as a treason — one simply did not go around explaining any member of the clan. To do that was to weaken all.

It is easier to comprehend if we think of the Rockefellers or the Fords, or any other gathering of wealth. Exposure by any member of such families is odious to the rest because their power — to themselves at least, as a reflection perhaps of their guilt — rests on a fragile base. Let us assume the same for our own Establishment. They came into being almost by accident for they began as left-wing militants interested in literary criticism, and attracted more or less nonradical literary scholars and critics of special stature like Trilling and Kazin and Dupee only when their politics — isolated from both the Left Wing and support of the American war effort in the forties — became so encysted, that it was politics literally of the cyst, it nourished nothing without, it was a politics without price, danger, or engagement — except for such extremes of pacifism and anarchism as provided by Lowell and MacDonald. Later, in the postwar forties and early fifties, the Establishment was to run — we may hope unwittingly — as sweepers for the CIA. From some unclassifiable brand of Trotskyism, The Family had pushed on to more or less total anti-communism as a political position. It was a position of much empty power and much empty polemic, a literary equivalent of congressional junkets, and left the Establishment on sterile ground after twenty-five years of existence — no major critic and no major novelist had developed from their influence. Of course, Trilling was quite possibly a major critic if one did not pose him too comparatively against Wilson, but he would have been that kind of major critic without The Family, he was a literary man first. Others — MacDonald, Kazin, and Howe most notably — were first-rate but they did not grow over the years, no schools of criticism developed from them, no seminal ideas, no ferments — just an endless series of brilliant but tactical papers. They were guardians rather than catalysts. Any number of members of The Family were enormously impressive in fragments, and Harold Rosenberg and Meyer Schapiro and Clement Greenberg all in quite separate ways had large even commanding effect on the New York art world, Paul Goodman was later to have as much to do with the formation of the New Left as any writer about, but in the fifties he was alienated from The Family — their only poet, Robert Lowell, was a poet without them and before them; their house novelist, Mary McCarthy, had fled to Newport in search of real stimulation, and their big novelist, Saul Bellow, who was later to justify his reputation, had been advanced to glory in the mid-fifties on the basis of *Augie March* which was absurd in its parts, unconvincing along its whole, overcooked, overstuffed, unfelt, heaps of literary bull-bull. If the Establishment had been wiped out in the late fifties by a bomb, the verdict of history might have found them destructive of more talent than they liberated.

It was in the sixties that much began to happen. Kennedy's desire to weld the separate establishments of America's cultural, social, and political life together, gave The Family opportunity to inherit new power — the vertices of their plots were found now in parties at Plimpton's and forums with Schlesinger — after the birth of the *New York Review* the Establishment had real power which ran to many a connection in many a corner of America. If the war in Vietnam had forced the Establishment to sever its connection with the Administration, there was still Bobby Kennedy to serve as Pope of Avignon and an extraordinary mixture of positions everywhere from just left of the ADA to just right of Black Power there to be taken on every issue of the minute. This Establishment once ogreish, fearful, arid, poisonous, proud, insular, scholarly, slavish, tyrannical, and cold, was now hip, slick, mercurial, Camp, evasive, treacherous, Pop, militant, and chic — yet wonder of wonders it was the same Establishment, same not because the people were similar (so many had gone, so many were new) but because its essential presentation of itself to the world was the same. The Establishment had begun as a put-on, and it was continuing as a put-on.

Let us quote three times quickly from Jacob Brackman's article on "The Put-On" in the *New Yorker*, June 24, 1967.

Irony is unsuccessful when misunderstood. But the put-on, *inherently*, cannot be understood.

Not holding any real position (the put-on) is itself invulnerable to attack.

He (the put-on artist) doesn't deal in isolated little tricks; rather, he has developed a pervasive style of relating to others that perpetually casts what he says into doubt. The put-on is an *open-end* form. That is to say it is rarely climaxed by having the "truth" set straight — when a truth, indeed, exists. "Straight" discussion, when one of the participants is putting the others on, is soon subverted and eventually sabotaged by uncertainty. His intentions, and his opinions remain cloudy.

Who can fail to recognize what a superb description this is of the Early Establishment and the Late. The love of ambiguity in the early Establishment, the endless theses so intricately structured in the syntax of their own jargon that parodies of the old *Partisan Review* style used to deliver insights, willy-nilly, as good as the original; indeed how better than by the logic of the put-on to explain the extraordinary scholarly apparatus of the old articles which produced theses so arcane and intimately rubbed with sorcerer's garlic that no one can remember a single one of the theses today. But they were not to be remembered — the articles, the magazines, the Establishment itself existed as a way of life which would generate a kind of power and position for itself without necessity for a product which might be consumed and criticized. The old *Partisan Review* used to sit on coffee tables like a magic object, not to be examined, certainly not to be enjoyed, but to be received, an emanation.

The new Establishment, neater, niftier, swift, puts working drawings of Molotov cocktails on the cover of the *New York Review of Books* — the put-on is merely more timely. Is it revolution they are advocating with the drawing, no, it is news. Is that really news? No, but it is an attitude. What's an attitude? That's for you to define, but why are you upset by the drawing? So the new Establishment is ultra-Left, yet not very left. They will talk of going to Hanoi to sit in cafés to be bombed, but they do not sign income tax protests against the war nor are they ready to put their names to a number of causes which could land them in jail. They are indifferent to power, they are resourceful at gathering it. In fact, they have no attitude to power, goes the put-on, why do you? Where the old Establishment was often supercilious about literary values, beating every writer to death with the standard of Henry James until the moment came when the critic would say, "I can't bear Henry James, can you?" so the new Establishment is supercilious about power, success, and money. Success is not its dirty little secret, but its ball of mercury. Do not trap the mercury, it would say — my powers of locomotion depend on its ability to keep me moving — I am a dead man once I stop!

That is the anxiety of all Establishments. Stripped of

all British wickedness, their talents they believe are revealed as second-rate, they are but flowers pressed in a book. So they will play the shell game, do the dance of the veils, adore the put-on, elevate Camp, praise Pop, rush to install plastic in fashions, and avoid like demons and witches confrontation upon a point.

Can that be why *Making It* was so abominable to them? Because Podhoretz was blind to the defenses of the put-on and had the idiocy or the suicidal strength to move to the center of the stage, open his box, exhibit his tricks? If mercury is your god, then self-exposure is like sand, like sand up your ass, like bogging the armies of your friends in swamps of sand — it was with all the fury of a military betrayal that the Establishment turned on Podhoretz.

Yes. For indeed this Establishment began some thirty or thirty-five years ago when a few timid intellectuals fierce in the power of their minds took a set of uncompromising attitudes on literary standards, and discovered to their surprise that more than a few in America — that bowl of the great undefined soup — listened to them as authorities, followed them as though they might be high priests with an ear to the murmur in the void.

It had begun as a put-on. No one knew as much as they claimed to know, no one could have passed through the galaxies of experience they were ready to judge, authority was a mask they assumed as the bravest assertion of their life (the ills and the terrors of the ghetto still clinging to some of their toes) and the triumph of the assertion was in the continuing life of their put-on, their life became a put-on where a stand would never be taken, for by a stand might they be judged and the mask stripped; no, they galloped and growled and huffed and puffed (nimble all the while) and stayed alive as comedians of the highest order, and were followed as their Establishment developed into another, by further newer younger practitioners of the put-on, young literary executives who would not be caught dead making a remark with their back to the wall or the ball of their foot off the ball of mercury, there was even a vaster anxiety to keep the put-on alive in this younger Establishment, for it was less well educated than the old, less seasoned, less tempered, the young were inheritors of power they had not gained by withstanding a siege. So they were somewhat appalled by their power and utterly aghast at the forces which confronted them across the gulf of America.

5

Of course, we are a severed land. We have grown too fast and never consumed our wastes. They bloat our gut, stupefy our mind, and wash the art of communication from Right Wing to Left with the St. Vitus Dance of the put-on. If the Left Establishment, now conscience of America, sits in terror before the muscle and body of that Right Wing which gained America with its fists (and its money), rest assured the Right Wing sits in its own terror before judgment, listening like Lennie to any George's speech about the rabbits, floundering in its own vast rotting cabbage of sentimental mortgages, poisoned fertilizer, ideological dustbowls, and put-ons so monumental you cannot shovel them away. The Kingfish of the put-on speaks:

> "Sad but steady — always convinced of his cause — he stuck it out," Mr. Johnson said of President Abraham Lincoln. "Sad but steady, so will we," he added.
> — *New York Times*, February 13, 1968

It's the tragedy of us all that the consummate moment of affirmation, outright confession, or sheer renunciation now appears out of a mirror whose first question becomes: Is this noble act the work of a whack or the superbest put-on of all?

Four
Prefaces

Deaths for the Ladies

Deaths for the Ladies was written through a period of
fifteen months, a time when my life was going through
many changes including a short stretch in jail, the
abrupt dissolution of one marriage, and the beginning of
another. It was also a period in which I wrote very little,
and so these poems and short turns of prose were my
lonely connection to the one act which gave a sense of
self-importance. I was drinking heavily in that period,
not explosively as I had at times in the past, but steadily
— most nights I went to bed with all the vats loaded,
and for the first time, my hangovers in the morning were
steeped in dread. Before, I had never felt weak without a
drink — now I did. I felt heavy, hard on the first steps of

middle age, and in need of a drink. So it occurred to me it was finally not altogether impossible that I become an alcoholic. And I hated the thought of that. My pride and my idea of myself were subject to slaughter in such a vice.

Well, this preface is not to recount the story of those years and how I may have come out of them; no, we are here to give a crack of light to the little book which follows. I used to wake up in those days, as I have just remarked, with a drear hangover, and the beasts who were ready to root in my entrails were prowling outside. To a man living on his edge, New York is a jungle, and such mornings were full of taboo. It was often directly important whether the right or left hand was crossed with water first.

One modest reality used to save such hours from dipping too quickly into too early a drink. It was the scraps of paper I would find in my jacket. There were fragments of poems on the scraps, not poems really, little groupings of lines, little crossed communications from some wistful outpost of my mind where, deep in drink the night before, it had seemed condign to record the unrecoverable nuance of a moment, a funny moment, a mean moment, a moment when something I might always have taken for granted was turned for an instant on its head.

Some of those curious little communications which came riding in on the night through an electrolyte of deep booze were fairly good, many were silly, the best were often indecipherable. Which would feel close to tragic. Almost always the sensation of writing a good poem in the dark of early morning was followed in the daylight by the knowledge I had gone so deep I could not find my eyes. My handwriting had temporarily disintegrated in the passion of putting down a few words. Somebody had obviously been down in the rapture of the depths.

It was not so very funny. In the absence of a greater faith, a professional keeps himself in shape by remaining true to his professionalism. Amateurs write when they are drunk. For a serious writer to do that is equivalent to a professional football player throwing imaginary passes in traffic when he is bombed, and smashing his body into parked cars on the mistaken impression that he is taking out the linebacker. Such a professional football player will feel like crying in the morning when he discovers his ribs are broken.

I would feel like crying too. My pride, my substance, my capital, were to be found in my clarity of mind or — since my mind is never so very clear — let us say found in the professional cool with which the brain was able to contend with the temptations and opportunities each leap of intuition offered. It was criminal to take these leaps like an amateur, steeped in drink, wasteful, wanton. To be hearing the inspirations of the angel when one is kissing the flames is a condition so implicit with agony that it took eighteen centuries of Christendom before Kierkegaard could come back alive with the knowledge that such moments not only existed but indeed were the characteristic way modern man found a knowledge of his soul — which is to say he found it by the act of perceiving that he was most certainly losing it.

I would go to work, however, on my scraps of paper. They were all I had for work. I would rewrite them carefully, printing in longhand and ink, and I would spend hours whenever there was time going over these little poems, these sharp dry crisp little instants, some of them no more and hopefully no less possessed of meaning than the little crack or clatter of an autumn leaf underfoot. Something of the wistfulness in the fall of the wind was in those poems for me. And since I wasn't doing anything else very well in those days, I worked the poems over every chance I had. Sometimes a working day would go by, and I might put a space between two lines or remove a word. Maybe I was mending. As the sense of work grew a little clearer and the hangover receded, there was a happiness working mornings on *Deaths for the Ladies* which I had not felt for years. I loved *Deaths for the Ladies,* not because it was a big book — I knew my gifts as a poet were determined to be small — but because I was in love with its modesty. The modesty of *Deaths for the Ladies* was saving me. Out of the bonfire I seemed to have made of my life, these few embers were to be saved and set — not every last part of one's memories would have to be consumed. Besides, I wanted to give pleasure. It seemed to me that *Deaths for the Ladies* would give more simple pleasure than any book I had ever written, it was pure, it was modest, it was sad, and it was funny — it was so very modest — how could one not like it? And it had even one innovation to offer poets — so I thought. There was no music or prosody or command or rush of language in the book, no power, not much meter, not at all, much of it was poetry only by the arbitrary insistence of the short line, but *Deaths for the Ladies* was something else, I thought — it was a movie in words. I set it with the greatest care. Every line was placed on the page by me. The spaces were chosen with much deliberation, the repetitions of phrases were like images in a film. The music of the poem as a whole — if it had any — was like the montage of a film. I felt that all of *Deaths for the Ladies* made up one poem, not at all a great poem, never in any way, but still a most modern poem about a man loose in our city, for one cannot talk of New York without saying *our* city, there, majestic, choking in its own passions, New York, the true capital of the twentieth century. And *Deaths for the Ladies* was like a small sea breeze running through some of those electronic canyons where a myriad of fine moments were forever dying in the iridescence of foam.

Of course, if you fall in love with a book, you may be certain it will drown, suffocate, or expire all alone on an untended bed. *Deaths for the Ladies* came out in modest edition and sank without a sound. It was only reviewed three or four places, and the one good review it received (the Sunday *New York Times*) was six months late. Poets, for the most part, resented it. Why should they not? I had dabbled in that life for which they were willing, if they were good enough, to starve and to lose love. They had studied their craft, I had just skipped about in it. They were dedicated to poetry, I was dedicated to climbing out of the hole I had dug for myself, and poetry was offering the first rung. Therefore, poets ignored the book, which was a pity, for a good poet might have done something with my little innovation, my movie in words.

But to end on a note less altruistic to the interests of art, let us look at one review. I had had secret hopes, I now confess, that *Deaths for the Ladies* would be a vast success at the bar of poetry. The hopes got bounced. Here is the review in *Time,* March 30, 1962:

> *Ever*
> *see*
> *a drunk*
> *come on*
> *daring*
> *I mean*
> *drunk*
> *like*
> *daring*
> *was a*
> *sloppy*
> *entrechat?*
> *Mr M*
> *comes on*
> *with fourbucks*
> *of poems*
> *about sex*
> *not love*
> *that run*
> *down*

like this
only
not
lined up
neat.
Having less
than
fourbucks
fun
a reader
counted
the words
and concluded
Mr M
is making up
for his
first book
which had
too many.
You
didn't
score
this
time
M
a
n
.
But hell you know that.

In a fury of incalculable pains, a poem was written in reply, sent to *Time* Magazine's column of letters, and printed there.

Poem to the Book Review at Time

You will keep hiring
        picadors from the back row
        and pic the bull back
        far back along his spine

> *You will pass a wine*
> *poisoned on the vine*
> *You will saw the horns off*
> *and murmur*
> *The bulls are*
> *ah, the bulls are not*
> *what once they were*
> *Before the corrida is over*
> *there will be Russians in the plaza*
> *Swine some of you will say*
> *What did we wrong?*
> *and go forth to kiss the conquerer.*

Now, on the comfortable flank of this reminiscence, I think I may have been fortunate to get so paltry a reception on *Deaths for the Ladies*. For if I had been treated well, I might have kept floating in a still little pond, and drowned my sorrow for myself in endless wine and scraps of paper and folios of further poems. Instead, the review in *Time* put iron into my heart again, and rage, and the feeling that the enemy was more alive than ever, and dirtier in the alley, and so one had to mend, and put on the armor, and go to war, go out to war again, and try to hew huge strokes with the only broadsword God ever gave you, a glimpse of something like Almighty prose.

The Short Fiction of Norman Mailer

It has been remarked that the short fiction of this author is neither splendid, unforgettable, nor distinguished, and I hasten hereby to join such consensus. A man may go his way, look for his education, grow cultivated, even become superb, yet he need never come in contact with a short story of mine. He will still seem almost perfect.

Nay, he will be almost perfect. Of course one would not want to chance this of a man ignorant of *An American Dream, The Deer Park, Barbary Shore,* or *The Naked and the Dead* — no, they should not be avoided. Why, others in fact might go on so far as to insist this highly cultivated fellow was directly hurting his appreciation of American rackets and letters by not catching up on the journalism, politics, essays, and general nonfiction of the author under examination. But, one place, there is agreement. The friends of the author, and his detractors, may argue over his position as novelist, philosopher, essayist, journalist, personality, cathartic, spark, or demiurge, but they hold hands on the short fiction. He's a journeyman there. And he agrees. The author agrees now twice. He does not have the gift to write great short stories, or perhaps even very good ones. In fact, he will confess he does not have the interest, the respect, or the proper awe. The short story bores him a little. He will admit he rarely reads them. He is, in secret, not fond of writers who work at short stories. Nor are they often, he suspects, fond of him. He has a private sneer for the reputations they have amassed. There is a terrible confession to make: he thinks the short story is relatively easy to write. You have only to be good for a day or a week — there is none of that arduous collaboration between character and passion, inspiration and ascetism, which goes into keeping one's balance on the teeter-totter of a novel where work goes on day after day through many a season into the years. Anyone can be good for a week, but who can be good for a year, or two, or three? So, while there may be admiration or affection for a few writers of the short story, for Chekhov, for Hemingway, for Isaac Bashevis Singer, for James T. Farrell — the list is really not that long. One does not really want to include de Maupassant, Steinbeck, or Katherine Mansfield. If Maugham always gave pleasure, and A. Conan Doyle and Edgar Allan Poe, Hawthorne seemed unreadable.

While Joyce was admittedly a master in *Dubliners,* no one cared less. Katherine Anne Porter was an avatar of the art but dependably left you flat. Mary McCarthy — yes that lady wrote very good short stories, and there was Truman Capote, and one story by Paul Bowles, but: Eudora Welty — couldn't read her, Flannery O'Connor — somehow never did read her, John Cheever and John Updike — old Prince and young Prince of good old maggie, the *New Yorker* — why push on with the list? It is evident we are confronting the taste of a mucker. He obviously doesn't care about the short story. The man is telling the truth. His short stories show it. They have little in common. They do not give us a great many different facets and situations and glimpses of people in a very specific milieu as Isaac Babel's stories about the Red Cossacks did, nor do they have that private vision of the whole you can find in the short fiction of Hemingway, Singer, Farrell, Sholom Aleichem, or Scott Fitzgerald — another favorite, Fitzgerald. When one thinks of the charm which resides in even the worst of his quick commercial stories, it is painful to push one's own plain efforts so far forward. Yet we do it. Yes, for the bucks first, paperback reader! For the good wives and good kids; for the ego — that snake who won't die no matter how we beat it on the head — that ego is a *muscle.* Finally, it is done for a legitimate motive — to keep Renaissance man alive. Yes. You see every one of these stories is different from every other one. They are all excursions and experiments. We might just as well be in at the birth of science — Renaissance man is looking for his experimental method, which he encounters, let us suspect, by dramatic contrast.

Should we explain? Then shift the metaphor this round. The real short-story writer is a jeweler. Like most such craftsmen, he does not — unless knighted by genius, as Hemingway or Faulkner — do much else. No, he stays in his shop, he polishes those jewels, he collects craft, lore, confirms gossip, assays jeweler's rouge, looks to steal the tricks of the arcane, and generally disports like a medieval alchemist who's got a little furnace, a small retort, a cave, a handful of fool's gold, and a mad monk's will. With such qualifications, one in a hundred becomes an extraordinary writer, but on the other hand, the worst of this guild makes a life from kissing spiders.

Now consider the hearty protagonist who has collected his short fiction for your pleasure, entertainment, and approval; here is a big, brawny, nineteenth-century version of Renaissance man — a prospector, son. He's not looking for jewels, no, he's digging up buckets of ore, he's panning by all various vigors and methods. The truth is that he is seduced more by method than by gold or gem. He is, you see, possessed of extraordinary greed. He is a modern man like all nihilists. So he does not wish to pick up a nugget or two and reduce it to its proper wealth, its full sheen; rather he's impatient, ambitious, and obsessed with one idea — move on fast. Keep looking for the biggest mine of them all. He doesn't want to get caught in the refining and polishing. So he sticks in a shovel here, sets off dynamite there, diverts a fast stream, builds up a dam, slapdash, bang and boom, move on fast. Look to learn a little about everything. That is the instinct of the Renaissance — it speaks not only of the energies and techniques of that twentieth century which will eventually issue out of it, but gives a hint as well of the wastes which are also to follow.

Yes, these short stories are imperfect artifacts — various drillings, diggings, tests, and explosions on the way to finding a certain giant mine, well-advertised over the years by the prospector. If some show too little evidence of the craftsman, others are even overpolished. There is in fact a spectrum, nay, a panoply of fictional techniques: we can go all the way over from the total solid conventionality of the three war stories to the experiments in style of *Truth and Being, Nothing and Time;* or *Adver-*

tisements for Myself on the Way Out. We can travel on the scale of literary merit from the precisions of *Ministers of Taste* down to the casual, even slovenly, prose which mars the narrative tension of *The Last Night.* The point to this collection is found in its contrast. It is therefore not without value to the young college writer of the short story, for an exploration to a given fictional point is often done more than once, but by opposite means. So, for example, *Truth and Being, Nothing and Time,* and *The Killer* are both about the slow deadening of the self, and that is their last resemblance, for *The Killer* is vastly impersonal — one could not determine the author from the style — while the other could have been written by no one but the servant of letters here in the stocks. Yet both stories were done within a month of each other.

Look further: *A Calculus at Heaven* and *Advertisements for Myself on the Way Out* are about the deaths of two men, both murdered — it is just that the deaths are very different, for one is killed in war, and the other is slain criminally, although we do not know how. Also — they are written sixteen years apart.

Continue: *The Greatest Thing in the World* and *Maybe Next Year* are stories composed in college, so predictably are about people in trouble because they have no money. But the styles are searching for their object in opposite directions.

See here: three war stories, *The Paper House, The Language of Men,* and *The Dead Gook,* all complete with sturdy construction of atmosphere, are presented alternately with three humorous stories — one dry, *The Notebook* — one episodic, *The Patron Saint of Macdougal Alley* — one arch, *Great in the Hay.* The first five of these six stories were written in the same few weeks.

Now consider that *Great in the Hay* is followed by *The Last Night,* a treatment for a projected movie which bears no relation to *Great in the Hay.* No relation but the most umbilical one — guys like Bert are the guys who make movies like *The Last Night,* that is if you are lucky. From what I hear, guys like Bert are getting rare. Next, two extraordinarily short stories, *It* and *The Shortest Novel of Them All,* are set side by side for instant examination. (One dare not say more or the comment will be longer than the stories.) They are followed by two ventures in mixed genre. Short stories full of resonance, evocation, style, mood, horror, outrage, etc., which began nonetheless as something else — *Ministers of Taste* as a letter, then two letters; *The Locust Cry* as a commentary on *The Early Masters* by Martin Buber.

Finally, we have *The Time of Her Time* and *The Man Who Studied Yoga* — two subtle ways are here presented by which love may be made to women. Since, however, no bad taste is so seductive as to write about oneself with iron objectivity — we will not go on to talk of what is very good or even — now it is confessed — superior in *The Time of Her Time* and *The Man Who Studied Yoga.* It is enough to say they are superior to most good short fiction. (But then these last two are also short novels and were written with the idea that they were the beginnings of real, full-length novels, so the dedication was deeper. Which proves a previous point. But, at this stage, resolutely, we turn the book over to the reader. May he consider the introduction modest, too modest by far.

The Saint and the Psychopath

Many years ago I wished to write a book called *The Saint and the Psychopath* and in time that book swelled to such proportions in my mind that I thought of a magnum opus to bear the monumental name: *A Psychology of the Orgy.* Ah, my *Psychology of the Orgy* reduced itself to the dimensions of an essay. "The White Negro" came out of these titles and ambitions and those years of immersion in marijuana. Other years and other titles went by — I thought from time to time of *The Hip and the Square,* or *After the White Negro,* and with more time forgot all of the titles and thought of other things. I came to use the words existential and existentialism rather than Hip. Hip, I knew, would end in a box on Madison Avenue.

I, in turn, did my work. I thought, however, that many of my writings were excursions into existentialism. Now, the title comes back. It is a good fit — *The Saint and the Psychopath.* Because these are writings on two themes, violence and the mystical, writings about what is criminal and what is religious, and the root of my perception all those years ago (after marijuana first stole into the keep of my psyche and began to lower the bridges one by one) was that the saint and the psychopath were united to one another, and different from the mass of men. They were closer to existence. They shared a sense of the present so powerful that memory, caution, precedent, tradition, commonplace, project, and future enterprise were nerveless before the sense of the present in their mind and body. In their most incandescent states, they existed for their next breath, and so were indistinguishable from one another; saint and psychopath — a murderer in the moment of his murder could feel a sense of beauty and perfection as complete as the transport of the saint. (And indeed this was the root of the paradox which had driven Kierkegaard near to mad for he had the courage to see that his criminal impulses were also his most religious.)

It will be noticed that the titles to each part of this collection are not modest. "The Psychology of the Psychopath" — it calls for a massive work. And "The Existentialism of Death" — certainly that is a ten-volume study. But the tomes do not exist, not even the theory. To the knowledge of this author, Robert Lindner (quoted in "The White Negro") is the only psychologist or psycho-analyst to make an imaginative pass at the first problem, and no major existentialist, not Sartre, nor Heidegger, nor Nietzsche, nor even Dostoyevsky, has advanced an inquiry into the possible existence of existential states within death (which is to say: states of dramatic purposeful change) in the dying and in one's condition after death. So the titles are novel, and the ideas arrived to the author in the purest psychopathic form — a way to tell you that they came in some degree out of that precise naïveté of the psychopath which assumes his experience is so pure in its lightning and consequent thunder that no one, not no one, has ever had an intimation before. The psychopath is insulated from history — how can he not be? He assumes in the intensity of his moment that all history is his lungs and loins, breath and sex, all is contained in that mysterious sensuous dread quite ready to disclose itself whenever we adventure nearest to life. So the titles. And an excuse for the presumption. There are worse crimes than presumption. Without it, more than one interesting action would never have begun.

The End of Obscenity

The book in your hand is a quiet and essentially modest account of a legal revolution led by a few determined and extraordinary publishers. When I think of Barney Rosset and Walter Minton, I am reminded on the instant of Civil War generals: Sherman and Grant race to the fore. They are men who are determined to take a hill even if it takes all summer and chews up half their resources. It was thus Minton's and Rosset's great good fortune to have one of Lee's Lieutenants for their legal counsel, a Light Horse Harry named Charles Rembar, and the purpose of this foreword is not to take up the arguments of the book, but rather to relieve its modesty with an account of the author. Like Rembar, Light Horse Harry was a great cavalryman, and his strategy and tactics were bold, luminous, witty, and exceptionally well balanced, but men endowed with the combative graces do not often write about themselves. So I will repair the lack of personal memoir and give you an introduction not to the work (which stands agreeably by itself) but to the author.

He is my cousin, Mr. Charles Rembar, the son of my mother's oldest sister, and he is the closest to an older brother I will ever come. Since he is eight years older than me (although I fear he does not look it) he was very much an older brother all through my childhood, and I worshipped him (with enormous funds of love and envy) because he was a hero. He was one of the few people I've ever known who had a happy look on his face when he came to bat in the late innings with men on base, his side behind, and the need for a homer prominent in everyone's head. Indeed he had his smile because it was slightly better than even money he was going to hit that homer. In fact, he would. This is not hyperbole. If I saw him in a hundred baseball games, there must have been fifty late inning spots of exactly the sort I describe: he probably hit thirty-six homers out of fifty. In fact, we usually didn't believe it if the ball didn't rocket over the center fielder's head. Often as not, Cy Rembar's homers would land in the tennis court at the end of our playing field, for that after all was the place where he would pull out all the winning sets from all the tennis players who were more trained than he, more devoted, more fanatical, and less humorous. Ditto for football.

Ditto for getting the best-looking girls. Because of Cy Rembar, I used to believe in Jack Armstrong.

Those were Depression years. Much gloom abounded in everyone, but he was the bright spot. He was the only figure I encountered in my childhood who seemed to believe it was more natural to win than lose, and that life was therefore to be enjoyed rather than decried.

Since then, he's gotten a little older, not a great deal so far as I can see, and it's a shock to realize I'm as tall as he is today and weigh — I do not brag of this — thirty pounds more. But he's still the one man in all the world whose good opinion is gold to me, because Rembar is not only a winner, but a man with a subtle moral force. While he was never religious, probably never will be, and so far as I know evolved no elaborate set of ethics other than a profound respect for the law which served to house the architecture of his ability to reason, that particular ability in him precisely to reason has become a force which approaches the power of a mighty muscle, for in close tactical argument and debate on any subject improvised at the drop of a coin, he is doubtless one of the world's best and most brilliant quick reasoners. Which is to say he can be as bad as a boil if he beats you in a tactical brush on your favorite theme. But I have been led astray by Rembar's annoying power to reason. I was speaking of his moral force. It comes, I suppose, from a reliance on taste, a sort of implicit sense that manners, if they are excellent enough, can serve as a substitute for metaphysics. (Doubtless they so serve because exquisite manners call upon that reservoir of natural grace and animal philosophy which existentialists like myself are always trying to chart.) No matter how, he's a modest moral force in any room in which he finds himself because he's a clean man, and looks for clean issues to complex problems, and does it with good will. Consider what a recommendation is this when the man has been my lawyer for twenty years and charges solid fees. But it is true. He looks for moral issues in his activities. And still plays baseball. And still might take a girl away from me if he chose to. Although I hope the odds have closed.

And I take pleasure in this book by him because I had a little to do with the commencement of his interest in these problems, yes, back years ago with *The Deer Park*, and years before, we used to argue (since it was a matter of direct moment to me) about the defense of serious works of literature which were on the face of their language or situation obscene, and I used to fulminate against those thumbscrews of the law which required the defense to engage respectable witnesses who had then all but to perjure themselves in order to swear that the particular erotic work was moral and aroused them not at all. I would cry out, "Why can't a novel just once be defended as erotic and valuable as well?" and Rembar would give me a short lecture, most clearly presented, about the subtle if sometimes retarded relation of the law to reality, and how perhaps the time was coming.

Well, it has come. A war has been won. Writers like myself can now in America write about any subject; if it is sexual, and we are explicit, no matter, the American writer has his freedom. Rembar has done as much as any lawyer alive to forge that freedom in several most historic cases. We can all congratulate ourselves.

He is, however, as I would remind you, a moral man, and so I was pleased to see as I read through these pages that he is troubled just a hint by the liberties won, just indeed as I am troubled. For back of the ogres of censorship and the comedies of community hypocrisy, there still rests the last defense of the censor, a sophisticated argument which might urge that sex is a mystery and men explore it and detail it and define it and examine it and eventually disembowel it of privacy at their peril. It is the argument of tradition against the power of reason. Rembar — we will repeat — personifies the positive attractions of the life of reason, but he is sufficiently instinctive as a gent to waste no time congratulating himself on heroic victories. Like the noblest (one revenges oneself on an older brother by drowning him in superlatives) yes, like the noblest of Lee's Lieutenants, he wonders privately and with concern if his cause is altogether just. So, too, do I. It is my cause as well. And like many another American writer, about to embark on a literary trip through some of the aesthetic territory Rembar's cases have given sanction to enter, I brood too about undue exposure of the mystery, and console myself with the second argument — that the inroads of science and industry, advertising, bad art, industry, and commerce, also invade the mysteries of existence. And thus the poet must be there as well to trim the lamp and anoint that numbing of the flesh which serves the technician's electrodes and probes. The novelist may help to sink the ship of sex before all is done, but it might be even worse without a literary exploration or two. For next to the mystery is the disease. It is the disease of the twentieth century, that ill so ubiquitously spawned by the anomalies of reason and the maceration of instinct, all the promiscuous pills of all of that labyrinthine and technological vat. So when I question the value of the inquiry I now have real freedom to make, I lave the edge of my doubt with the certainty that some one of us artists must manage to be there to arrest the doctor when he also marches into the door of the mystery. Because the doctor takes flashbulbs into the womb, whereas we — if we are good enough — will take the herbs of some of the good words and balm the helpless exposure of the girl with aromatics and spice. Perhaps life continues on a certain irreducible minimum of art. Without that, no life. That is the *modus operandi* of the advocate whose opinions and deeds you are now ready to encounter. Welcome to the writing racket, Cousin Cy.

An
Imaginary
Interview

INTERVIEWER: Well, here I am again.

MAILER: Nobody has seen you since *Cannibals and Christians*.

INTERVIEWER: If you want to know the truth, I'm a little annoyed about that. You feel you can call me when you want me, and then need never invite me back for a cup of coffee in between.

MAILER: I want you to learn about social life. It is built entirely on the instrumentalities we offer each other.

INTERVIEWER: Then today it seems I'm of use to you.

MAILER: On occasion, you are of use to me.

INTERVIEWER: Yes, really, you bet. Today! Why didn't you get another interviewer? Someone with a name?

MAILER: Well, you always manage to get my remarks right.

INTERVIEWER: You can also filter and select your questions.

MAILER: Leave me my pride. I am not afraid of questions. A man who can't answer questions shouldn't run for President.

INTERVIEWER: Are you really still running?

MAILER: Only for President of the literary world.

INTERVIEWER: Well, even there you've got a way to go. There's opposition, Mr. Mailer, considerable opposition.

MAILER: Still, I think I'm the best candidate around. It's a modest remark, believe me, because the best isn't necessarily that good. At any rate, I'm prepared to wait for office.

INTERVIEWER: You think you're better than Burroughs or Nabokov or Malamud?

MAILER: They have very large talents, but their nose is not on the presidency. I concentrate more than they do on that.

INTERVIEWER: What about Bellow and Algren?

MAILER: They are capital fellows. But no one from Chicago can ever become chief executive of the literary world. The East would be in insurrection.

INTERVIEWER: What about William Styron?

MAILER: He's the only Southern writer I know who's the living embodiment of the New York Yankees. I suspect the Establishment would be hopelessly lonely without him, for then they would not have much else but me. And I derive from the Brooklyn Dodgers.

INTERVIEWER: You don't think Styron is a marvelous writer?

MAILER: He has a very fragrant if slightly redolent breath; but so far as I know, a dangerous idea has never infiltrated his brain. His mind is happy as a virgin oyster. Oysters taste wonderful if you like them, but they stir no foundations.

INTERVIEWER: Whereas you, sir, are a foundation shaker?

MAILER: I do my humble best.

INTERVIEWER: There are some — I am one of them — who would say that the foundation manages to shake you up considerably more than you shake it. That photograph of you, for example, on the back of your new book, with a black eye as big as a fist on your face — well, you may think it's funny, but there's low appeal concealed in it. What you are really saying is, "Don't get too mad at me! I'm just America's No. 1 literary clown."

MAILER: I didn't see it that way, or I wouldn't have used such a picture. No, I was trying to perform a public service. You see, people go around all the time saying, "That Norman Mailer — I'd like to see him get punched in the nose." Well, it's no good for Americans to walk around with so much anger botttled up. Most charitably, I was trying to relieve them.

INTERVIEWER: Or were you trying to relieve the anger a lot more Americans are going to feel for paying $4.95 for your novel *Why Are We in Vietnam?* when it's hardly two hundred pages long and has nothing to do with Vietnam?

MAILER: Do we have to rush into a discussion of my book so quickly?

INTERVIEWER: I would expect you to prefer not to talk about it too much.

MAILER: You dislike it?

INTERVIEWER: I think it's dreadful. It's the most cooked-up phony piece of I don't know what. I hated it.

MAILER: Maybe I shouldn't have called you for an interview. We're a considerable distance apart, and I was hoping I might find you in the middle. You see, there are times when I read *Why Are We in Vietnam?* and it displeases me too, but there are other times when I decide it's one of the ten funniest books written since *Huckleberry Finn.*

INTERVIEWER: You are suffering from prepublication schizophrenia with accompanying megalomania on the manic side of the moon.

MAILER: Not the first author to be so afflicted. Look, I don't know what to say of this book. Sometimes I think it's the best two hundred pages I've yet done, the most American, certainly the two hundred pages least alienated from genius.

INTERVIEWER: You are daring to say you are a genius?

MAILER: Be careful. This is one of the ways I get my terrible reputation. I didn't say I was a genius, I rather said in effect that the positive half of my prepublication schizophrenia looked now and again upon this new novel with the sentiment that my prose was here less alienated from genius than in my other works.

INTERVIEWER: What does the negative side of this schizophrenia have to say?

MAILER: That the book was written to fulfill a contract.

INTERVIEWER: You sit there and say you wrote this book to fulfill a contract? Your cynicism would make hardened politicians walk the plank.

MAILER: I wrote the book to fulfill a contract. What's so exceptional about that? My expenses are, to me, huge. I write to make a living. That does not obligatorily inhibit the work from rising above itself. I did *An American Dream* in installments because I was in debt and had to make a small fortune in a hurry. That didn't make it a bad book. I think it's my best book. I confess I still believe sentence for sentence *An American Dream* is one of the better-written books in the language.

INTERVIEWER: And *Vietnam,* which was written in . . . ?

MAILER: Four months.

INTERVIEWER: . . . is thereby twice as good?

MAILER: I started with a cynical motive which was first burned through and then burned out by the rush of the impulse. The pages came to me faster than any book since *The Naked and the Dead.*

INTERVIEWER: But you still have a divided mind on its merit?

MAILER: Some books come to you. As *The Naked and the Dead* came to me. They are bonuses, gifts. You do not have to kill some little part of your flesh to dredge them up. This is a fatal shade mystical, but it is almost as if you are serving as agent for a book which wants to get itself written. So the author never knows what to think of such books when he is done. His real fondness — since writing books is the closest men ever come to childbearing — is more for those books he delivered out of his own flesh, torn and deadened by the process, but able at least to use all art and craft, all accumulated lore. Whereas *Why Are We in Vietnam?* came through like a storm, writing itself — I enjoyed the work, I was full of energy when I was done, but the work was by the same token impersonal. So I do not know if I love the new novel or am indifferent to it.

INTERVIEWER: Let us go back to the idea that you were serving as an agent for a book which wanted to get written. What then is this book saying?

MAILER: I'm afraid it is saying that America enters the nightmare of its destiny like a demented giant in a half-cracked canoe, bleeding from wounds top and bottom, bellowing in bewilderment, drowning with radio transmitters on the hip and radar in his ear. He has a fearful disease, this giant.

INTERVIEWER: What is it?

MAILER: Greed. Vanity.

INTERVIEWER: What else?

MAILER: The Faustian necessity to amass all knowledge, to enslave nature.

INTERVIEWER: And what is the first vice of this giant who, in your words, symbolizes America, and has now become the metaphor *pro tem* of your new novel, *Why Are We in Vietnam?*, a work — at least I can get this in — about some Texans who go off on a hunting trip in Alaska. What is the first vice of this giant who symbolizes America?

MAILER: Arrogance. Half the people in this country think they are possessed of genius. It is no accident, you see, that I run for President of the literary world. (*Sighs.*) I wish you liked my book more. Then I could open up and tell you all sorts of interesting little things about it. But as it is . . . oh, well, (*the faintest strain of self-pity appears*) they say Beethoven talked to himself.

A
One-Act
Play

A Fragment from Vietnam

(The staging is obviously free. As first performed in Provincetown in the summer of 1967 with Rip Torn playing D.J., Beverly Bentley as Hallie Lee Jethroe and Dan Durning as Dr. Rothenberg, it was effective to let D.J. walk up and down the main aisle and address the audience intimately while, on stage, Hallie Lee lay on a couch and Rothenberg sat behind her, each frozen in tableau during D.J.'s long opening speech.)

D.J.: "He's evil," said Mrs. Jethroe, *(D.J. points to Mrs. Jethroe — he will, within quotation marks, imitate her voice.)* the mother of this extraordinary late adolescent, *(D.J. points to himself)* the one who calls himself D.J., who is eighteen and sometimes appears to be twice eighteen, (*wink*) or thirty-six. "Why, he's evil. What am I going to do with D.J.? The boy needs to be spanked. I would just as soon spank a puma! He's evil," said Mrs. Jethroe to her psychiatrist, (*D.J. points to the psychiatrist*) who is a Jewish fellow, nothing other, working his ass off in Dallas, which means so to speak that he must spend eight to ten clammy periods of fifty minutes each listening to Dallas matrons complain about the sexual habits of their husbands, all ex–hot rodders, hunters, cattlemen, oil riggers, corporation gears, and insurance finks, zap! Well, like every one of these bastards (as Mrs. Jeth — call her Death-row Jethroe — might say when her breath is big! like the bottom of a burnt-out bourbon barrel) well, every one of these bastards has the sexual peculiarities of red-blooded men, which is to say that one of them can't come unless he's squinting down a gunsight, and the other won't produce unless his wife sticks a pistol up his ass — that man is of course a cop. If the psychiatrist wasn't such a fink and such a nice Jewish fellow type as to be working for the general good and wheel of society, and if he wasn't afraid of drilling a little career-and-cancer piss right into the heart of Texas, he would write this book about the ejaculatory jump habits of cops, big ass Southern redneck cops all bullwhipped and bullshitted up into putteez, son, they come more ways — I froth at the mouth, said the killer, but don't think it's spit. Well, what's to say, D.J.'s mother, Death-row Jethroe, is the prettiest little blond you ever saw (looks like a draw between young Katherine Anne Porter and young Clare Booth Luce, whew) all perfume snatchy poo, appears twenty-five, is actually forty-five, airs, humors, curl to her mouth, half Texas ass accent, half London wickedness, trill and thrill, she's been traveling around the world, Heartache House in Bombay and Freedom

House in Bringthatpore, shit, she's been getting cunt-tickled and fucked by all the Class I Dongs in Paris and London, not to mention the upper dedicated pricks of Rome and Italy while her hus, big daddy Rusty Jethroe, is holding up the corporation end all over the world including Dallas, Big D, D.J.'s father, Big Daddy, old Rusty, has got the dynamite. He don't come, he explode, he's a geyser of love, hot piss, shit, corporation pus, hate and heart, baby, he blasts, he's Texas willpower, hey yay!

Yeah, D.J.'s father, the cream of corporation corporateness, Rutherford David Jethroe Jellicoe Jethroe, came back to Dallas after spending twelve years off and on moving around the world for Central Consolidated Chemical and Plastic, CCCP being what the boys called it till they found out the Red-ass Russians had their Communist Party initials CCCP, this was a terrible day in Texas the night they found out, so they changed the name, they called it Central Consolidated *Combined* Chemical and Plastic, the new coagulation of title now being CCCCP or as the team began to say, 4C and P, which is an unhappy conjunction since how much do you have to foresee before you got — well, they say people in the Corporate life shoot their urine straighter than a '03 Springfield, y'hear Rangoon? So back came Rusty after twelve big years in the foreign ass vineyards out where the reindeer run and the flying fishes try out their flying CIA fucks past Mandalay.

Back came Rusty to Dallas to head Pew Rapports — the filter with the purest porosity of purpose — and Rusty was a heroic-looking figure of a Texan, six feet one-half inch, 194, red-brown lean keen of color, eyes gray-green-yellow-brown which is approved executive moderate shit hue color for eyes if you want to study corporation norms, mores, and tempos of shift and success in massive organizational configurations, and since he was big exec, what do you think he look and talk like? Well Clara, go to the rear of the line, he look like a high-breed crossing between Dwight D. Eisenhower and Henry Cabot Lodge, what the buns do you think a corporation exec is going to look like if he got the time to make his face grow the way he want it to grow during all the fifties while he's overseas, I mean what face did he ever see more of than Dwight D., and Henry C. working his ax at the U.N., these corporation eggzex are full of will, man, they're strong as bulls these hide-ass Waspy mules with their silvy-rim specs, I mean they go direction they want to go, their hair too curly they go bald, their nose too long, they sniff it up, their lips too fat, forget it, we're talking about the wrong man, they tie that nice dry-oiled West Point ramrod to their back just like they're a tomato plant on a stick, I mean they grow into a bat's ass if it help our astronauts along. Rusty can zip that corporation fly working as executive, and/or director, and/or special adviser and/or consultant and/or troubleshooter and/or organizer and/or associate of, and/or paid employee for the 4c and P, the CIA, the C of C, the FBI, the ADA, the ADA?, the Policemen's Benevolent Society, the John Birch, natch, the Dallas Citizens Council for Infighting and Inflicting Symphonic Music, the Benevolent Order of Oilwell Riggers Drillers and Roughnecks, the Warren Commission Boosters, the President's Thousand Dollar Club, the Gridiron Club, the UIA and 4A of D, that is the Underwriters, Insurance Agents and Actuarial Agents Association of America and Dallas, the RELM Cons — the Rotary, Elks, Lambs, Masons Consolidated for corporation studs who jes ain't got the time to spread out so they put it all in one dead fuck building — and the Republican Party, not to mention the Second Congregated Anglo Episcopal and Conjoint Presbyterian Clutch and Methodist Church of Maltby Avenue, Dallas (that's St. Martin's, you faggot!) and the Gourmet Wine and Pate

Plate and Fork Society. Forget the country clubs unless you like to read lists, the Dallas Elm and Tree Club, the Dallas Cowboy Turtle Creek Cheering and Chowder, TCU Boosters, SMU Boosters, Gala Ring and Ranch, Loretta Noodlehad's Country Club, take it from D.J., forget this shit. If Rusty was to run around all year, which he does, he still couldn't get his dick in every door for which he's got a card, you know, Diners Club, Carte Blanche, American Express, Budget Rent-A-Car, Rusty's a pig! he's a real pig, man! It was all that dried-out sun-baked smoked jerkin of meat his cowboy fore-ass bears used to eat, I mean, man, they used to use that hide for everything before they'd eat it, they'd swab out their mare's dock with it, wipe their own ass with it, pick up the pus from the corner of their eye, blow their nose, mop the piss off their boots, even use that dry old piece of meat to wrap around their skinny old dick for stuffing when they want to sodomize a real big cow, why they repair holes in their chaps with it, they used to have to beat it with a hoe handle before they could even cook it and fry it in axle grease. I mean, man, they were kind of tough. So, no wonder Rusty's a pig. His cells are filled with the biological inheritance and trait transmissions of his ancestors, all such rawhide, cactus hearts, eagle eggs, and coyote. Now, Rusty rolls that Château Lafite-Mouton-Rothschild around his liver-loving lips, and he can tell '49 from '53 from '59, all the while thinking of sixty and nine. He sings the song of the swine, D.J.'s daddy, nice fellow actually. Also forgot to mention he's an unlisted agent for Luce Publications, American Airlines Overseas Division, and the IIR — the Institute for International Research — shit!, Spy Heaven they ought to call it.

Does this idyll of family life whet your curiosity, flame your balls, or sour your spit? But hush you now. Think no longer of Rusty. The real stuff is turning on.

Her princess-ship. Alice Hallie Lee Jethroe is speaking to her Doc, Clam Fink, the Texas Hebe, actually his name is Leonard Levin Fichte Rothenberg, pronounced by all big-mind Texans as Linnit Live'n Fixit Rottenbug.

HALLIE: Lionhard, will you jes take a fix on what D.J. has to say. It's enough to make a mother wipe up Aunt Jemima's puke. He's out of his mind. Poor sad little fellow.

HALLIE (*with maternal pride*): He read the Marquis de Sade at the age of fifteen.

ROTHENBERG: Alice Hallie Lee Jethroe, I saw Ranald at your request, he was recalcitrant, charming, gracious, anti-Semitic, morally anesthetized, and smoldering with presumptive violence, a host of incence, I mean incest fixes, murder configurations, suicide sets, disembowelment diagrams and diabolism designs, mandalas! Face into the eye of the real, Hallelujah, he's a humdinger of a latent homosexual highly over-heterosexual with onanistic narcissistic and sodomistic overtones, a task force of libidinal cross-hybrided vectors.

HALLIE: He has high-breed vectors all right, he's got the cunningest ancestry, in fact, cause we're on my mother's side from the Norloins.

ROTHENBERG: New Orleans?

HALLIE: Yis, from Norlins, the Norlins Frenchy Montesquious and the Bat Fartsmotherers. (*Seeing that Levin Fichte is living on her word, she just knocks over a bottle of one of his urine specimens, adieu albumin!*) Mon Doo Rottenbug, you're sure full of shit for a doctor, don't y'know there are no fine Southern families called Fartsmotherer? Lord knows we ain't that fucking stupid, why even British county stock wouldn't be called Fartsmotherer, maybe Assknocking, but not the other, you can't analyze me, Living Fichte, if you don't know things like that, oh, poo, I wish you was an Italianate Jew, all earthy and Levantine and suave and had a cunt-tickler of a moustache, instead of your clammy cold Lithuanian brow, what are you, a Talmud hokum? speak up, ass, I just wish you was good enough to kiss my sweet perfumed powdered old pooty-toot, hey Linnit? am I getting out my egressions now?

ROTHENBERG: I would not call them aggressions so much as identity crises.

HALLIE: Oh, poo, let me tell you about the Montesquious. Half-Portuguese, half-French, all that hot crazy blood packed one-quarter into me, for the other half of my mother was just straight Arkansas mule, the Mulies, why they the richest family in Arkansas then, hot out of Peezer, Arkansas, and they used rat paper for tar paper on the Chic Sale, that's how benighted was their latrine, Army folk of course, the MacArthurs used to kiss their ass. And my daddy, well he was just a lover of a husband to my ma, and he must have had a dick on him like a derrick, do I shock you, Dr. Jew?

ROTHENBERG: To my cornplasters.

HALLIE: Oh, Linnit, you'll be the death of me yet. Listen to this old hen cackle. Well, Daddy was Indian for sure, and he had a personal odor like hot rocks in the sun which is in me all mixed with the fine sauces of Franco-Portuguese Montesquiou rut — I mean you should smell my armpits, noxious to some, a knockout to others, I keep them perfumed of course, we want no barmaid's fatal scent on Hallie Jethroe, so I wash, Dr. Rothenberg, three times a day, I don't want nothing but a soupçon of my good sweet crazy full-blooded woman's scent on the breeze off my knees, just enough for to keep the breed alive, talk of high-breed vectors, they're all marshals, and bastards and cowboys, and one desperado, and one railroad tycoon, and one professor at Harvard, first Texas professor they ever had in Clamsville, which is what I call Harvard, Linnit tell me straight and clear what am I going to do with Ranald, he's insane, that boy, tell me, you Talmud hokum, you clammy Have-it grit, I suppose I now have to pony up my fifty dollars for the hour.

ROTHENBERG: Madam, you owe me eleven hundred and fifty.

HALLIE: You'll have to bust a nut to get it, Rottenbug.

ROTHENBERG: I'll torture you, I love torturing Gentile females. All that white buttermilk flesh. Yum, yum. Yum, yum, yum.

D.J.: Hey, hey, they really talk that way? That little blond lady, Hallie-perfume and powder on the poo — she talk that way? And Rottenbug going yum yum yum — is he out of his fucking skull? Wait and see. Nobody's got any OK patience anymore, just cannibals asking for chocolate on their stick. Wait and see? You know what they're doing. They're talking about Tex, Tex Hyde, Gottfried "Texas" Hyde Junior, that's D.J.'s best friend, and know what, get that drop of cream off your jeans before you grow hair in your hand, this is the pitch, Tex is half-German and half-Indian on his father's side, Redskin and Nazi all in one paternal blood, and his mother, well, bless his mother, Tex Hyde's mother is jes old rawhide Texas ass family running back thru fifty-two shacks, right back to the Alamo where all old saddlesore real Texas ass families run back to, why lick the scab on LBJ's knee if one-tenth of all the Dallas ass families that go back to the Alamo was really there, they'd have all drowned in shit they were so congested and Santa Anna could have thrown his marijuana seed on the top and there'd be a forest of hemp now right in the heart of Texas.

Well, Tex Hyde, he's a mother fucker, sell you pot was grown on human shit, and he nothing but D.J.'s best friend. And they are terrible together. Listen to Halleloo. Her tone is full of hell right now, Line It With Hot Bugs is shifting in horror in his seat, cause Halleloo is talking in her bitchy boozy voice which means don't come near unless you can steer your prick like a whip and French tickler all in one, worm! women know which man has got the spring and who and which is the unfortunate dead ass, here is her words:

HALLIE: Tex Hyde is the son of an *undertaker,* I mean think of that, a Montesquiou Jellicoe Jethroe a-whopping around with a Kraut mortician's offspring, and all that bastard Indian Hyde blood in the background, firewater and dirty old engine oil, Indians unless they're descended from my daddy's line, and never you mind what it was, don' ask if it's Navajo, Apache, or any of those shit questions, you anthropologist manqué, you fuckless wonder listening to the sex'l habits of all us mule-ass Texans, ought to get your ears wiped out Dr. Fink Lenin Rodzianko whateva your name is, an Indian don't tell the secret of his name in a hurry to strangers like you, Clam Grits from Harvard Square, why, honey, that Tex Hyde don't have Eenyen blood like my daddy and my Rusty's daddy's daddy, no, it's just the sort of dirty vile polluted cesspool Eenyen blood like Mexican — you know just a touch of that Latin slicky shit in it, vicious as they come, and mated up, contemplez-vous, to fatty Bavarian oonshick and poonshick jawohl furor lemme kiss your dirty socks my leader, can you imagine? the filthiest of the Indians and the slimiest of red-hot sexy-ass Nazis intercoursing each other, mating and breeding to produce Tex Hyde who grows up in his daddy's big booming business which is stuffing corpses and doing God knows what to their little old pithy bowels and their dropped stomachs and whatever else corpses got which must be plenty or why pay thousands of dollars for a funeral unless it's a fumigation, hey Tonto? and that boy growing up there comes out like a malevolent orchid in a humus pile, or a black panther, that's what he is, black panther with all his black panther piss, I'm dreaming of him, Linnit, and so is my son, the black puma, he's got my son who's just as beautiful as George Hamilton and more clean-cut swearing by him, the puma and the panther, I think they took the vow of blood, cut their thumbs and ran 'em around the rim of some debutante's pussy, after the way these kids now live there ain't much left for them but to gang-fuck tastefully wouldn't you say, speak up, Linnit?

ROTHENBERG: Now, Hallie, I know you're not going to listen to me.

HALLIE: But I am, my dear. I full intend to, Linnit?

ROTHENBERG: Yes, milady.

HALLIE: Tell me I've been ladylike. I know I haven't. I know I've been outré and spouting great clouds of baloney from inner space, I mean you might think my language was the proper vocabulary for a roughneck or a driller, but I adore you, Linnit, cause you got a kind Jewish heart and I always said when Hitler killed the Jews, half the kindness went out of the world.

(*He begins to laugh. He laughs so hard he cannot reply for many a second.*)

ROTHENBERG (*gasping*): Maybe he shoulda killed the other half.

(*They spend an apocalyptic minute laughing together.
When Hallie cools, her voice is ice.*)

HALLIE: Heh, heh, heh, heh. Gallows humor, Linnit.

D.J.: My poor old Dad. He got all the burden of one
man's family. Yeah, what poor old Rusty has to brood
about. (*Transforms himself into Rusty.*) Yeah, the
time is soon coming when fornication will be professional athletics, and everybody will watch the national eliminations on TV. Will boys like D.J. and
Tex be in the finals with a couple of Playboy bunnies
or black-ass honeys? well, shit-and-sure, fifty thousand major league fuckers will be clawing and cutting
to get in the big time to present their open flower-petal
pussy, or hand-hewn diamond tool and testicles in
happy magnification by Color Vision RCA. Only thing
holding this scheme back is the problems of integration. What if the Spades run away with the jewels?
Not to mention all the wet pussy in America. Think
of that in color TV — all the purple majesty, if they
do, America'll really be looking for a white hope, huh.
  Of course, I'll be having to watch. Oh, the ignominy.
Just stick my middle-age dick against the screen.
Yeah, the twentieth century is breaking up the ball
game: (1) The women are free. They bed down with
too many to believe one man can do the job. (2) The
Niggers are free, and the dues they got to be paid is
no Texas virgin's delight. (3) The Niggers and the
women are tooling each other. (4) The Yellow races
are breaking loose. (5) Africa is breaking loose. (6)
The adolescents are breaking loose including my own
son. (7) The European nations hate America's guts.
(8) The products are no fucking good anymore. (9)
Communism is a system guaranteed to collect dues
from all losers. (9a) More losers than winners in the
world. (9b) and out: communism is going to defeat
capitalism, unless promptly destroyed. (10) a. Sexual

intercourse is king. b. Jerk-off dances are the royal
road to sexual intercourse. c. I am no great jerk-off
dancer. d. I am thereby disqualified from playing
King Fuck. (11) Therefore, I am fucked.

ROTHENBERG: Hallie, are you saying you've got to separate those boys?

HALLIE: I know, I know. But they're stuck to each other
like ranch dogs. Hunting together, playing football
together, holding hands while they ride, studying
karate together, I bet they can't even get their rocks
off unless they're put-putting in the same vaginal
slime. I hope at least D.J. has got the taste and sentiment to be putting it in the young lady's vagina rather
than going up her dirt track where old Tex Hyde belongs (after all those bodies he helped his fat growing
rich daddy embalm). Kiss the lint from my navel,
Linnit, a mother can't even be sure of that anymore,
because, I even heard of a debutante knock-up case
where the boy who had to accept the onus of parent-
hood was the one who had addressed himself to the
fore, his buddy's lawyer got him to admit that cardinal
fact by the following examination, "Would you, Son,
be so filthy and so foul as to address yourself to a
young lady's dirt track." "Of course I wouldn't go near
her anus," said this idiot called Son, "do you think I'm
a pervert?" "Well, my client *is* a pervert," said the
lawyer, "so you are the proud papa, the Brains rest,"
end of case.

ROTHENBERG: Take the undertaker out of it, that's what
disturbs your sense of peers and social compeers. A
mortician is at a social disadvantage in stable struc-
turification of society, but it's not to be calibrated on
a final scale. If Tex Hyde were the son of a normal
occupation father, for instance if Gottfried Hyde
Senior was straight corporation exec like Rusty.

HALLIE: No, no, no, Rottenbug, you're thinking like a tick again.

ROTHENBERG: Tell me why, pie.

HALLIE: Because Tex grew up an undertaker's son, fool! plunging his hands into dead people's vitals, picking up through his fingertips all sorts of black occult steamy little grimes of things, swamp music and black lightning and soundless thunder — purple wonders, it's like sleeping the night in a rotten old stump — who knows what song the maggots sing, and what aromatic intuitions inflame the brain. Herbs are the nerve to a fearsome underworld — listen, baby, I didn't get fucked by Aleister Crowley for nothing, those passes at the Black Masses . . . (*putting a gloved finger up to her dear chin*)

D.J.: She is incidentally now lying her ass off because she's too young to know Aleister Crowley, but she's like her son, D.J., she's got to brag, better believe it.
  Well this has gone on long enough. Cause you ought to know who had produced this material. This has been D.J. presenting to you the private scene of his mother being psychoanalyzed by that clammy little fink, with occasional odd spotlights on his father, and if the illusion has been conveyed that my mother, D.J.'s own mother, talks the way you got it here, well, dear audience, you're sick in your own drool, because my mother is a Southern lady, she's as elegant as an oyster with powder on its ass, she don't talk that way, she just thinks that way. Do we understand each other now, son? You've had fun long enough. The serious shit soon starts. You're contending with a genius, D.J. is his name, only American alive who could outtalk Cassius Clay, that's lip, duck the blip, Orlando, it's right on your radar screen. Oueep, oueep!

A Translation from Lorca by Susan and Norman Mailer

Lament for Ignacio Sánchez Mejías

The Wound and the Death

At five in the afternoon
It was five on the dot of the afternoon.
A boy brought the white sheet
at five in the afternoon.
A basket of lime all prepared
at five in the afternoon.
The rest was death and death alone
at five in the afternoon.

The wind carried away the cottonwool
at five in the afternoon.
And the oxide planted crystal and nickel
at five in the afternoon.
The dove and the leopard were fighting
at five in the afternoon.

And a thigh with a desolate horn
at five in the afternoon.
The bass-string was plucked
at five in the afternoon.
Arsenic in the bells and smoke
at five in the afternoon.
Gangs of silence in the corners
at five in the afternoon.
And the bull alone, his heart held high
at five in the afternoon.
While the sweat of snow was coming in
at five in the afternoon.
while the bullring was covered with iodine
at five in the afternoon.
death put eggs to the wound
at five in the afternoon.
At five in the afternoon.
At five on the dot of the afternoon.

A coffin on wheels is the bed
at five in the afternoon.
Bones and flutes sound in his ear
at five in the afternoon.
The bull moans at his forehead
at five in the afternoon.
The room is shuddering with agony
at five in the afternoon.
From a distance gangrene is coming
at five in the afternoon.
The horn of the lily in the young groin
at five in the afternoon.
Wounds burned like suns
at five in the afternoon.
and the people were breaking the windows
at five in the afternoon.
At five in the afternoon.
Oh what a brutal five o'clock
It was five on all the clocks!
It was five in the shade of the afternoon.

The Spilled Blood

I do not want to see it!

Tell the moon to come
for I do not want to see the blood
of Ignacio on the sand.

I do not want to see it!

The moon is full.
Horses of the quiet clouds
and the gray bullring of sleep
with willows on the barrera.

I do not want to see it!
for memories burn.
Go tell the jasmines
with their delicate white, that

I do not want to see it!

The cow of the old world
was passing her sad tongue
over a snoutful of blood
spilled on the sand,
and the bulls of Guisando
near to death and near to stone
moaned like two centuries
sick of stamping the earth

No.

I do not want to see it!

Up by the highest bleachers goes Ignacio
with his death on his shoulders.
He was looking for the dawn
and the dawn was not there.
He was looking for his fine profile
and his sleep led him away.
He was looking for his beautiful body
and found his flowing blood.
Do not ask me to see it!
I do not want to feel the spurt

with less force each time;
this spurt of blood which illumines
the tiers of seats and pours
over the corduroy and leather
of that thirsty mob
who cries out for me to look!
Do not ask me to see it.

His eyes did not close
when he saw the horns near,
but the terrible mothers
raised their head.
And across all the ranches
was an air of secret voices
who cried out to celestial bulls,
herders of the pale fog.
There was not a prince in Seville
who could compare to him,
not a sword like his sword
nor a heart so real.
Like a river of lions
was his marvelous strength
and like a torso of marble
his fine-drawn restraint.
The air of Andalusian Rome
gilded his head
his laugh was a spikenard
of salt, a gardenia of intelligence.
What a great bullfighter in the plaza!
What a mountaineer for the hills.
How deft with the thorns!
How hard with the spurs!
How tender with the dew!
What brilliance at the fiesta!
What magnificence with the banderillas of the dusk.

Now he sleeps without end.
Now the moss and the grass
open with sure fingers
the flower of his skull.
And his blood comes singing now
singing by marshes and meadows,

slipping past numb horns
rootless and uncertain in the mist
stumbling over a herd of hooves
like a long, dark sad tongue
making a mudhole of agony
near the Guadalquivir of the stars.
Oh white wall of Spain!
Oh black bull of sorrow!
Hard blood of Ignacio!
Nightingale of his veins!
No.
I do not want to see it!
For there is no chalice to contain it,
no swallows to drink it,
no glitter of morning frost to freeze it
no songs, no floods of white lilies
no crystal to cover the silver
No.
I do not want to see it!

The Body Before Us

Stone is a forehead where dreams cry out
never to hold the curve of water nor the ice of cypress.
The stone is a back to transport time
with arbors of tears and ribbons and planets.

I have seen gray rain run into the waves
raising its tender riddled arms
so it will not be imprisoned by the overhanging stone
who displays his bulk but never mops the blood.

Because the stone receives seeds and shadows
skeletons of larks, wolves of darkness
but stone gives no sound, nor crystal nor fire,
only bullrings and bullrings and rings without walls.

Already Ignacio, Ignacio of the good family, lies on the stone.
It is over; what is happening? Contemplate his face:
death has covered it with pallid sulphur
and has made his head from a dark minotaur.

It is over. The rain pours in his mouth.
The air like a madman in flight quits his sunken chest,
and Love, steeped with tears of snow
warms itself on the ridge of the bull ranches.

What do they say? A silence full of stench.
We are here with a body before us. That clear form
once made of nightingales is fading
and we see it is full of bottomless pits.

Who wrinkles the shroud? What it says is not true!
Here no one sings, nor cries by the corners
nor pricks with the spurs, nor frightens the serpent:
Here I want nothing but full eyes
to see that body without hope of repose.

Here I want to see the men with harsh voices.
Those who tame horses and rivers:
the men whose bones can be heard, men who sing
with the full mouth of sun and flint.

Here I want to see them. In front of the stone.
In front of this body with its broken reins.
I want them to show me the exit
for this captain bound by death.

I want them to show me a lament like a river
possessed of sweet mists and deep shores;
let them take Ignacio's body and let it be lost
without having to hear the quick panting of the bulls.

Let him disappear in the round bullring of the moon
which pretends in its youth to be a motionless horn:
let him be lost in the night without a song of the fish
lost in white briars of frozen smoke.

I do not want them to cover his face with handkerchiefs
so that he will make himself comfortable with death.
Go away Ignacio: Do not feel the hot bellow of the bull.
Sleep, fly, rest: the sea also dies.

Absent Soul

Neither the bull nor the fig tree know you,
nor horses, nor ants in your house.

The boy does not know you, nor the afternoon
because you have died forever.

The spine of the rock does not know you,
nor the black satin in which you fall apart.
Your mute memory does not know you
because you have died forever.

Autumn will come with winding staircases
grape of the mist and a range of hills.
But nobody will want to see your eyes
because you have died forever.

Because you have died forever
like all the dead of the Earth,
like all the dead who are forgotten
in a heap of chewed-up dogs.

Nobody knows you. No. But I sing of you.
I sing to the future of your profile and your grace.
Of your famous wisdom, connoisseur.
Your appetite for death and the taste of its mouth.
The sadness I had in your brave mirth.

It will be a long time, if ever, before there is born
an Andalusian so bright and rich in adventure.
I sing of elegance with words which weep
and remember a sad breeze by the olive trees.

An
Interview

Excerpts from *Playboy*

PLAYBOY: How do you feel about being interviewed?

MAILER: I start with a general sense of woe.

PLAYBOY: Why?

MAILER: The interviewer serves up 1 percent of himself in the questions and the man who answers has to give back 99 percent. I feel exploited the moment I step into an interview. Of course, once in a while there is such a thing as a good interview; but even then, the tape recorder eats up half the mood. It isn't the interview I really dislike so much as the tape recorder.

PLAYBOY: What do you think is the best way to conduct an interview?

MAILER: There's no good way. It's just a matter of grinding through — that's all.

PLAYBOY: If you feel so negative about being interviewed, why did you consent to this one?

MAILER: About every two or three years, I feel I have to have a psychic housecleaning, go through my ideas in general, even brutal form — the brutal form of the interview — just to see about where I stand. Because most of the time, I spend my time thinking privately. Without this kind of psychic housecleaning, I might get too infatuated with some ideas. It's a way, I suppose, of exposing ideas that are weak. After that, you can either discard them or think about them a little harder.

PLAYBOY: As you talk about housecleaning your ideas — disregarding, changing or improving them — we're reminded of your sentence in *The Deer Park* about growth: "There was that law of life, so cruel and so just, that one must grow or else pay more for remaining the same." Yet you've been charged by many critics with dissipating the potential growth of a major talent in American fiction by wearing so many hats. They point out that there's Mailer the politician, who once seriously considered running for mayor of New York City: there's Mailer the journalist, who writes about the maladies in American life and about the political brutalities; there's Mailer the celebrity, who grabs headlines by booze brawls and other acts of public violence. How do you answer that criticism?

MAILER: Moving from one activity to another makes sense if you do it with a hint of wit or a touch of grace — which I don't say I've always done; far from it —

but I think moving from one activity to another can give momentum. If you do it well, you can increase the energy you bring to the next piece of work. Growth, in some curious way, I expect, depends on being always in motion just a little bit, one way or another. Growth is not simply going forward; it's going forward until you have to make a delicate decision either to continue in a difficult situation or to retreat and look for another way to go forward. The pattern that this creates — no, pattern is a poor word — the line of the movement reveals the nature of form.

More to the point, I've been accused of having frittered many talents away, of having taken on too many activities, of having worked too self-consciously at being a celebrity, of having performed at the edges and, indeed, at the center of my own public legend. And, of course, like any criminal in the dock, I can sing a pretty tune; I can defend myself; I'm my own best lawyer; the day when I'm not will be a sad day. The defense I'll enter today depends on my favorite notion: that an expert, by definition, is opposed to growth. Why? Because an expert is a man who works forward in one direction until he reaches that point where he has to use all his energy to maintain his advance; he cannot allow himself to look in other directions.

PLAYBOY: Is all this related to *The Naked and the Dead* and the celebrity that followed in its wake?

MAILER: Yes. Being well known at twenty-five created a chain of legend for everything I did. If I left a party early, it wasn't because I might have been sleepy; it was because I had put down the party. Every little thing I did was exaggerated. Lo! There was a feedback that had little to do with me. It was as if — if you will — every one of my actions was tuned to an amplifier.

PLAYBOY: Is this what you meant when you once remarked that your success at twenty-five was "like a lobotomy"?

MAILER: It cut me off from my past. I felt like someone who had been dropped onto Mars.

PLAYBOY: Did you dig your sudden fame?

MAILER: Of course I dug it. I had to dig it. I mean, to be brutally frank for all our swell *Playboy* readers out there: it enabled me to get girls I would not otherwise have gotten.

PLAYBOY: You make a distinction between the legendary Mailer in the spotlight whose acts were scrutinized and gossiped about and the Mailer who wanted to grow in his own sweet time. Could you contrast the two Mailers a bit more?

MAILER: Well, contrasting two Mailers might have value in a novel, but to talk about it would end up being tiresome. This is the point I want to make: I had some instinctive sense — right or wrong — that the best way to grow was not to write one novel after another but to move from activity to activity, a notion that began with Renaissance man; it's not my idea, after all. My personal celebrity was an obstacle to any natural ability to move quickly and easily. For years, it was a tremendous obstacle; and I ended up having a very dull, dogged personality that sought to wrestle with the legend, and that tried to say, "Look, fellows, I'm really simple, honest, hardworking; I'm as close to Abe Lincoln as Arthur Miller is."

The hoarseness of this confession is not to enlist sympathy but to prepare the ground for my boast: I learned how to accept and live with my legend. The legend becomes your friend, the beard, a front man, a pimp, a procurer of new situations. You live with a ghost who is more real to people than yourself; every single action you take with another person is part of a triangle. Every girl you talk to is not only in love with you or disappointed in you but also is in love with or hating your legend — who, incidentally, is more real to her than you. There are times, therefore, when you beef up your legend, perform some action to support it; times when you draw credit back from your legend, like cashing in the desire of somebody else to do something nice for you. Either way, you don't pretend — as I did for years — that the legend ain't there; it *is*.

PLAYBOY: One of your celebrated experiments with growth was your experience with drugs. You were on marijuana, Benzedrine, and sleeping pills for a few years and were addicted to Seconal. Later, you said that a man on drugs will pay for it by "a gutted and burned-out nervous system." How do you feel about that topic today?

MAILER: Drugs are a spiritual form of gambling. This is a poetic equation that can be carried right down to the end of its metaphor, because on drugs you're even bucking the house percentage — which for a drug like marijuana is probably something like 30 to 40 percent.

PLAYBOY: Would you expand this?

MAILER: Marijuana does something with the sense of time: it accelerates you; it opens you to your unconscious. But it's as if you're calling on the reserves of the next three days. All the sweets, all the crystals, all the little decisions, all the unconscious work of the next three days — or, if the experience is deep, part of the next thirty days, or the next thirty years — is called forward. For a half hour or two hours — whatever is the high of the pot — you're better than you are normally and you get into situations you wouldn't get into normally, and generally more happens to you. You make love better, you talk better, you think better, you dig people better. The point is, you've got to get in pretty far, because you're using up three days in an hour — or whatever the particular ratio is for any particular person. So unless you come back with — let us say — seventy-two hours in one hour, you lose. Because you have to spend the next three or four days recovering. You might ask: what happens to the guy who smokes pot all the time? I don't know. But I do know something is being mortgaged; something is being drawn out of the future. If his own future has already been used up in one or another mysterious or sinister sense, then maybe the pot is drawing it out of the very substance of what I may as well confess I call God. I suspect God feeds drug addicts the way a healthy body feeds parasites.

PLAYBOY: How do you mean?

MAILER: Well, if God has great compassion, He may not be willing to cut the drug addict off from Him. During the time the addict has some of his most intense and divine experiences, it is because he is literally imbibing the very marrow and nutrient of existence. But since I do not believe that God is necessarily inexhaustible, the drug addict may end up by bleeding Him.

PLAYBOY: Do you think this happens on LSD?

MAILER: I don't think you have a mystical experience on chemicals without taking the risk of exploiting something in the creation. If you haven't paid the real wages of love or courage or abstention or discipline or sacrifice or wit in the eye of danger, then taking a psychedelic drug is living the life of a parasite; it's drawing on sweets you have not earned.

PLAYBOY: What is the danger of this parasitical self-exploitation on LSD?

MAILER: I'm not going to say that LSD is bad in every way for everyone, but I'm convinced it's bad if you keep taking it. Any drug is bad finally in the same way that being a confirmed gambler is bad. A confirmed gambler ends up losing all his friends because he blows their money and blows their trust. A gambler will tell any lie to get back into the action. By the same token, if you stay on any drug for too long, then you have a habit; you're a victim; to anticipate something, you're a totalitarian.

Let me put it this way: LSD is marvelous for experts to take when they get too frozen in their expertise. Let's suppose they've driven deep into something impenetrable, some obstacle that was bound to trap them because of the shortsighted nature of their expertise. Although they work and work manfully as experts, at this point they're similar to soldiers who have pushed far into enemy territory but are now up against a resistance they cannot get through. Their only action is to retreat, but they don't know how to, because they have no habits of retreat. They're experts; they know only how to move forward to amass more knowledge and put more concentration upon a point. When this concentration does not succeed in poking through the resistance of the problem, the expert is psychically in great trouble. He begins to live in increasing depression; he has to retreat and doesn't know how: he wasn't built to retreat.

My guess is: on LSD, you begin to die a little. That's why you get this extraordinary, even divine sense of revelation. Perhaps you taste the odor and essence of your own death in the trip; in excess, it's a deadly poison, after all. Therefore, what's given to the expert is a broader vision: dying a little, he begins to retreat from his expertise and begins to rejoin his backward brothers. Hallelujah! So that LSD taken a few times could be very good, I would imagine. But before very long, if the expert keeps taking LSD, he can become nothing but an expert on LSD.

PLAYBOY: What do you think of Timothy Leary?

MAILER: Well, I wonder who we were just talking about.

PLAYBOY: More of an answer, please.

MAILER: I never met him. Perhaps I'd like him if I did. Many of my friends like him. But I have heard him speak, and he is then nought but simple shit.

PLAYBOY: Alcohol seems to be another way by which you've tried to grow or "move forward." One of the characters in your stage version of *The Deer Park* declares: "A man must drink until he locates the truth." How does alcohol help a man do that?

MAILER: I'm going to offer one fundamental equation: A man who drinks is attempting to dissolve an obsession.

PLAYBOY: What's the obsession?

MAILER: Talk first about what an obsession *is*. I've thought about obsession a great deal, but I'm not sure I know the answer. Everybody talks about obsessions; nobody's ever really explained them. We can define them, but we don't really know what we're talking about. An obsession, I'd suggest, is not unlike a pole of magnetism, a psychic field of force. An obsession is created, I think, in the wake of some event that has altered our life profoundly, or perhaps we have passed through some relation with someone else that has altered our life drastically, yet we don't know whether we were changed for good or for bad; it's the most fundamental sort of event or relation. It has marked us, yet it's morally ambiguous.

PLAYBOY: What kind of event?

MAILER: Suppose a marriage breaks up. You don't know if it was finally your fault or your wife's fault or God's fault or the Devil's fault — four uncertainties. Let's reduce them to two: a man or his wife. Put it this way: People move forward into the future out of the way they comprehend the past. When we don't understand something in our past, we are therefore crippled. Use the metaphor of the Army here: If you move forward to attack a town and the center of this attack depends upon a road that will feed your attack, and this road passes through a town, yet you don't know if your people hold that town or someone else holds it, then, obviously, if you were a general, you'd be pretty obsessive about that town. You'd keep asking, "Will you please find out who owns that town?" You'd send out reconnaissance parties to locate the town, enter it, patrol it. If all sorts of mysterious things occurred — if, for example, your reconnaissance platoon didn't return — you'd feel so uncertain you might not move forward to attack. The obsession is a search for a useful reality. What finally did occur? What is real?

PLAYBOY: You haven't told us yet how drink helps dissolve an obsession.

MAILER: Well, if a man's drink takes him back to an earlier, younger state of sensitivity, it is then taking him to a place back of the place where he originally got into the impasse that created the obsession. If you can return to a state just preceding the one you were in when these various ambiguous events occurred, you can say to yourself, "Now, I'm approaching the event again. What really did happen? Who was right? Who was wrong? Let me not miss it this time." A man must drink until he locates the truth. I think that's why it's so hard for people to give up booze. There's an artwork going on with most serious drinkers. Usually, it's a failed artwork. Once again, one's playing against the house percentage: one drinks, one wrecks one's liver, dims one's vision, burns out one's memory. Drinking is a serious activity — a serious moral and spiritual activity. We consume ourselves in order to search for a truth.

PLAYBOY: In terms of your concept of growth, you've made in *An American Dream* and other writings a brilliant, dazzling, and rather puzzling remark concerning the possibility that God Himself may be involved in a process of growth. You've said that you have an "obsession with how God exists," and you've argued for the possibility that He may be a God whose final nature is not yet comprehended, even by Himself. Could you comment on this?

MAILER: I think I decided some time ago that if there is a God and He's all-powerful, then His relation to us is absurd. All we can see in our human condition are thundering, monumental disproportions, injustices of such dimension that even the conservative notion of existence — which might postulate that man is here on earth not to complain but to receive his just deserts and that the man who acts piggishly on earth will be repaid in hell, regardless of whether he was rich or poor — yes, even this conservative vision depends on a God who is able to run a world of reasonable proportions. If the only world we have is one of abysmal, idiotic disproportions, then it becomes too difficult to conceive of an all-powerful God who is all good. It is far easier to conceive of a God who died or who is dying or who is an imperfect God. But once I think of an imperfect God, I can begin to imagine a Being greater than ourselves, who nonetheless shares

His instinctive logic with us: we as men seek to grow, so He seeks to grow; even as we each have a conception of being — my conception of being, my idea of how we should live, may triumph over yours, or yours over mine — so, in parallel, this God may be engaged in a similar war in the universe with other gods. We may even be the embodiment, the partial expression of His vision. If we fail, He fails, too. He is imperfect in the way we are imperfect. He is not always as brave or extraordinary or as graceful as He might care to be. This is my notion of God and growth. The thing about it that gives me sustenance is that it enables me to love God, if you will bear these words, rather than hate Him, because I can see Him as someone who is like other men except more noble, more tortured, more desirous of a good that He wishes to receive and give to others — a torturous ethical activity at which He may fail. Man's condition is, then, by this logic, epic or tragic — for the outcome is unknown. It is not written.

PLAYBOY: Could you talk a bit more about the relationship between a man and this God who is still involved in discovering His own nature?

MAILER: In capsule: There are times when He has to exploit us; there are times when we have to exploit Him; there are times when He has to drive us beyond our own natural depth because He needs us — those of us, at least, who are working for Him: We have yet to talk of the Devil. But a man who talks about his religion is not to be trusted. Who knows — I may be working for the Devil. In fact, I sometimes suspect every novelist is a Devil's helper. The ability to put an eye on your own heart is icy.

A
Speech

Accepting the
National Book Award

On Monday when queried by Mr. Raymont of the *Times* about my reaction to winning one of the National Book Awards, I was sufficiently ungracious to say, "There's something obscene about a middle-aged man who wins an award. Prizes are for the young and the old." Writers are notoriously double- and triple-layered — like color film they have their yellow base, their blue-green, their slice of sensitivity to red. Who knows what was meant? It could have been bitterness, or the growl of a curmudgeon kicking at the edge of his pleasure.

At any rate, standing on this podium, your speaker is here to state that he likes prizes, honors, and awards and will accept them. He will accept them. The honorable

Jean-Paul Sartre, an author it is impossible not to esteem, refused the Nobel Prize a few years ago with the remark — let this approximate his words — that he wished the bourgeoisie to know him as Jean-Paul Sartre, not Jean-Paul Sartre, Nobel Prize Winner. Respectful of his integrity, one could nonetheless disagree with his decision. The most bourgeois elements in French society had been speaking of him for years as Jean-Paul Sartre, perverted existentialist, and would continue to do so. How much better for the final subtleties of their brain if they had been obliged instead to think of him as Jean-Paul Sartre, perverted existentialist *and* Nobel Prize Winner. An entrance might have been made into the complexity of his vision. It might have introduced that bourgeoisie to the vertiginous schizophrenia of the modern condition, a clifflike species of cultural dislocation.

We are a savagely mechanical society poised upon the lip, no, the main of a spiritual revolution which will wash the psychic roots of every national institution out to sea. We are on the brink of dreams and disasters. We are entering a world in which the value systems of the stoutest ego will spin like a turning table, the assertions of the inner voice go caroming through vales of electronic rock.

So it is nice to have awards and to accept them. They are measures of the degree to which an Establishment meets that talent it has hindered and helped. So it is a measure, an historic bench mark, as each of us, one by one, gives up his grip on the old rail of established winning procedure and proceeds to whirl down the turns into that new future, airless, insane, existential, and bright, which beats in the pulse on our neck. And as we go whirling and twisting into the future, which by God we could swear we did not make, how sweet, how charming, how comic and nice that on a given year to a given man, there came an award which was a measure of the plasticity of taste, the volatility of status, and the essential good spirit of the literary world as it readied its tools, old sweet simple pencil in hand, to meet the obliterating Armageddons of technology, the last five centuries of guilt, and the electric dread at the center, for no longer do we know where we go nor whom we fight. So three cheers for good marks, that remonstrance of devoted parents and modest schools, and bless us all as we explore the night. Thank you.

Letters

(April 28, 1966)

To the Editors:

In Richard G. Stern's picaresquely written "Report from the MLA," which included an account of the Cheever-Ellison-Mailer festivities (Feburary 17) he also reported the following sentence about me —

In the carful of goggling professors, sloshing his drink, he [Mailer] called out "Nine" as the elevator hurtled from Ten, and when released at Seven, he fired genially at the uniformed auntie from his fortress of licensed clowning, "You Jew," and rollicked like a sailor down the mirrored corridor, leaving behind a small carnage of titillated shock.

Note: James Yuenger giving an account of the same event in the *Chicago Tribune Magazine,* February 6, 1966 —

> As the 12th floor flashed by, Mailer suddenly said, "Stop — right — HERE." It was on 10 already, and stopped at 7, and Mailer said: "O, boy, you're a real pearl."

A man I have never met happened to read these two somewhat separate versions, then told my friend, Robert Lucid, that as between pearl and Jew, I must have said to the elevator operator, "Oh, boy, you're a jewel." In fact, it is also my conclusion. I think Stern is wrong. I think I said, "Sweetheart, you're a real jewel." But I had a bit to drink (not a slosh — Stern writes like a man who has never held a glass), yes, a bit to drink in celebration, having read my paper to the ASA of the MLA, so I cannot be certain finally what I said. The elevator operator was, I recollect, one Wasp lady who could play tackle for the John Birch Society if and when they field a team, sallah! so I could indeed have said, "You pearl, you Jew," much as once I said, "You Communist," to a redneck Miami sheriff who was making us fight writers show our fight credentials in our hand as he passed us through. Which tradition encourages me to say now, "Stern, how could you, a Jew, do this to me, a fellow son of Samuel — you Ginzo, you Mafia, you Wop."

Norman Mailer

Brooklyn, New York

To the *Saturday Review*

(*April 20, 1971*)

Gentlemen:

Over the years, an author collects horseflies under the tail of his self-esteem. I know the editors of the *Saturday Review* will be pleased to hear that *Time* and their own magazine are my favorite horseflies, and God willing, will go back some day to their own true natural food out in the fields.

Since it is the character of a horsefly to try its sting on every material before it, I suppose one need not be surprised at the combination of inaccuracy and unattributed reporting in the following quotation from Stuart Little's piece, "What Happened at *Harper's*."

> At one get-together later in Morris's apartment, Mailer, reportedly rather pleased that his article was in the center of controversy, urged resignations on the editors, but some resented his surrogation of their moral decision. "Well, Norman," one of them is reported to have said stormily, "I may have done a lot of bad things, but I've never sold to *Life* for a million dollars an idea ["Of a Fire on the Moon"] Willie Morris gave me."

Since in two sentences Little manages to make four errors, let me tell Little what he could have learned by inquiring into my version of the events.

(1) I was not pleased that "The Prisoner of Sex" was "in the center of controversy." I was sick at the thought that this piece I had written in the great editorial freedom of *Harper's* (a climate not easy to describe to *Satur-*

day Review editors) had contributed to smashing that same editorial freedom. But then who reported I was pleased?

(2) I didn't urge resignations on the editors. In my outrage on first hearing the news, I blurted out, "Well, I guess the editors will all resign now," passing insensitively over the fact that they had families, commitments, and need for salaries, and resignation would cost them much. But I did not *urge* them. I merely spoke once, too quickly, and without the right.

(3) I didn't *sell* "Of a Fire on the Moon" to *Life*. The *Life* editors approached me. Aware that Willie Morris had suggested the same idea two months before, he was the first man I called after accepting *Life*'s offer. It was at a time when finances were pressing, and Morris recognizing the inevitable, sighed mightily and agreed that under the circumstances I had small choice.

(4) It was not for a million dollars. This is nothing but slovenly or invidious reporting. Everybody in publishing knows by now that the true figure is $450,000, and only a small fraction of that sum was paid by *Life*. The rest, as the reporter and editors of *Saturday Review* have to be aware, was hard-cover, paperback, serial rights, and foreign rights. But a horsefly is a horsefly. Its need is to sting.

Cheers, gents, and regards to Stuart Little for getting all those facts so straight. There's nothing like reporting what a guy said he heard another guy tell him somebody said.

Norman Mailer

To the
New York Times Book Review

(June 13, 1971)

Toward the end of Brigid Brophy's generous review of
The Prisoner of Sex (May 23), she lights upon my
phrase "politics rendered every pride" and concludes it is
a malapropism. " 'Surrendered' does he mean," asks
Miss Brophy, "or 'rent'?" Well, I guess a number of us
know something about the kitchen that Brigid don't.
"Render" is used to describe that process where fat
heated upon a fire is returned to oil and clarified of its
impurities. So too can the hot and compromising hands
held in politics melt pride on occasion down to shame.
But how was it ever possible that the modest manifestos
of *The Prisoner of Sex* could yet have rendered Brophy's
nectar into surrenders of vinegar and rents of urea's hot
torrent? Brave and broiling Brigid. We must find a man
good enough to kiss her hem. Ahem! Yours, and cor-
dially,

Norman Mailer

Capsule
Entertainments

An Appreciation of Henry Miller

Henry Miller was in Edinburgh for the festival in 1962, and, being present myself, I had the chance to see a bit of him for a week and never the good luck to see him again. Therefore, if I write about Miller now, it is not as an expert but an admirer. And in fact I admire not only his work, which I do, enormously (his influence has been profound on a good half of all living American writers), but I admire his personality. He has one of the best personalities I ever met. It is all of a piece, all composed, the way a fine cabinetmaker or a big-game hunter or a tightrope artist has a personality which is true to itself all the way through. No neurotic push-pull, no maggots in the smile, no envies, no nervousness. It is the kind of composure which suggested he was ready for anything which came on next — did a lion escape from the zoo and walk suddenly into the room, you had the feeling Henry Miller would say, "Say, fellow, you look pretty big coming in here out of the zoo. How's it feel to stretch your legs?"

It is, you see, a personality which is extraordinarily gentle without being the least bit soft, and after a while you get the feeling that Miller always tells the truth, and does it as simply as possible, in a minimum of words, and tempers it only with the desire to be as kind as he can in the circumstances. In that sense, a poet without talent who has asked him to read his work would probably bother Henry Miller more than the lion, but he would tell the truth, in that slightly rough, slightly humorous voice of his, with the gutty hint of Brooklyn still in the pipes.

So there is Miller, a man of medium size, trim, jaunty in his dress (knickers and a cap in Edinburgh), with a good tough face, big nose, near bald head, looking for all the world like Marx's noble proletarian, like some bricklayer, let us say, you started talking to on a train, and then it turned out he had eighty-two kids and worked at his hobby in spare time — it was translating Sophocles. Then you wonder at the gulf which forever exists between an artist's personality and his work — here particularly the violent, smashing, fuck-you gusto of *Tropic of Cancer* and the strong, benign, kindly mood of the man today — and decide that writing is also the purge of what is good and bad in yourself, and the writers who write sweet books, pastorales, idylls, and hymns to the human condition, end up snarling old beasts in their senility, whereas Henry, after years of saying out every black thought he had in his head (and some silver ones too), is now forced to defend himself against the allegation that he is angel or saint.

An Appreciation of Cassius Clay

I'm working on something else now, so don't want to get started writing about Muhammad Ali, because I could go on for a book. Suffice it that the most interesting original talented and artistic prizefighter to come along in at least a decade has been cut off by the bully-boy mentality of the American sporting world. A great athlete is almost always an extraordinary man, but a mediocre athlete has a character which is usually no prettier than the lifestyle of a mediocre writer. The sort of mugs and moguls who run our amateur and professional sports and write about them are invariably mediocrities, second-rate athletes, rich boys — they gravitate to running sports and writing up the canons of sports, and they ran Muhammad Ali right out of boxing. Their basic reflex is, after all, to kiss ass (it is their connection to the primitive) and patriotism is thus their head-on sublimation for such kissing. Therefore we are all deprived of an intimate spectacle which was taking place in public — the forging of a professional artist of extraordinary dimensions. Yes, I could write a book about Cassius: he was bringing a revolution to the theory of boxing, and bringing it into that monarchical spook-ridden class where every theory runs into a bomb — the heavyweights. Those who don't know boxing don't know the frustration one feels that he couldn't have the run of his own true career, for the knowledge he offered was mint.

Two Oddments from *Esquire*

Modern is Our Temper

"I don't know what to do. The last time I needed some money I wrote to my parents and told them I had to have an abortion. But that was only three months ago. I wonder if it isn't too soon to tell them I need another."

"Tell them that this time it's a Negro."

"That's a good idea."

Putting Culture on to Culture

Several years ago, visiting a friend who was sick, I was introduced to his hobby. He happened to be an actor, but his temperament was not unlike a jeweler's or a collector's. He saved quotations. Whenever he came across something he liked particularly well in a book or poem he would set it down in a notebook he kept for the purpose, a handsome notebook of good paper covered with red leather. His idea of course was not novel; most of us have started such notebooks more than once. What separated his collection from others was that he kept it going for years, and he used it. If he found himself in a profound depression he would turn to the notebook (it was of course in several volumes by now) and try to read his way out of the depression. Indeed, he would succeed as often as not. His depression encountering the precision or poetry of a good sentence would shift to sorrow or melancholy or open into anger. Conversely, he would also pick up his notebook on those nights when he could not sleep for excitement or anticipation of the day to come, and would calm himself by the contrast of one salient thought upon another.

I started to keep a notebook for myself. And I found there was a subtle, almost insidious magic to the sequence of quotations. Sometimes I would put down two or three in an hour from one book or several books, sometimes months would go by between insertions, and yet when I would open the notebook and pass through it, the collision of one thought enjoyed at a particular moment in the past situated next to another thought taken from an altogether different moment seemed to produce a shift in one's memory, a clarification of the past, and the chronology of small events took shape again so that I would remember the sequence of details in a specific episode even if the quotations I was reading bore no other relation to the event than to be near it in time.

At any rate — and I hope this is not a mistake — I thought I'd put down some of these quotations now, and see if I could induce any of you to begin your private book. In fact, if it's not too presumptuous of me, any of you are welcome to start your book with any of the quotations that follow. Be certain, however, to give credit to the correct author. Because that is the critical part of the notebook's value.

Telling the truth makes us burn with the desire to convince our audience, whereas telling a lie affords ample leisure to study the result.   — Oscar Wilde

So the blind will lead the blind and the deaf shout warnings to one another until their voices are lost.
                                         — Herman Melville

Have you forgotten? Do you remember how the poorest of the poor used to be driven to the room where they were given death by gas?   — Albert Camus

[266]

"You ripped her kimono," I told him.
"Yeah, I got to buy her another."   — Mickey Spillane

Talent is in its infancy.   — G. B. Shaw

To be forced to admire what one instinctively hates,
and to hate all which one would naturally love is the condition of our lives in these bad years, and so is the cause
beneath other causes for our sickness and our death.
                                        — Leo Tolstoy

Why is my brain always so alive when I'm too drunk
ever to do anything about it?   — F. Scott Fitzgerald

The essence of spirit, he thought to himself, was to
choose the thing which did not better one's position, but
made it more perilous. That was why the world he knew
was poor, for it insisted morality and caution were iden-
tical. He was so completely of that world, and she was
not. She would stay with him until he wanted her no
longer, and the thought of what would happen afterward
ground his flesh with pain as real as a wound.
                                        — D. H. Lawrence

He held her to him, and fondled her hair, feeling a
sense of protection which bid her to stop here and ask no
more; for of all the distance she had come, and he had
helped her to move, and there were times like this when
he felt the substance of his pride to depend upon exactly
her improvement as if she were finally the only human
creation in which he had taken part, he still knew that he
could help her no longer, nor could anyone else, for she
had come now into that domain where her problems
were everyone's problems and there were no answers and
no doctors, but only that high plateau where philosophy
lives with despair.   — John Galsworthy

[267]

The woe of his life washed up on him at all he had not done, and all that he would never do, and he wept, he wept the harsh tears of a full-grown man.

— Ford Madox Ford

As socialists we want a socialist world not because we have the conceit that men would thereby be more happy — those claims are best left to dictators — but because we feel the moral imperative in life itself to raise the human condition even if this should ultimately mean no more than that man's suffering has been lifted to a higher level, and human history has only progressed from melodrama, farce, and monstrosity, to tragedy itself.

— Trotsky

Good style is the record of powerful emotion reaching the surface of the page through fine conscious nets of restraint, caution, tact, elegance, taste, even inhibition — if the inhibition is not without honor.

— Arthur Quiller-Couch

That many of you are frustrated in your ambitions, and undernourished in your pleasures, only makes you more venomous. Quite rightly. If I found myself in your position, I would not be charitable either.

— Thoreau

He felt the kind of merriment men know when events have ended in utter disaster.

— Jack London

Nobody could sleep . . . all through the ship, all over the convoy, was the knowledge that in a few hours some of them were going to be dead.

— Ernest Hemingway

I assure you, doctor, it is a relatively simple matter for a weathered charlatan like myself to keep up interest in so small a carnival as this.

— Nietzsche

One
Book
Review

Rush to Judgment by Mark Lane

On May 14, 1964, when J. Edgar Hoover testified before the Warren Commission, he said about Marguerite Oswald: "The first indication of her emotional instability was the retaining of a lawyer that anyone would not have retained if they really were serious in trying to get down to the facts." Well, Bill Terry once asked if the Dodgers were still in the league, and J. Edgar Hoover revealed this day an even more massive incapacity to judge certain kinds of underdogs and men, for Mark Lane, the lawyer retained, has come up with four hundred pages of facts on the Warren Commission's inquiry into the murders of President John F. Kennedy, Officer J. D. Tippit, and Lee Harvey Oswald, and they are somewhat staggering facts. If one-tenth of them should prove to be significant, then the work of the Warren Commission will be judged by history to be a scandal worse than Teapot Dome.

Rush to Judgment is of course a defense attorney's brief, and it seeks to make its case as best it can, wherever it can. Those looking for a comprehensive explanation of the mystery of the assassination will not find it, not here. There is no single overall explanation of the unspoken possibilities, nor is one even offered. Lane is attempting to prove that Oswald most certainly could not have committed the crime alone, and that the odds are great he did not commit either murder. Lane's attempt, therefore, is to disprove the case brought in by the prosecution — it is a small continuing shock to recognize, as Lane fortifies his arguments in the most interesting detail, that the Warren Commission served as an agent of gentlemanly prosecution rather than a commission of inquiry. That this was not head-on evident when the Report came out is due to the lucidities and sweet reasonable tone of the style in which the Warren Commission Report is written. But the gentlest of men often write in a bad harsh voice, and many a quiet calculating brute has acquired the best of good tones in prose. Yes, the Warren Commission Report convinced a majority of Americans by the reasonableness and modesty of its style — what casual study did not show, however, was that when the Commission was being most reasonable in stating that something could not be proved, it was neglecting to say that the preponderance of unexplored leads to new evidence was pointed resolutely in the opposite direction from their conclusion. The scandal of the Warren Commission was twofold — it did not look into some of the most interesting and fascinating matters before it, and it distorted its hard findings. As Hugh Trevor-Roper points out in a fine British introduction to *Rush to Judgment*, "A pattern was made to emerge out of the evidence, and having emerged, seemed to subordinate the evidence to it." It was not enough to read the Report; one was obliged, Trevor-Roper points out, to read the twenty-six volumes of "Hearings." "To follow the same question through the three successive levels of 'Hearings,' 'Report,' and 'Summary and Conclusions' is to see sometimes a quiet transformation of evidence."

But one may ask: was the Warren Commission in conspiracy to hide the truth, all those fine, separate, august, and honorable gentlemen? And the answer is: of course not. They were not in conspiracy, they never needed to be, no more than a corporation has to be in conspiracy to push out a product which is grievously inferior to the product they are potentially equipped to make, nor the head of General Motors need hire private detectives to hound Ralph Nader. Products come from processes, and a commission's report is a reflection of a method of inquiry. Edward Jay Epstein's book demonstrated even to Fletcher Knebel's satisfaction that the Warren Commission did not work very hard. Walter Craig, president of the American Bar Association, appointed as "protector" of Oswald's interests, attended two out of fifty-one sessions of the Commission — he was perhaps not the kind of lawyer Mr. Hoover would have recommended to Mrs. Oswald; the only Commission member to be present much more than 50 percent of the time was Allen Dulles of the CIA — perhaps he had the most to protect.

No, for the large part, the seven members of the Commission were abstracted and often distant. The established lawyers who pursued the investigation as the Commission's professional assistants were busy in private practice, and usually absent. So the work passed on down to junior assistants, bright young lawyers with careers to make. They were forced to contend every day with agents, investigators, and detectives who knew more about criminal investigation than they did and were also presumably possessed of more physical strength, more martial arts, as well as endowed with that dead, muted, fanatical intensity which wins much in negotiation across a table. The investigation seemed to push at every turn against the likelihood of inefficiency, corruption, collusion, or direct involvement in the case by the Dallas police, and, in more complex fashion, the CIA and the FBI. The Secret Service, having done a poor job, had their own reputations to protect. In such a situation, what overworked young lawyer is going to continue to make a personal crusade of his own investigation against the revelatory somnolence of the Commission members, and the resistance of the FBI, especially when a routine performance satisfactory to the Commission gives assurance of a happy and accelerated career?

What becomes oppressively evident is that the Warren Commission from the beginning had no intention of trying to find any other assassin than Oswald. Whether from pure motives or from intentions not so clear (it will be remembered that before the Commission began to sit, the chief justice was speaking already of information which could not be divulged for seventy-five years), whether from honest bias or determined obfuscation, the evidence fitted a bed of Procrustes. Everything was enlisted to satisfy the thesis that Oswald, half mad, had done the job alone, and Ruby, half mad, had done his particular job alone. So a witness, Brennan, who had poor eyesight, was credited by the Commission with identifying Oswald in a sixth-story window — his eyes, went the unspoken assumption, could see better at one time than another; whereas a man with excellent eyesight named Rowland who saw two men in the window was considered unreliable because his wife told the Commission her young husband was prone to exaggerate the results of his report cards.

Besides, it was a game of experts. The expert always plays a game in which his side is supposed to win — the expert has a psychic structure which is umbilically opposed to finding the truth until the expert finds out first if the truth is good for his side. We have prosecuting attorneys and defense attorneys because a legal case is first a game — each side looks for its purchase of the truth, even if the search carries them into almost impossible assumptions. It is why a fact-finding commission cannot by its nature make discoveries which are as incisive as the evidence uncovered by the monomaniacal, the Ahab-like search of a dedicated attorney. In contrast to him, the totalitarians look to find their truth in consensus. You and I are more likely to find it beneath a stone.

So Lane's book provides the case for the defense. Like all lawyers' briefs, it is not wholly satisfactory as a book. One wishes that the strongest evidence of Oswald's guilt provided by the Warren Commission were presented at least in summary, if only to be demolished, or that admission were made by Lane that certain crucial damaging points cannot be refuted, but Lane's intent is to do the best for his dead client, and that is what he does. If *Rush to Judgment* accomplishes nothing else, it will live as a classic for every serious amateur detective in America. Long winter nights in the farmhouse will be spent poring over the contradictions in the twenty-six volumes of "Hearings" with Lane's book for a guide, and plans will be made and money saved to take a trip to Dallas, which will become a shrine for all the unborn Baker Street Irregulars of the world. Because Lane's book proves once and forever that the assassination of President Kennedy is more of a mystery today than when it occurred.

Well, then — what finally does Lane produce? He presents a thousand items of clear-cut doubt in four hundred pages, material sufficient for five years of real investigation by any fair country commission. He makes it clear that most of the witnesses to the assassination thought the shots came not from the Texas Book Depository Building but from behind a fence on a knoll above and in front of the Presidential limousine. And that autopsy which could clarify whether the President was shot from the front, from behind, or from both separate positions — well, that autopsy is mired in massive confusion which the Commission did not dissolve and in fact interred, for X-rays and photographs taken at the autopsy have not been published. The bullet which shattered the President's skull almost certainly had to be a soft-nosed lead round to explode so large a wound; Oswald's gun fired hard-nosed metal-jacketed rounds. The questions raised by Edward Jay Epstein in *inquest* about the bullet which was alleged to strike the President and Governor Connally are explored again and point to the same conclusion — one bullet could not have entered where it did, and come out where it came out.

Nor has any satisfactory explanation ever been offered, Lane shows in detail, as to how the police were able to send out a call to apprehend Oswald fifteen minutes after the assassination, nor why the two officers who discovered the rifle on the sixth floor described it in careful detail as a "7.65 Mauser bolt-action equipped with a 4/18 scope, a thick leather brownish-black sling on it . . . gun metal color . . . blue metal . . . the rear portion of the bolt was visibly worn. . . ." But the Mauser turned into a pumpkin and became a 6.5 Mannlicher-Carcano. Of course, Marina Oswald, on hearing of the assassination over the radio, went out to the garage to see if Oswald's Mannlicher-Carcano was in place. It was there. It was there? "Later," she said, "it turned out that the rifle was not there . . . I did not know what to think." The Dallas police came in soon to search the garage and later reported that they found an empty blanket upon a shelf. It was that empty blanket, they declared, which Marina had mistaken for the rifle. So the rifle on the sixth floor altered from a 7.65 Mauser bolt-action to a 6.5 Mannlicher-Carcano carbine, a point in the shade of

Sherlock Holmes, for unless the police in Texas are such unnatural Texans as to be innocent of rifles, they would know a 7.65 Mauser bolt-action, since the Mauser is the most beloved and revered of bolt-actions, whereas the 6.5 Mannlicher-Carcano rests among the more despised of shooting irons. It is curious; one repeats: it is curious that the Commission taking testimony from the very same officer who discovered the original rifle which he had declared a Mauser did not choose to show this police officer the Mannlicher-Carcano and ask if he might be in error, or if, horror beyond belief, the guns were switched.

Roll call of these unexplored details continues. The Mannlicher-Carcano had the same scope as the nonexistent Mauser, but Marina Oswald had never seen a scope on a rifle. (She was a woman, after all.) So the suggestion intrudes itself — was the 4/18 scope on the Mauser switched in a great private frantic hurry to the Mannlicher, installed in fact so quickly that the telescopic sight was unrelated to the line of fire! Certainly we have it on record that the scope had to be reset with shims before three masters of the National Rifle Association could even aim it. This, the rifle supposed to have killed Kennedy? And when they fired for test, these three masters, six shots each in groups of two at three fixed targets, eighteen shots in total by three masters, they did not fire nearly so quickly nor so well at fixed targets as Oswald had fired at moving targets from a more difficult and certainly more extraordinary position. In fact the Mannlicher dispersed its shot group so widely (an estimated twelve inches at one hundred yards) that no one of the experts in all their collective eighteen shots succeeded in striking the head or neck of the fixed target. Nonetheless, the Commission decided that the Mannlicher-Carcano had done the job. Oswald, of course, had no great record as a rifleman, but perhaps his bad aim, the moving car, the crazy banged-up scope, the inaccurate barrel, and the very heavy trigger pull came together in the vertigo of the moment, to funnel in two hits out of three. Perhaps. Perhaps there is one chance in a thousand. But a Zen master, not a rifle expert, must be consulted for this.

Questions arise here and everywhere. The package of curtain rods in which Oswald was supposed to have concealed the Mannlicher-Carcano was too small (on the account of both witnesses who had seen it) to contain the disassembled rifle. But the size of the bag remains moot because it was ruined in the FBI labs while being examined for fingerprints. Another bag was put together — thirty-eight inches in length. The witnesses seemed to think it was about ten inches longer than the original. (The Mannlicher disassembled is almost thirty-five inches.) The Commission decided the witnesses "could easily have been mistaken in their estimate." So could the FBI, unless there were affidavits on the dimensions of the original bag before it had been subjected to fingerprint tests.

Move on. The only eyewitness to the murder of Tippit was a woman named Mrs. Markham. She was certain the killing took place at 1.06 P.M. The Commission was not able to get Oswald to the spot before 1.16 P.M. So the Commission decided Mrs. Markham was correct in her identification of Oswald, but wrong in her placement of the time. Mrs. Markham, however, in an interview with Lane, described Tippit's killer as "a short man, somewhat on the heavy side, with slightly bushy hair." The description she gave the police was "about thirty, five feet eight, black hair, slender."

Tippit leads to Ruby. Among the many potential witnesses who were not called were a variety of people who had been associated with Ruby for years. They made a general collective estimate that Ruby knew personally more than half the officers on the Dallas police force. Ruby kept begging the Warren Commission to get him out of the Dallas jail and into Washington. "I want to tell the truth," he said, "and I can't tell it here. . . . Gentlemen, unless you get me to Washington you can't get a fair shake out of me." Of course, many witnesses were intimidated in mysterious ways. Two reporters who visited Ruby's apartment just after he killed Oswald were later murdered, one in his Dallas apartment as the victim of a karate attack (where are you, Charlie Chan?). The Commission did not seem to explore this. Another witness, Warren Reynolds, was shot through the head, but recovered. He had seen a man whom he did not identify as Oswald (until many tribulations and eight months later) fleeing the scene of the Tippit murder, pistol in hand. Two months elapsed before Reynolds was questioned. He then told the FBI that he could not identify the fugitive as Oswald — although he had followed the man on foot for one block. Two days after the interview, Reynolds was shot through the head with a rifle and somehow survived. The prime suspect, Darrel Wayne Garner, was arrested by Dallas police, and later admitted he had made a call to his sister-in-law and "advised her he had shot Warren Reynolds," but the charges were dropped because Garner had an alibi in the form of a filed affidavit by Nancy Jane Mooney, a stripteaser who had been employed once at Jack Ruby's Carousel. Eight days later, Miss Mooney was arrested by Dallas police for fighting with her roommate, "disturbing the peace." Alone in her cell — less than two hours after arrival — Miss Mooney hanged herself to death, stated the police report.

Item: In January 1964, Reynolds told the FBI that the man he saw was not Lee Harvey Oswald.

Item: In July 1964, Reynolds — who now owned a watchdog, took no walks at night, and whose house was ringed with floodlights — testified that he now believed the man was Oswald. The Commission, in reporting the changed statements, omitted to mention at that precise point the attempt on Warren Reynolds's life.

Item: Information given by Nancy Perrin Rich to the Warren Commission that Jack Ruby brought money to a meeting between various agents and one U.S. Army officer for smuggling guns to Cuba, and refugees out, was stricken from the record by the Warren Commission.

Item: A communication from the CIA in response four months late to a Commission inquiry: "An examination of Central Intelligence files has produced no information on Jack Ruby or his activities." Indeed. Which files? The Balkan files? The Ipcress file?

Item: William Whaley, Oswald's alleged cab driver, was killed in an automobile collision on December 18, 1965.

Item: Albert G. Bogard, an automobile salesman who tried to sell a car to a man calling himself Lee Oswald, was beaten up by some men after testifying and was sent to a hospital. The Warren Commission determined that the man buying the car could not be Oswald, but it did not inquire further. That someone might be impersonating Oswald before the assassination was a matter presumably without interest to the Commission.

Item: On Wednesday, January 22, a call came to J. Lee Rankin, general counsel for the Warren Commission. It was from the attorney general of Texas who told Rankin he had learned that the FBI had an "undercover agent" and that agent was none other than Lee Harvey Oswald. After much discussion that evening and much resolution that evening to conduct an independent investigation of this charge, the Commission nonetheless ended months later with this verdict: "Nothing to support the speculation that Oswald was an agent, employee, or informant of the FBI," citing as its basis the testimony of Hoover, his assistant, and three FBI agents, plus reference to some affidavits signed by various other FBI agents. That proved to be the limit of the "independent investigation." There is nothing to show that the attorney general of Texas was ever asked to give testimony as to how he heard the rumor.

So there we are left in this extraordinary case, and with this extraordinary Commission which looks into the psychic traumas of Oswald's childhood and Jack Ruby's mother's "fishbone delusion," but does not find out by independent investigation which Dallas cop might have let Jack Ruby into the basement, or whether Oswald could ever have been an undercover agent for the FBI, the CIA, the MVD, MI-5, Fair Play for Cuba, JURE, Mao Tse-tung, the John Birch Society, the Nazi Renaissance Party, or whether indeed an agent for all of them. The word of Mr. Hoover is good enough for the Commission. Mr. Hoover is of course an honorable man, all kneel.

No, what we are left with, after reading this book, is an ineradicable sense of new protagonists — the Dallas police — and behind them, opposed to them, for them, beneath them, on every side of them; another protagonist or protagonists. But first, foremost, the police.

Criminals fall into two categories — good criminals and bad. A bad criminal is the simplest of people — he cannot be trusted for anything; a good criminal is not without nobility, and if he is your friend he is a rare friend. But cops! Ah, the cops are far more complex than criminals. For they contain explosive contradictions within themselves. Supposed to be law enforcers, they tend to conceive of themselves as the law. They are more responsible than the average man, they are more infantile. They are attached umbilically to the concept of honesty, they are profoundly corrupt. They possess more physical courage than the average man, they are unconscionable bullies; they serve the truth, they are psychopathic liars (no cop's testimony is ever to be trusted without corroboration); their work is authoritarian, they are cynical; and finally, if something in their heart is deeply idealistic, they are also bloated with greed. There is no human creation so contradictory, so finally enigmatic, as the character of the average cop, and these contradictions form the keel of the great American mystery — who killed President Kennedy?

Yet even that oppressive sense of the Dallas police does not satisfy all the resonance of this mystery. For the question remains: was Oswald some sort of agent? We are getting uncomfortably close to the real heart of the horror. So it is time to offer a new hypothesis (or at least offer the beginnings of a working hypothesis), even to make it out of whole cloth without a "scintilla of evidence." Call it a metaphor. So I will say the odds are indeed that Oswald was an undercover agent. He was too valuable not to be. How many Americans, after all, knew Soviet life in the small intimate ways Oswald had known it? And indeed how was it so possible for him to arrange his return? If you, sir, were the head of an espionage service, would you not wish to make Oswald work for you as the price of his return? If you were in Russian intelligence, would you not demand that he serve as some kind of Soviet agent in exchange for his release? A petty undercover agent for two services or three, a man without real importance or any sinister mission, he may still have been in so exposed a position that other services would have been attracted to him. Espionage services tend to collect the same particular small agents in common, for most of their operations are only serious as a game, and you need a pocket board on which to play. Oswald may have been just such a battered little pocket board.

Worked over and played over until he metamorphosed from playing board to harried rat, he may even have nibbled at the edge of twenty Dallas conspiracies. It was all comedy of the most horrible sort, but when Kennedy was assassinated, the espionage services of half the world may have discovered in the next hour that one little fellow in Dallas was — all pandemonium to the fore — a secret, useless, little undercover agent who was on their private lists. What nightmares must have ensued! What nightmares on the instant! What quiet little mind in some unknown council-of-war room, thinking of the exceptional definition of the game which might soon be given by a rat harried past the point of no return, a rat let loose in a courtroom, cried out in one or another Ivy League voice, "Well, can't something be done, can't we do something about this man?" and a man getting up saying, "See you in a while," and a little later a phone call made and another and finally a voice saying to our friend Ruby, "Jack, I got good news. There's a little job . . ." Is it so unreasonable that the tiny metaphorical center of a host of espionage games should be killed by that precise intersection of the Mafia, the police, the invisible government, and the striptease business which Jack Ruby personified to the point.

No, there may have been no formal master plan to murdering Kennedy, just coincidences beyond repair and beyond tolerance, as if all things came together in a blaze of one huge existential moment, and nothing left but wreckage, paranoia, and the secret bewildered sense in every cop, criminal, and agent of the western hemisphere that something beyond anyone's ken had occurred; now the evidence had to be covered. So Kennedy may have been killed by a conspiracy which was petty to its root; certainly he must have been killed by a very petty conspiracy with a few good Texas marksmen in it, but the power of several master conspiracies may then have been aroused to protect every last one of us against the possibility of discovery, against the truth, for no one in power in America knew what that truth was. Not any longer. So the case was fertilized and refertilized — it grew into a thicket. And the Commission was obliged to cut a tidy path through the thicket and this laid the ground for future scandals and disasters out of measure.

If in the next few years some new kind of commission

does not establish in hard and satisfactory fashion the known and unknown boundaries of the case, then the way is open to a series of surrealistic political machinations. On that unhappy — let us hope impossible — day when America becomes a totalitarian government of Left, Center, or Right, the materials are now at hand for a series of trials of high government figures which will make the Moscow trials of 1936 to 1938, following upon the assassination of Kirov, seem like modest exercises in domination, for the wealth of contradictory evidence now upon us from the rot-pile of Dallas permits any interpretation, any neat little path, to be cut through the thicket. From any direction to any direction. The Right may now convict the Left. The Left may now stifle the Right. The Center may eat them both. The cannibal's pure totalitarianism is near.

So one would propose one last new commission, one real commission — a literary commission supported by public subscription to spend a few years on the case. There are major intellectuals in this country who are old now and have never been able to serve in American life. Not ever. It is time for that. Time for the best of intellectuals to serve. I would trust a commission headed by Edmund Wilson before I trusted another by Earl Warren. Wouldn't you? Would you not estimate that Dwight Mac-Donald, working alone, could nose out more facts and real contradictions than could twenty crack FBI investigators working together? Laugh, angels, pass the drinks, make this the game for the week. Pick your members of the new commission. It is very funny. And yet the small persisting national need is for a few men who can induce, from contradictory evidence, a synthesis. The solution to President Kennedy's murder will come not from legal or government commissions, but from minds deeply grounded first and last in the mysteries of hypothesis, uncorrupted logic, tragedy, and metaphor. In the meanwhile, waiting for such a literary commission, three cheers for Mark Lane. His work is not without a trace of that stature we call heroic. Three cheers. Because the game is not yet over. Nor the echo of muffled drums. Nor the memory of the riderless horse.

PART THREE

GRIPS
ON
THE
AESTHETIC
OF
THE
STREET

Black
Power

Looking for the Meat and Potatoes —
Thoughts on Black Power

> "You don't even know who you are," Reginald had said.
> "You don't even know, the white devil has hidden it from
> you, that you are of a race of people of ancient civiliza-
> tions, and riches in gold and kings. You don't even know
> your true family name, you wouldn't recognize your true
> language if you heard it. You have been cut off by the
> devil white man from all true knowledge of your own
> kind. You have been a victim of the evil of the devil
> white man ever since he murdered and raped and stole
> you from your native land in the seeds of your fore-
> fathers. . . ."
>
> — *The Autobiography of Malcolm X*

In not too many years, we will travel to the moon, and on
the trip, the language will be familiar. We have not had

our education for nothing — all those sanitized hours of orientation via high school, commercials, corporations and mass media have given us one expectation: no matter how beautiful, insane, dangerous, sacrilegious, explosive, holy or damned a new venture may be, count on it, fellow Americans, the language will be familiar. Are you going in for a serious operation, voting on the political future of the country, buying insurance, discussing nuclear disarmament, or taking a trip to the moon? You can depend on the one great American certainty — the public vocabulary of the discussion will suggest the same relation to the resources of the English language that a loaf of big-bakery bread in plastic bag and wax bears to the secret heart of wheat and butter and eggs and yeast.

Your trip to the moon will not deal needlessly with the vibrations of the heavens (now that man dares to enter eschatology) nor the metaphysical rifts in the philosophical firmament; no poets will pluck a stringed instrument to conjure with the pale shades of the white lady as you move along toward the lunar space. Rather, a voice will emerge from the loudspeaker. "This is your pilot. On our starboard bow at four o'clock directly below, you can pick out a little doojigger of land down there like a vermiform appendix, and that, as we say good-bye to the Pacific Coast, is Baja California. The spot of light at the nub, that little bitty illumination like the probe bulb in a cystoscope or comparable medical instrument is Ensenada, which the guidebooks call a jeweled resort."

Good-bye to earth, hello the moon! We will skip the technological dividend in the navigator's voice as he delivers us to that space station which will probably look like a breeding between a modern convention hall and the computer room at CBS. Plus the packaged air in the space suits when the tourists, after two days of acclimation in air-sealed moon motels, take their first reconnoiter outside in the white moon dust while their good

American bowels accommodate to relative weightlessness.

All right, bright fellow, the reader now may say — what does all this have to do with Black Power? And the author, while adept at dancing in the interstices of a metaphor, is going to come back straight and fast with this remark — our American language is not any more equipped to get into a discussion of Black Power than it is ready to serve as interpreter en route to the moon. The American language has become a conveyer belt to carry each new American generation into its ordained position in the American scene, which is to say the corporate technological world. It can deal with external descriptions of everything which enters or leaves a man, it can measure the movements of that man, it can predict until such moment as it is wrong what the man will do next, but it cannot give a spiritual preparation for our trip to the moon any more than it can talk to us about death, or the inner experiences of real sex, real danger, real dread. Or Black Power.

If the preface has not been amusing, cease at once to read. What follows will be worse: the technological American is programmed to live with answers, which is why his trip to the moon will be needlessly God-awful; the subject of Black Power opens nothing but questions, precisely those unendurable questions which speak of premature awakenings and the hour of the wolf. But let us start with something comfortable, something we all know, and may encounter with relaxation, for the matter is familiar:

. . . think of that black slave man filled with fear and dread, hearing the screams of his wife, his mother, his daughter being *taken* — in the barn, the kitchen, in the bushes! . . . *Think* of hearing wives, mothers, daughters, being *raped!* And you were too filled with *fear* of the rapist to do anything about it! . . . Turn around and look at each other, brothers and sisters, and *think* of

this! You and me, polluted all these colors — and this
devil has the arrogance and the gall to think we, his victims, should *love* him!

— *The Autobiography of Malcolm X*

"Okay," you say, "I know that, I know that already. I
didn't do it. My great-grandfather didn't even do it. He
was a crazy Swede. He never even saw a black skin. And
now for Crysake, the girls in Sweden are crazy about
Floyd Patterson. I don't care, I say more power to him.
All right," goes the dialogue of this splendid American
now holding up a hand, "all right, I know about collective responsibility. If some Scotch-Irish planter wanted
to tomcat in the magnolias, then I'll agree it's easier for
me than for the victim to discern subtle differences between one kind of Wasp and another, I'll buy my part of
the ancestral curse for that Scotch-Irish stud's particular
night of pleasure, maybe I'm guilty of something myself,
but there are limits, man. All right, we never gave the
Negro a fair chance, and now we want to, we're willing
to put up with a reasonable amount of disadvantage, in
fact, discomfort, outright inequality and inefficiency. I'll
hire Negroes who are not as equipped in the productive
scheme of things as whites; that doesn't mean we have to
pay iota for iota on every endless misdemeanor of the
past and suffer a vomit bag of bad manners to boot.
Look, every student of revolution can tell you that the
danger comes from giving the oppressed their first liberties. A poor man who wins a crazy bet always squanders
it. The point, buddy, is that the present must forgive the
past, there must be forgiveness for old sins, or else progress is impossible." And there is the key to the first door:
progress depends upon anesthetizing the past. What if,
says Black Power, we are not interested in progress, not
your progress with packaged food for soul food, smog for
air, hypodermics for roots, air conditioning for breeze —
what if we think we have gotten strong by living without

progress and your social engineering, what if we think that an insult to the blood is never to be forgotten because it keeps your life alive and reminds you to meditate before you urinate. Who are you to say that spooks don't live behind the left ear and ha'nts behind the right? Whitey, you smoke so much you can't smell, taste, or kiss — your breath is too bad. If you don't have a gun, I can poke you and run — you'll never catch me. I'm alive 'cause I keep alive the curse you put in my blood. Primitive people don't forget. If they do, they turn out no better than the civilized and the sick. Who are you, Whitey, to tell me to drop my curse, and join your line of traffic going to work? I'd rather keep myself in shape and work out the curse, natural style. There's always white women, ahem! Unless we decide they're too full of your devil's disease, hypocritical pus-filled old white blood, and so we stay black with black, and repay the curse by drawing blood. That's the life-giving way to repay a curse."

"Why must you talk this way?" says the splendid American. "Can't you see that there are whites and whites, whites I do not begin to control? They wish to destroy you. They agree with your values. They are primitive whites. They think in blood for blood. In a war, they will kill you, and they will kill me."

"Well, daddy, I'm just putting you on. Didn't you ever hear of the hereafter? That's where it will all work out, there where us Blacks are the angels and honkies is the flunky. Now, let me take you by the tail, white cat, long enough to see that I want some more of these handouts, see, these homey horseballs and government aid."

The splendid American has just been left in the mire of a put-on and throwaway. How is he to know if this is spring mud or the muck of the worst Negro Hades?

The native's relaxation takes precisely the form of a muscular orgy in which the most acute aggressivity

and the most impelling violence are canalised, transformed and conjured away. . . . At certain times on
certain days, men and women come together at a given
place, and there, under the solemn eye of the tribe,
fling themselves into a seemingly unorganized panto-
mime, which is in reality extremely systematic, in
which by various means — shakes of the head, bending of the spinal column, throwing of the whole body
backwards — may be deciphered as in an open book
the huge effort of a community to exorcise itself, to lib-
erate itself . . . in reality your purpose in coming together is to allow the accumulated libido, the hampered
aggressivity to dissolve as in a volcanic eruption. Sym-
bolical killings, fantastic rites, imaginary mass murders
— all must be brought out. The evil humours are un-
dammed, and flow away with a din as of molten
lava. . . .

      — Frantz Fanon, *The Wretched of the Earth*

 Here is the lesson learned by the struggles of present-
day colonial countries to obtain their independence: a
war of liberation converts the energies of criminality, assassination, religious orgy, voodoo, and the dance into
the determined artful phalanxes of bold guerrilla armies.
A sense of brotherhood comes to replace the hitherto
murderous clan relations of the natives. Once, that pro-
pensity to murder each other had proved effective in
keeping the peace — for the settler. Now, these violent
sentiments turn against the whites who constrain them.
Just as the natives upon a time made good servants and
workers for the whites, while reserving the worst of their
characters for each other, now they looked to serve each
other, to cleanse the furies of their exploited lives in open
rude defiance against the authority.
 This is the conventional explanation offered by any
revolutionary spokesman for the Third World — that
new world which may or may not emerge triumphant in
Latin America, Asia, and Africa. It is a powerful argu-

ment, an uplifting argument, it stirs the blood of anyone who has ever had a revolutionary passion, for the faith of the revolutionary (if he is revolutionary enough to have faith) is that the repressed blood of mankind is ultimately good and noble blood. Its goodness may be glimpsed in the emotions of its release. If a sense of brotherhood animates the inner life of guerrilla armies, then it does not matter how violent they are to their foe. That violence safeguards the sanctity of their new family relations.

If this is the holy paradigm of the colonial revolutionary, its beauty has been confirmed in places, denied in others. While the struggles of the NLF and the North Vietnamese finally proved impressive even to the most gung-ho Marine officers in Southeast Asia, the horrors of the war in Biafra go far toward proving the opposite. The suspicion remains that beneath the rhetoric of revolution, another war, quite separate from a revolutionary war, is also being waged, and the forces of revolution in the world are as divided by this concealed war as the civilized powers who would restrain them. It is as if one war goes on between the privileged and the oppressed to determine how the productive wealth of civilization will be divided; the other war, the seed contained within this first war, derives from a notion that the wealth of civilization is not wealth but a corporate productive poisoning of the wellsprings, avatars, and conduits of nature; the power of civilization is therefore equal to the destruction of life itself. It is, of course, a perspective open to the wealthy as well as to the poor — not every millowner who kills the fish in his local rivers with the wastes from his factory is opposed to protecting our wilderness preserve, not at all, some even serve on the State Conservation Committee. And our First Lady would try to keep billboards from defacing those new highways which amputate the ecology through which they pass. Of course, her husband helped to build those highways. But then the rich, unless altogether elegant, are inevitably comic. It is in the worldwide militancy of the underprivileged, undernourished, and exploited that the potential horror of this future war (concealed beneath the present war) will make itself most evident. For the armies of the impoverished, unknown to themselves, are already divided. Once victorious over the wealthy West — if ever! — they could only have a new war. It would take place between those forces on their side who are programmatic, scientific, more or less socialist, and near maniac in their desire to bring technological culture at the fastest possible rate into every backward land, and those more traditional and/or primitive forces in the revolution of the Third World who reject not only the exploitation of the Western world but reject the West as well, in toto, as a philosophy, a culture, a technique, as a way indeed of even attempting to solve the problems of man himself.

Of these colonial forces, black, brown, and yellow, which look to overthrow the economic and social tyrannies of the white man, there is no force in Africa, Asia, or Latin America which we need think of as being any more essentially colonial in stance than the American Negro. Consider these remarks in *The Wretched of the Earth* about the situation of colonials:

"The colonial world is a world cut in two. The dividing line, the frontiers are shown by barracks and police stations." (Of this, it may be said that Harlem is as separate from New York as East Berlin from West Berlin.)

". . . if, in fact, my life is worth as much as the settler's, his glance no longer shrivels me up nor freezes me, and his voice no longer turns me into stone. I am no longer on tenterhooks in his presence; in fact, I don't give a damn for him. Not only does his presence no longer trouble me, but I am already preparing such efficient ambushes for him that soon there will be no way out but that of flight." (Now, whites flee the subways in New York.)

". . . There is no colonial power today which is capable of adopting the only form of contest which has a chance of succeeding, namely, the prolonged establishment of large forces of occupation." (How many divisions of paratroops would it take to occupy Chicago's South Side?)

The American Negro is of course not synonymous with Black Power. For every Black militant, there are ten Negroes who live quietly beside him in the slums, resigned for the most part to the lessons, the action, and the treadmill of the slums. As many again have chosen to integrate. They live now like Negroid Whites in mixed neighborhoods, suburbs, factories, obtaining their partial peace within the white dream. But no American Negro is contemptuous of Black Power. Like the accusing finger in the dream, it is the rarest nerve in their head, the frightening pulse in their heart, equal in emotional weight to that passion which many a noble nun sought to conquer on a cold stone floor. Black Power obviously derives from a heritage of anger which makes the American Negro one man finally with the African, the Algerian, and even the Vietcong — he would become schizophrenic if he tried to suppress his fury over the mutilations of the past.

The confrontation of Black Power with American life gives us then not only an opportunity to comprehend some of the forces and some of the style of that war now smoldering between the global rich and the global poor, between the culture of the past and the intuitions of the future, but — since Black Power has more intimate, everyday knowledge of what it is like to live in an advanced technological society than any other guerrilla force on earth — the division of attitudes within Black Power has more to tell us about the shape of future wars and revolutions than any other militant force in the world. Technological man in his terminal diseases, dying of air he can no longer breathe, of packaged food he can just about digest, of plastic clothing his skin can hardly bear, and of static before which his spirit has near expired, stands at one end of revolutionary ambition — at the other is an inchoate glimpse of a world now visited only by the primitive and the drug-ridden, a world where technology shatters before magic and electronic communication is surpassed by the psychic telegraphy of animal mood.

Most of the literature of Black Power is interested entirely, or so it would seem, in immediate political objectives of the most concrete sort. Back in 1923, Marcus Garvey, father of the Back-to-Africa movement, might have written, "When Europe was inhabited by a race of cannibals, a race of savages, naked men, heathens and pagans, Africa was peopled with a race of cultured black men, who were masters in art, science, and literature, men who were cultured and refined; men who, it was said, were like the gods," but the present leaders of Black Power are concerned with political mandate and economic clout right here. Floyd McKissick of CORE: the Black Power Movement seeks to win power in a half-dozen ways. These are:

"1. The growth of Black *political* power.
"2. The building of Black *economic* power.
"3. The improvement of the *self-image* of Black people.
"4. The development of Black *leadership.*
"5. The attainment of *Federal law enforcement.*
"6. The mobilization of Black *consumer power.*"

These demands present nothing exceptional. On their face, they are not so different from manifestos by the NAACP or planks by the Democratic Party. A debater with the skill of William F. Buckley or Richard Nixon could stay afloat for hours on the lifesaving claim that there is nothing in these six points antithetical to conservatives. Indeed, there is not. Not on the face. For example, here is Adam Clayton Powell, a politician most respected by Black Power militants, on some of these points. Political power: "Where we are 20 percent of the voters, we should command 20 percent of the jobs, judgeships, commissionerships, and all political appointments." Economic power: "Rather than a race primarily of consumers and stock boys, we must become a race of producers and stockbrokers." Leadership: "Black communities . . . must neither tolerate nor accept outside leadership — black or white." Federal law enforcement: "The battle against segregation in America's public-school systems must become a national effort, instead of the present regional skirmish that now exists." Even consumer protest groups to stand watch on the quality of goods sold in a slum neighborhood are hardly revolutionary, more an implementation of good conservative buying practices. *Consumers Digest* is not yet at the barricades.

Indeed, which American institution of power is ready to argue with these six points? They are so rational! The power of the technological society is shared by the corporations, the military, the mass media, the trade unions, and the Government. It is to the interest of each to have a society which is rational even as a machine is rational. When a machine breaks down, the cause can be discovered; in fact, the cause must be capable of being discovered or we are not dealing with a machine. So the pleasure of working with machines is that malfunctions are correctable; satisfaction is guaranteed by the application of work, knowledge, and reason. Hence, any race problem is anathema to power groups in the technological society, because the subject of race is irrational. At the very least, race problems seem to have the property of repelling reason. Still, the tendency of modern society to shape men for function in society like parts of a machine grows more powerful all the time. So we have the paradox of a conservative capitalistic democracy, profoundly entrenched in racial prejudice (and hitherto profoundly attracted to racial exploitation) now transformed into the most developed technological society in the world. The old prejudices of the men who wield power have become therefore inefficient before the needs of the social machine — so inefficient, in fact, that prejudiced as many of them still are, they consider it a measure of their responsibility to shed prejudice. (We must by now move outside the center of power before we can even find General Curtis LeMay.)

So the question may well be posed: if the demands formally presented by Black Power advocates like McKissick and Powell are thus rational, and indeed finally fit the requirements of the technological society, why then does Black Power inspire so much fear, distrust, terror, horror, and even outright revulsion among the best liberal descendants of the beautiful old Eleanor Roosevelt bag and portmanteau? And the answer is that an intellectual shell game has been played up to here. We have not covered McKissick's six points, only five. The sixth (point number three) was "the improvement of the *self-image* of Black people." It is here that Black hell busts loose. A technological society can deal comfortably with people who are mature, integrated, goal-oriented, flexible, responsive, group-responsive, etc., etc. — the word we cannot leave out is white or white-oriented. The technological society is not able to deal with the self-image of separate peoples and races if the development of their self-image produces personalities of an explosive individuality. We do not substitute sticks of dynamite for the teeth of a gear and assume we still have an automotive transmission.

McKissick covers his third point, of course: "Negro history, art, music and other aspects of Black culture . . . make Black people aware of their contributions to the American heritage and to world civilization." Powell bastes the goose with orotundities of rhetorical gravy:

"We must give our children a sense of pride in being black. The glory of our past and the dignity of our present must lead the way to the power of our future." Amen. We have been conducted around the point.

Perhaps the clue is that political Right and political Left are meaningless terms when applied conventionally to Black Power. If we are to use them at all (and it is a matter of real convenience), then we might call the more or less rational, programmatic, and recognizably political arm of Black Power, presented by McKissick and Powell, as the Right Wing, since their program can conceivably be attached to the programs of the technological society, whether Democrat or Republican. The straight-out political demands of this kind of Black Power not only can be integrated (at least on paper) into the needs of the technological society, but must be, because — we would repeat — an exploited class creates disruption and therefore irrationality in a social machine; efforts to solve exploitation and disruption become mandatory for the power groups. If this last sentence sounds vaguely Marxist in cadence, the accident is near. What characterizes technological societies is that they tend to become more and more like one another. So America and the Soviet Union will yet have interchangeable parts, or at least be no more different than a four-door Ford from a two-door Chevrolet. It may thus be noticed that what we are calling the Right Wing of Black Power — the technological wing — is in the conventional sense interested in moving to the left. Indeed, after the Blacks attain equality — so goes the unspoken assumption — America will be able to progress toward a rational society of racial participation, etc. etc. What then is the Left Wing of Black Power? Say, let us go back to Africa, back to Garvey.

We must understand that we are replacing a *dying* culture, and we must be prepared to do this, and be absolutely conscious of what we are replacing it with. We are
sons and daughters of the most ancient societies on this
planet. . . . No movement shaped or contained by
Western culture will ever benefit Black people. Black
power must be the actual force and beauty and wisdom
of Blackness . . . reordering the world.

— LeRoi Jones

Are you ready to enter the vision of the Black Left? It
is profoundly anti-technological. Here are a few remarks
by Ron Karenga:

"The fact that we are Black is our ultimate reality. We
were Black before we were born.

"The white boy is engaged in the worship of technology; we must not sell our souls for money and machines.
We must free ourselves culturally before we proceed po-
litically.

"Revolution to us is the creation of an alternative . . .
we are not here to be taught by the world, but to teach
the world."

We have left the splendid American far behind. He
believes in speaking his mind; but if LeRoi Jones — insults, absolute rejection, and consummate bad-mouthing
— is not too much for him, then Karenga will be his
finish. Karenga obviously believes that in the root is the
answer to where the last growth went wrong — so he believes in the wisdom of the blood, and blood-wisdom
went out for the splendid American after reading *Lady
Chatterley's Lover* in sophomore year. Life is hard
enough to see straight without founding your philosophy
on a metaphor.

Nonetheless the mystique of Black Power remains.
Any mystique which has men ready to die for it is never
without political force. The Left Wing of Black Power
speaks across the void to the most powerful conservative
passions — for any real conservatism is founded on re-

gard for the animal, the oak and the field; it has instinctive detestation of science, of the creation-by-machine. Conservatism is a body of traditions which once served as the philosophical home of society. If the traditions are now withered in the hum of electronics; if the traditions have become almost hopelessly inadequate to meet the computed moves of the technological society; if conservatism has become the grumbling of the epicure at bad food, bad air, bad manners; if conservatism lost the future because it enjoyed the greed of its privileged position to that point where the exploited depths stirred in righteous rage; if the conservatives and their traditions failed because they violated the balance of society, exploited the poor too savagely and searched for justice not nearly enough; if finally the balance between property rights and the rights of men gave too much to the land and too little to the living blood, still conservatism and tradition had one last Herculean strength: they were of the marrow, they partook of primitive wisdom. The tradition had been founded on some half-remembered sense of primitive perception, and so was close to life and the sense of life. Tradition had appropriated the graceful movements with which primitive strangers and friends might meet in the depth of a mood, all animal in their awareness: lo! the stranger bows before the intense presence of the monarch or the chief, and the movement is later engraved upon a code of ceremony. So tradition was once a key to the primitive life still breathing within us, a key too large, idiosyncratic, and unmanageable for the quick shuttles of the electronic. Standing before technology, tradition began to die, and air turned to smog. But the black man, living a life on the fringe of technological society, exploited by it, poisoned by it, half rejected by it, gulping prison air in the fluorescent nightmare of shabby garish electric ghettos, uprooted centuries ago from his native Africa, his instincts living ergo like nerves in the limbo of an amputated limb, had thereby an experience unique to modern man — he was forced to live at one and the same time in the old primitive jungle of the slums, and the hygienic surrealistic landscape of the technological society. And as he began to arise from his exploitation, he discovered that the culture which had saved him owed more to the wit and telepathy of the jungle than the value and programs of the West. His dance had taught him more than writs and torts, his music was sweeter than Shakespeare or Bach (since music had never been a luxury to him but a need), prison had given him a culture deeper than libraries in the grove, and violence had produced an economy of personal relations as negotiable as money. The American Black had survived — of all the peoples of the Western world, he was the only one in the near seven decades of the twentieth century to have undergone the cruel weeding of real survival. So it was possible his manhood had improved while the manhood of others was being leached. He had at any rate a vision. It was that he was black, beautiful, and secretly superior — he had therefore the potentiality to conceive and create a new culture (perchance a new civilization), richer, wiser, deeper, more beautiful and profound than any he had seen. (And conceivably more demanding, more torrential, more tyrannical.) But he would not know until he had power for himself. He would not know if he could provide a wiser science, subtler schooling, deeper medicine, richer victual, and deeper view of creation until he had the power. So while some (the ones the Blacks called Negroes) looked to integrate into the super-suburbs of technology land (and find, was their hope, a little peace for the kids), so others dreamed of a future world which their primitive lore and sophisticated attainments might now bring. And because they were proud and loved their vision, they were warriors as well, and had a mystique which saw the cooking of food as good or bad for the soul. And taste gave the hint. That was the Left of Black

Power, a movement as mysterious, dedicated, instinctive, and conceivably bewitched as a gathering of Templars for the next Crusade. Soon their public fury might fall upon the fact that civilization was a trap, and therefore their wrath might be double, for they had been employed to build civilization, had received none of its gains, and yet, being allowed to enter now, now, this late, could be doomed with the rest. What a thought!

> When the *canaille roturière* took the liberty of beheading the high *noblesse,* it was done less, perhaps, to inherit their goods than to inherit their ancestors.
> — Heinrich Heine

But I am a white American, more or less, and writing for an audience of Americans, white and Negro in the main. So the splendid American would remind me that my thoughts are romantic projections, hypotheses unverifiable by any discipline, no more legitimate for discussion than melody. What, he might ask, would you do with the concrete problem before us. . . .

You mean: not jobs, not schools, not votes, not production, not consumption. . . .

No, he said hoarsely, law and order.

Well, the man who sings the melody is not normally consulted for the bylaws of the Arrangers' Union.

Crap and craparola, said the splendid American, what it all comes down to is: how do you keep the peace?

I do not know. If they try to keep it by force — we will not have to wait so very long before there are Vietnams in our own cities. A race which arrives at a vision must test that vision by deeds.

Then what would you do?

If I were king?

We are a republic and will never support a king.

Ah, if I were a man who had a simple audience with Richard Milhous Nixon, I would try to say, "Remember when all else has failed, that honest hatred searches for responsibility. I would look to encourage not merely new funding for businessmen who are Black, but Black schools with their own teachers and their own texts, Black solutions to Black housing where the opportunity might be given to rebuild one's own slum room by room, personal idiosyncrasy next to mad neighbor's style, floor by floor, not block by block; I would try to recognize that an area of a city where whites fear to go at night belongs by all existential — which is to say natural — law to the Blacks, and would respect the fact, and so would encourage Black local self-government as in a separate city with a Black sanitation department run by themselves, a Black fire department, a funding for a Black concert hall, and most of all a Black police force responsible only to this city within our city and Black courts of justice for their own. There will be no peace short of the point where the Black man can measure his new superiorities and inferiorities against our own."

You are absolutely right but for one detail, said the splendid American. What will you do when they complain about the smog our factories push into their air?

Oh, I said, the Blacks are so evil their factories will push worse air back. And thus we went on arguing into the night. Yes, the times are that atrocious you can hardly catch your breath. "Confronted by outstanding merit in another, there is no way of saving one's ego except by love."

Goethe is not the worst way to say good-night.

Contribution to a
Partisan Review Symposium

Allow a symposiast to quote from himself. The following is out of *The Armies of the Night.*

Not for little humor had Negroes developed that odd humorless crack in their personality which cracked each other into laughter, playing on one side an odd mad practical black man who could be anything, wise chauffeur, drunken butler, young money-mad Pullman porter, Negro college graduate selling insurance — the other half was sheer psychopath, rocks in the ice-cube, pocket oiled for the switchblade, I'll kill you, Whitey, burn baby, all tuned to a cool. These Blacks moved through the New Left with a physical indifference to the bodies about them, as if ten Blacks could handle any hundred of these flaccid Whites, and they signaled to each other across the aisles, and talked in quick idioms and out, an English not comprehensible to any ear which knew nothing of the separate meanings of the same word at separate pitch (Maoists not for nothing these Blacks!) their hair carefully brushed out in every direction like African guerrillas or huge radar stations on some lonely aisle, they seemed to communicate with one another in ten dozen modes, with fingers like deaf and dumb, with feet, with their stance, by the flick of their long wrist, with the radar of their hair, the smoke of their will, the glide of their passage, by a laugh, a nod, a disembodied gesture, through mediums, seeming to speak through silent mediums among them who never gave hint to a sign. In the apathy which had begun to lie over the crowd as the speeches went on and on (and the huge army gathered by music, now was ground down by

words, and the hollow absurd imprecatory thunder of
the loudspeakers with their reductive echo — you must
FIGHT . . . *fight* . . . fight . . . fite . . . ite . . . ,
in the soul-killing repetition of political jargon which
reminded people that the day was well past one o'clock
and they still had not started) the Blacks in the roped-
in area about the speaker's stand were the only sign
of active conspiracy, they were up to some collective
expression of disdain, something to symbolize their
detestation of the White Left — yes, the observer was
to brood on it much of the next day when he learned
without great surprise that almost all of the Negroes
had left to make their own demonstration in another
part of Washington, their announcement to the press
underlying their reluctance to use their bodies in a
White War. That was comprehensible enough. If the
Negroes were at the Pentagon and did not preempt the
front rank, they would lose face as fighters; if they
were too numerous on the line, they would be beaten
half to death. That was the ostensible reason they did
not go, but the observer wondered if he saw a better.

There is an old tendency among writers of the Left when
apologists for one indigestible new convulsion or another
— they go in for a species of calculated reduction which
attempts to introduce comfortable proportions into historic phenomena which are barbaric, heroic, monstrous,
epic, and/or apocalyptic. (*New Republic* and *Nation*
writers please stand!) So we may remember there was
never much of a famine in the Ukraine, just various
local dislocations of distribution; never real Moscow
trials, rather the sort of predictable changing of the
guard which accompanies virile epochs of history. The
American labor unions were never really in danger of
leaving the Left, just being led down the garden path by
unscrupulous but limited leadership. Et cetera. So forth.

Now, Black Power. We are bound to hear before we
are done that Black Power is merely a long-due cor-

rective for premature and administratively betrayed efforts at integration — an indispensable period of self-development which will result in future integrations at a real level.

Like all such Left perspectives, it is wishful, pretty, programmatic, manipulable by jargon, and utterly stripped of that existential content which is indispensable to comprehending the first thing about Black Power.

The first thing to say, pretty or no, is that the Negro (that is the active volatile cadres of every militant Negro movement, SNCC, Black Muslims, etc., plus those millions of latently rebellious black masses behind them — which is what we will refer to when we speak of the Negro), yes, this Negro does not want equality any longer, he wants superiority, and wants it because he feels he is in fact superior. And there is some justice on his side for believing it. Sufficiently fortunate to be alienated from the benefits of American civilization, the Negro seems to have been better able to keep his health. It would take a liberal with a psychotic sense of moderation to claim that whites and Negroes have equally healthy bodies; the Negroes know they have become on the average physically superior, and this *against all the logic of America's medical civilization* — the Negroes get less good food ostensibly, no vitamins, a paucity of antibiotics, less medical care, less fresh air, less light and sanitation in living quarters. Let us quit the list — it is parallel to another list one could make of educational opportunities vs. actual culture (which is to say — real awareness of one's milieu). The Negro's relatively low rate of literacy seems to be in inverse relation to his philosophical capacity to have a comprehensive vision of his life, a large remark whose only support is existential — let us brood, brothers, on the superior cool of the Negro in public places. For the cool comes from a comprehensive vision, a relaxation before the dangers of life, a readiness to meet death, philosophy, or amusement at any turn.

Commend us, while we are on lists, to the ability of the Negro to police himself, as opposed to the ability of the White to police others. At the civil rights march on Washington in 1963 with over a hundred thousand Negroes in town, no episodes of violence were reported — in the riots in the years which followed, fascinating patterns of cooperation among the rioters emerge. One may look, as government commissions do, for patterns of a plot; or one may do better to entertain the real possibility that the Negroes have psychic powers of mass impromptu collaboration which are mysterious, and by that measure, superior to the White.

What the Negro may have decided at this point, as Black Power emerges, is that he has gotten the worst and the least of civilization, and yet has been able to engage life more intensely. It is as if the cells of his body now know more than the white man — so his future potentiality is greater. Whether this is true, half-true, or a species of madness is beyond anyone's capacity to know in this year, but the psychological reality is that breaking through his feelings of vast inferiority, a feeling of vast superiority is beginning to arise in the black man, and the antennae of this superiority lead not to developing the Negro to a point where he can live effectively as an equal in white society, but rather toward developing a viable modern culture of his own, a new kind of civilization. This is the real and natural intent of Black Power; not to get better schools, but to find a way to educate their own out of textbooks not yet written; not to get fair treatment from the police, but grapple instead with the incommensurable problem of policing one's own society — what will Black justice be? Ergo, not to get a fair share of hospitals, but an opportunity to explore Black medicine, herbs in place of antibiotics, witchcraft for cancer cures, surgical grace with the knife in preference to heart transfers. In parallel: not to get into unions, but to discover — it is far off in the distance — Black notions of labor, cooperation, and the viability of hip in production methods; not housing projects, but a new way to build houses; not shuttle planes, but gliders; not computers — rather psychic inductions.

Black Power moves then, obviously, against the technological society. Since the Negro has never been able to absorb a technological culture with success, even reacting against it with instinctive pain and distrust, he is now in this oncoming epoch of automation going to be removed from the technological society anyway. His only salvation, short of becoming a city brigand or a government beggar, is to build his own society out of his own culture, own means, own horror, own genius. Or own heroic, tragic, or evil possibilities. For there is no need to assume that the black man will prove morally superior to the white man. Schooled in treachery, steeped in centuries of white bile, there are avalanches and cataracts of violence, destruction, inchoate rage, and promiscuous waste to be encountered — there is well a question whether he can build his own society at all, so perverse are the conduits of his crossed emotions by now. But the irony is that the White would do well to hope the Black can build a world, for those well-ordered epochs of capitalism which flushed the white wastes down into the Black heart are gone — the pipes of civilization are backing up. The irony is that we may even yet need a Black vision of existence if civilization is to survive the death chamber it has built for itself. So let us at least recognize the real ground of Black Power — it is ambitious, beautiful, awesome, terrifying, and has to do with nothing so much as the most important questions of us all — what is man? why are we here? will we survive?

A Consequent Exchange: Letters

Sirs:

In your Spring 1968 issue Norman Mailer writes:

Sufficiently fortunate to be alienated from the benefits of American civilization, the Negro seems to have been better able to keep his health. It would take a liberal with a psychotic sense of moderation to claim that whites and Negroes have equally healthy bodies; the Negroes know they have become on the average physically superior, and this *against all the logic of America's medical civilization.* . . .

In the *New York Times,* May 19, 1968, there appears the following:

Poor Americans are four times as likely to die before the age of 35 as the average citizen. Negro women in Mississippi die six times as often in childbirth as white women and in some urban ghettos of the North one child in ten dies in infancy. The life expectancy of an American Negro at birth is 61 years, that of a white American is 68.

In citing these figures Dr. H. Jack Geiger of Tufts–New England Medical Center said recently that the health of the poor in this country "is an ongoing national disaster."

The effects of racial discrimination and economic disadvantage begin before birth, Dr. Geiger said. . . . Poor women obtain prenatal care less often than others. In the maternity wards of public hospitals 45 percent of the mothers have had no such care. This increases three-fold their likelihood of bearing children prematurely. Mental retardation occurs ten times more often in very small premature babies than in those born at full term. . . .

The health gap between rich and poor is growing. In 1940 the infant mortality rate for nonwhites was 70 percent higher than that for whites. In 1962 the rate was 90 percent greater.

We all know that "the poor" includes a vast number of Negroes and often is used as a euphemism for Negroes. Now then, who is right — Dr. Geiger or Dr. Mailer?

Irving Howe

Mr. Mailer replies:

I was not aware of Dr. Geiger's figures when I wrote the piece from which Irving Howe quotes, or I would have attempted to use his statistics to fortify my case, particularly the relation of the following two sentences: "The life expectancy of an American Negro at birth is 61 years, . . . of a white American . . . 68" and "in 1962 the [infant mortality rate for nonwhites] was 90 percent higher.

Now a few figures from a book by J. I. Rodale, *Are We Really Living Longer?* (Emmaus, Pa., 1955). In 1850, the life expectancy of a white male at birth was 38.3 years; in 1947 it was 65.16 years. But "in 1850, white men who lived to be forty years old could expect on the average to live 27.9 years longer or to a total age of 67.9 . . . in 1947 it [life expectancy] had only increased to 30.6 (total age 70.6). In 100 years, therefore, the life expectancy had only increased 2.7 years *after forty years of age* [italics mine]." In fact, a man reaching the age of 60 in the year 1850 had a slightly longer life expectancy than a man of 60 in 1947.

Evidently, the medical gains are to be found in infant mortality rates. Infants and children who would have died one hundred years ago are kept alive today by medical science.

Now, Negro infants obviously receive inferior medical

care. So their mortality rate by the Geiger figures is 90 percent higher. Yet note that every time an infant dies, someone else must live to the age of seventy in order to have an average life expectancy for the two of 35 years. If, then, the American Negro's life expectancy at birth is *so high* as 61 years (after incorporating an infant mortality rate 90 percent higher than the white man's) and the white American's life expectancy (after the advantage of his reduced infant mortality rate) is still *so low* at birth as 68 years, the inference can hardly be ignored that if the American Negro can manage to get through the rigors of his infancy, his future life expectancy — poor medical care and all — is going to be higher than the white's. And indeed after the age of 65, the contemporary Negro, despite all early obstacles, has a greater life expectancy than the white man.

Perhaps the logic of America's white medical civilization is to keep the babies alive and debilitate the men.

Regards to Dr. Howe.

Sirs:

Your readers may recall the exchange between Norman Mailer and myself in the last *Partisan Review* concerning health, physical condition, etc., among Negroes and whites in America. Since my letter was based on a report by Dr. H. Jack Geiger, I thought it might be useful to submit the Howe-Mailer exchange to him and see what he thought. Which I did. Dr. Geiger then wrote me the following letter, asking that it be submitted to *Partisan Review* for publication. Which I do.

Irving Howe

Dear Mr. Howe:

Your letter of August 5 has just been forwarded to me in Mississippi, where most of my work is now focused. I am pleased at your thoughtfulness in sending me the exchange of correspondence between yourself and Norman Mailer in the *Partisan Review*. I think the issue is a most important one.

First of all, I have to point out an error which occurred either in your letter, or in the *Times* of May 19. The quote should have said "and in some urban ghettos of the North one child in ten dies in infancy."

With regard to Mr. Mailer's reply, it is inaccurate. I do not want to bore you, or him, or the readers of *Partisan Review*, with a long and statistical analysis, but the fundamental error is in the application to whole populations of the idea that "every time an infant dies someone else must live to the age of 70 in order to have an average life expectancy for the two of 35 years." In a sample of two people, life may be divided between 0 years and 70 years to reach an average of 35; but in the large Negro population of the United States it is not 50 percent that dies under one year of age but only approximately 4 percent — even though this is a rate 90 percent higher than the white rate. The fact of the matter is that most but not all of the seven-year differential in life expectancy between Negroes and whites in the United States is accounted for by infant mortality. It is worth emphasizing the "not all." While it is quite true, as Mr. Mailer points out, that there has been very little progress for life expectancy beyond age 40 (regardless of race) in the last 50 years, the fact is that at *almost every age* from 0 to 65, including the ages past 40, the Negro has a lower life expectancy in the United States than the white. Put more bluntly, a Negro in the United States at any age is likelier to die sooner than a white man of the same age. The death rates for virtually every major grouping of diseases, at any age, is higher for Negroes than for whites in the United States.

This is obviously in very large measure — if not entirely — due to the circumstances of life for the Black American — that is, miserable housing, overcrowding, inadequate nutrition, greater exposure to infectious disease, discrimination, social and psychological stress, and all the rest of the dreary litany that is so familiar to us.

It is just not true in the United States that Negroes and whites have equally healthy bodies; at any age, the Negro is likelier to suffer illness — or at least to die from the illnesses he suffers. I do not know what Mr. Mailer means by "the Negroes have become on the average physically superior. . . ." What is the criterion of physical superiority? It cannot be in growth and development; inadequate nutrition and faulty medical care have seen to that. It cannot be in life expectancy. The implication is that there is some sort of intrinsic or genetic physical superiority in Negroes, however obscured it may be by the effects of environment and faulty medical care. On the basis of our present knowledge, this is as ridiculous as the contention that Negroes are intrinsically inferior and whites superior. There is just no scientific support for claims of racial superiority and inferiority, no matter which race we are talking about.

The most profound admiration for American Negroes — for the ability to survive, somehow, to some extent, in the face of brutalizing, bitter, discriminatory biological, social, and physical environment — does not require statistical manipulation nor genetic mythology. It would be tragic if we let anything obscure our confrontation of the slow and systematic damage our social order wreaks on Black Americans, just as it would be foolish if we made longevity the test of the quality of a social order. After all, whites in North Dakota live longer than anybody in the United States, and I doubt that Mr. Mailer would be interested in the thesis that rural North Dakota represents the epitome of Western civilization.

Finally, I do not know what Mr. Mailer means by "America's medical civilization." Discrimination and injustice in medical care are a significant and disgusting feature of American life, but the basic harm that is done to Blacks in the United States has nothing to do with medicine; it has to do with the social order of which medicine is only a part.

H. Jack Geiger, M.D.
Tufts University School of Medicine

Mr. Mailer replies:

One point I wished to make in my answer to Irving Howe: With the exception of infant care, our medical civilization (by which I mean techniques, pharmacopia, hospitals, etc.) deprive people of more health than they furnish. Dr. Geiger's letter with its corrected statistics — statistics, mind you, which had to be corrected after passing through three reliable sources, Dr. Geiger, the *New York Times* and Irving Howe — admits that even with the corrected statistics, Negro life expectancy is almost as great as white. The Negro's greater mortality, as Dr. Geiger points out quite justly, is due to leading lives of such abysmal economic misery that Black health is affected. Obviously their slightly greater rate of adult mortality is due not to insufficiency of medical care, but to a lack of the most basic requirements of life, food, and shelter. It seems to me that the true test of the argument might be to study Negro communities which have decent food and shelter but not enough income to afford any expensive medical care against prosperous white samples who receive all the medical care in the world. Then we might see whose body was voting for longevity. I do not wish to make a fetish of longevity in and of itself. It was the others, after all, who first brought it up. I would rather point out that my attack was made upon the conditioned reflexes of the liberal stance which rushes to claim that he who does without professional medical care is automatically damned, and damned unhealthy, whereas I would rush to assume that one of the roots of the twentieth-century disease is the over-proliferation of medical techniques and medical drugs without in some

— or by now is it in most? — cases rudimentary studies of their ultimate effects.

In none of this have I mentioned once that the physical superiority of the Negro appears most evident in the extraordinary number of Negroes who make superb athletes. Let Irving Howe say that the reason for athletic eminence is because nothing else is open to the talented Negro — I would suggest he watch a few of their moves. The resources of an emerging culture can sometimes be glimpsed in the passage of a figure. (Or is that what modern dance has been trying to tell me all these years?)

White
Politics

An Open Letter to Richard Nixon

Dear Mr. President-Elect:

Years ago, talented sportswriters like Jimmy Cannon used to write columns which began: "You're Ray Robinson and you used to be the greatest welterweight in the world. Now, you're older, and trying to make it back as a middleweight." Mr. Cannon was employing a subtle literary form: exhortation by the insinuation of the second person. It is a style of literary address used for speaking to children, monarchs, champions, union workers, and chiefs, so it is hardly a routine tense to employ for open correspondence with a President. We are a republic, after all, and it is incumbent on us to venerate the Presidency. Only a fool, fanatic, lout, or very wicked fellow would presume to speak in the Insinuative Exhortative to his Commander-in-Chief.

Yet, as you have been the first to remark, we live in times so divisive that the most affecting moment of your campaign was the sight of a sign, BRING US TOGETHER, which a young girl held up at the edge of the crowd as evening came on. We are all hungry for honest sentiment to nourish the marrow of our raddled psychology, so hungry one would feel demonic to suggest that we cannot be certain of the precise occasion of any fact. Yet it is impossible in the age of the Avenue of the Madison not to suspect that the girl and the sign could have been the bright idea of a bright young executive with horn-rimmed glasses who simply set out to design that scene, and converted the meaning of the sign, therefore, from sentiment to a computation of the techno-structure.

Well, we could never know. In the horror of our modern times, there is nothing more difficult to verify than the root of a fact. It may be incumbent on us, therefore, to trust your Presidency until that day we are certain you do not mean what you say. It is happier to believe that you do, that you are a man who has made a remarkable return from an abysmal political defeat, and that your passion is to bring peace and justice to this country, to unite us, drain our running wounds, and flesh us a vision of some creative future. Nothing less would entitle you to be called a great President; nothing less than a great President might be ready to satisfy our need.

Of course your detractors in the Democratic Party, even writers so elegant as Mr. Schlesinger and Mr. Galbraith, expect you to entertain policies they think detestable: a search for nuclear superiority, a program of law and order with increments of local police force too large for democratic balance, even a certain cynicism about the rate of unemployment, a flirtation with depression rather than inflation, a bending of the tax structure to cushion the corporations and the rich; they are blunt to fear that you are a man of paranoid disposition, unstable temperament in crisis, and not above striking a low blow. Of course these two gentlemen might today admit that the same description of personality could fit Lyndon Johnson. Yet if any writer had suggested such a syndrome in 1964, Schlesinger and Galbraith would have wished to dispatch him to an institution. So we do not have to accept their view of your character, especially since they have already certified themselves as fine fellows, but abominably off the point on occasion in their judgments of men. Of course, they are Democrats, and the Democratic Party has much to bewilder it today. It is a party of the people which lately does not find a candidate the people desire. Dump the Hump! It is a party which has become all program and no coherent philosophy. Its approach to every social, moral, and spiritual ill of man is to inject money; so it has the psychology of the pusher: in trouble? — take a fix! People, in fact, are so addicted to voting for the Democratic Party that many pulled the lever for its last nominee even if the thought of him offered nausea.

Of course, many voted for you without enthusiasm either. It is conceivably part of your strength that you are well aware of this. One would hope so. For in that case, it could prove an attractive and powerful passion to demonstrate to America that it was wrong and that there are funds of imagination, decency, and creative politics open to you which will yet astound the nation. That is why one may hope the liberal intellectuals of the Democratic Party are mistaken in their assumption that you will look for nuclear superiority, massive dragoonings of law and order, policies of repression in the ghetto, and the engineering of all oxygen out of one's breath. There is a crisis in the world today which comes out of the massive over-development of the machine before we have comprehended its excesses, or even how to dispose of its wastes. This super-employment of machines is accelerated every instant by the promiscuities of electronic communication which strip the husk of new ideas as pervasively as paper money once uprooted the yeoman from his field and the craftsman from his bench. Now a new generation of rulers has entered our century. We are governed no longer by chieftains, statesmen, or princes — now managers, experts, and executives, members of what some have come to call the techno-structure, seem to rule society. You are a respectable member of that techno-structure, as was your Democratic opponent. Your political differences seemed no more separated philosophically than the discussion of two mechanics (with different religious affiliations) about the best way to repair a machine which had become hopelessly inefficient, if not downright sinister, since its fumes brought death to every breath of air, its wastes gave promise of destroying the fields and glutting the rivers, its plastic residue proved insoluble to departments of sanitation all over the world, and its ferocious coupling of new ideas thrust nihilism into every pore of intellectual and academic life.

Since it is obvious that you are still full of belief in the power of the techno-structure to solve the problems of society, one anticipates your Administration with heavy foreboding. Yet this sense of gloom might have been greater if either of your opponents had won, since the man to your Right could have brought on a civil war in the cities, and the man to your Left would have looked like nothing so much as a third-string tailback scurrying from sideline to sideline, first Left, then Right, never gaining a yard. Hysteria is the wild gallop of unleashed horses who never move, and if your opponents claim that you are unstable, any common witness would know that the candidate on your Left was hysterical.

Let us hope then, sir, that you are precisely unstable enough to move in ways unforeseen by any of your critics or supporters. If you are on the one hand a believer in the techno-structure, you are on the other a conservative, you believe or pretend to believe in the immanence of God, the nourishment of tradition, and the sanctity of nature. The technological society which you now begin to administer proceeds to destroy all three at a rate far greater than the worst Communism of your nightmares; you, like every other American, must look into the eye of a dilemma no smaller than the agony of the twentieth century. Nothing less than the artful balance of old dialogues and new, of revolutionary approaches to particular problems and the delicate restoration of tradition within other kinds of crisis can begin to awaken our world from the chimeras of destruction which now surround us. Once, on television, in a show called "Firing Line," the writer of this letter said to William F. Buckley that he thought Fidel Castro and Charles de Gaulle were the two greatest political figures alive today. It is the only time he ever saw Mr. Buckley's jaw fly open in a debate. If you feel a clue to the impact of that remark, then there is cause for optimism that you as President will be able to contribute an unforeseen thought or two to the political theatre of America and our dramatic sense of the democratic art. If, on the other hand, praise for two such existential leaders leaves you perplexed, one is forced to suggest that the health of a good society in evil times may come from the grace to recognize a merit in the most unlikely man. But here I am, sir, working for myself again, or is it tooling the trick for you?

Yours for an interesting and prosperous Administration,

Norman Mailer

An Instrument for the City

The New York Times *Magazine, May 18, 1969*

How is one to speak of the illness of a city? A clear day can come, a morning in early May like the pride of June. The streets are cool, the buildings have come out of shadow, and silences are broken by the voices of children. It is as if the neighborhood has slept in the winding-sheet of the past. Forty years go by — one can recollect the milkman and the clop of a horse. It is a great day. Everyone speaks of the delight of the day on the way to work. It is hard on such mornings to believe that New York is the victim "etherized upon a table."

Yet by afternoon the city is incarcerated once more. Haze covers the sky, a grim, formless glare blazes back from the horizon. The city has become unbalanced again. By the time work is done, New Yorkers push through the acrid, lung-rotting air and work their way home, avoiding each other's eyes in the subway. Later, near midnight, thinking of a walk to buy the *Times,* they hesitate — in the darkness a familiar sense of dread returns, the streets are not quite safe, the sense of waiting for some apocalyptic fire, some night of long knives, hangs over the city. We recognize one more time that the city is ill, that our own New York, the Empire City, is not too far from death.

Recollect: When we were children, we were told air was invisible, and it was. Now we see it shift and thicken, move in gray depression over a stricken sky. Now we grow used to living with colds all year, and viruses suggestive of the plague. Tempers shorten in our hideous air. The sick get sicker, the violent more violent. The frayed tissue of New York manners seems ready to splatter on every city street. It is the first problem of the city, our atrocious air. People do not die dramatically like the one-day victims of Donora, rather they dwindle imperceptibly, die five years before their time, ten years before, cough or sneeze helplessly into the middle of someone else's good mood, stroll about with the hot iron of future asthma manacled to their lungs. The air pollution in New York is so bad, and gives so much promise of getting worse, that there is no solution to any other problem until the air is relieved of its poisonous ingestions. New York has conceivably the worst air of any city in the universe today — certainly it is the worst air in the most technologically developed nation in the world, which is to say it is the air of the future if the future is not shifted from its program. Once Los Angeles was famous for the liver-yellow of her smog; we have surpassed her.

That is our pervasive ill. It is fed by a host of tributary ills which flow into the air, fed first by our traffic, renowned through the world for its incapacity to move. Midtown Manhattan is next to impenetrable by vehicle from midday to evening — the average rate of advance is, in fact, six miles an hour, about the speed of a horse at a walk. Once free of the center, there is the threat of hour-long tie-ups at every bridge, tunnel, and expressway if even a single car breaks down in a lane. In the course of a year, people lose weeks of working time through the sum of minutes and quarter hours of waiting to crawl forward in traffic. Tempers blow with lost schedules, work suffers everywhere. All the while stalled cars gun their motors while waiting in place, pumping carbon monoxide into air already laden with caustic sulphur dioxide from fuel oil we burn to make electricity.

Given this daily burden, this air pollution, noise pollution, stagnant transport, all but crippled subways, routes of new transportation twenty years unbuilt —

every New Yorker sallies forth into an environment which strips him before noon of his good cheer, his charity, his calm nerve, and his ability to discipline his anger.

Yet, beneath that mood of pestilential clangor, something worse is ticking away — our deeper sense of a concealed and continuing human horror. If there are eight million people in New York, one million live on welfare, no, the figure is higher now, it will be one million two hundred thousand by the end of the year. Not a tenth of these welfare cases will ever be available for work; they are women and children first, then too old, too sick, too addicted, too illiterate, too unskilled, too ignorant of English. Fatherless families and motherless families live at the end of an umbilical financial cord which perpetuates them in an embryonic economic state. Welfare is the single largest item in the city budget — two years ago it surpassed the figure we reserve for education, yet it comes down to payments of no more than $3,800 a year for a family of four. Each member of that family is able to spend a dollar a day for food, at most $1.25 a day.

Still, it is worse than that. If one of eight people in New York is on welfare, half as many again might just as well be on welfare because their minimum wage brings in no more than such a check. So the natural incentive is to cease working. Close to $1.5 billion is spent on welfare now. The figure will go up. Manpower Training, in contrast, spends about a twenty-fifth as much. Looking to skill the poor for work, it will train as many as 4,000 men a year, and place perhaps 10,000 men out of 100,000 applicants in bad jobs without foreseeable future, the only jobs indeed available for the untrained. Sometimes in the Job Corps it cost $13,000 to train a man for a job where he might be able to make $6,000 a year if he could find a job, but the skills he had learned were not related to the jobs he might return to at home. Poverty lies upon the city like a layer of smog.

Our housing offers its unhappy figures. If we have calculated that it is necessary to build 7,500 new low-
income apartments a year, merely to keep on the same
terms with the problem, we end in fact with 4,000 units
constructed. Never mind how most of it looks — those
grim, high-rise, new-slum prisons on every city horizon.
Face rather the fact that we lose near to the same number of units a year as old buildings which could have
been saved run down into a state requiring condemna-
tion. Of the $100,000,000 the city spends each budget
year for new housing, $20,000,000 goes into demolition.
If four times as much were spent by present methods on
low- and middle-income housing, 36,000 new and reha-
bilitated units could be provided a year, but housing
needs would still be huge and unmet — the average family could wait twenty-five years to benefit from the program.

Our finances are intolerable. If New York State delivers $17 billion in income tax and $5 billion in corporate taxes to the federal government, it is conservative to
assume that $14 billion of the total of $22 billion has
come from the people of New York City. But our city
budget is about $7.5 billion: of that sum only $3 billion
derives from the state and from Washington. New York
must find another $4.5 billion in real estate and other
local taxes. Consider then: We pay $14 billion in income
tax to the federal government and to Albany: back
comes $3 billion. We put out five dollars for every dollar
which returns. So we live in vistas of ironbound civic
poverty. Four of those lost five dollars are going to places
like Vietnam and Malmstrom in North Dakota where the
ABM will find a site, or dollars are going to interstate
highways which pass through regions we probably will
never visit. In relation to the federal government, the
city is like a sharecropper who lives forever in debt at the
company store.

Yes, everything is wrong. The vocations of the past disintegrate. Jewish teachers who went into the education system twenty years ago to have security for themselves and to disseminate enlightenment among the children of the poor, now feel no security in their work, and are rejected in their liberal sociological style of teaching. The collective ego of their life-style is shattered. They are forced to comprehend that there are black people who would rather be taught by other black people than by experts. The need for authenticity has become the real desire in education. "Who am I? What is the meaning of my skin, my passion, my dread, my fury, my dream of glories undreamed, my very need for bread?" — these questions are now become so powerful they bring the pumps of blood up to pressure and leave murder in the heart. What can education be in the womb of a dying city but a fury to discover for oneself whether one is victim or potential hero, stupid or too bright for old pedagogical ways? Rage at the frustration of the effort to find a style became the rage at the root of the uproar in the schools last year, and the rage will be there until the schools are free to discover a new way to learn. Let us not be arrogant toward the ignorant — their sensitivity is often too deep to dare the knowledge of numbers or the curlicue within a letter. Picasso, age of eleven, could still not do arithmetic because the figure 7 looked like a nose upside down to him.

Among the poor, genius may stay buried behind the mask of the most implacable stupidity, for if genius can have no issue in a man's life, he must conceal it, and protect it, reserve it for his seed, or his blessing, or, all else gone, for his curse. No wonder we live with dread in our heart, and the nicest of the middle class still padlock their doors against the curse. We are like a Biblical city which has fallen from grace. Our parks deteriorate, and after duty our police go home to suburbs beyond the city — they come back to govern us from without. And municipal employees drift in the endless administrative bogs of Wagnerian systems of apathy and attrition. Work gets done at the rate of work accomplished by a draft army in peacetime at a sullen out-of-the-way post. The Poverty Program staggers from the brilliance of its embezzlements. But, of course, if you were a bright young black man, might you not want to steal a million from the feds?

Here, let us take ourselves to the problem. It goes beyond the Durham gang. Our first problem is that no one alive in New York can answer with honesty the question: can New York be saved? None of us can know. It is possible people will emigrate from New York in greater and greater numbers, and administration will collapse under insufferable weights, order will be restored from without. Then, everyone who can afford it will redouble his efforts to go, and New York will end as the first asylum of the megacity of the technological future. We who leave will carry with us the infection of the cowardice and apathy, the sense of defeat of the terminal years. We will move into other cities similarly affected or into a countryside wary of us, for we are then packers and peddlers from an expiring social world. So our first problem is to find whether we can find a way to rally our morale.

Part of the tragedy, part of the unbelievable oncoming demise of New York is that none of us can simply believe it. We were always the best and the strongest of cities, and our people were vital to the teeth. Knock them down eight times and they would get up with that look in the eye which suggests the fight has barely begun. We were the city of optimists. It is probably why we settled so deep into our mistakes. We simply couldn't believe that we weren't inexhaustible as a race — an unspoken race of New Yorkers.

Now all our problems have the magnitude of junkie

[327]

problems — they are so coexistent with our life that New Yorkers do not try to solve them but escape them. Our fix is to put the blame on the Blacks and Puerto Ricans. But everybody knows that nobody can really know where the blame resides. Nobody but a candidate for mayor. It is the only way he can have the optimism to run. So the prospective candidate writing these words has the heart to consider entering the Democratic primary on June 17 because he thinks he sees a way out of the swamp: better, he believes he glimpses a royal road.

The face of the solution may reside in the notion that the Left has been absolutely right on some critical problems of our time, and the conservatives have been altogether correct about one enormous matter — which is that the federal government has no business whatever in local affairs. The style of New York life has shifted since the Second World War (along with the rest of the American cities) from a scene of local neighborhoods and personalities to a large dull impersonal style of life which deadens us with its architecture, its highways, its abstract welfare, and its bureaucratic reflex to look for government solutions which come into the city from without (and do not work). So the old confidence that the problems of our life were roughly equal to our abilities has been lost. Our authority has been handed over to the federal power. We expect our economic solutions, our habitats, yes, even our entertainments, to derive from that remote abstract power, remote as the other end of a television tube. We are like wards in an orphan asylum. The shaping of the style of our lives is removed from us — we pay for huge military adventures and social experiments so separated from our direct control that we do not even know where to begin to look to criticize the lack of our power to criticize. We cannot — the words are now a cliché, the life has gone out of them — we cannot forge our destiny. So our condition is spiritless. We wait for abstract impersonal powers to save us, we despise the abstractness of those powers, we loathe ourselves for our own apathy. Orphans.

Who is to say that the religious heart is not right to think the need of every man and woman alive may be to die in a state of grace, a grace which for atheists and agnostics may reside in the basic art of having done one's best, of having found some part of a destiny to approach, and having worked for the view of it? New York will not begin to be saved until its men and women begin to believe that it must become the greatest city in the world, the most magnificent, most creative, most extraordinary, most just, dazzling, bewildering, and balanced of cities. The demand upon us has come down to nothing less than that.

How can we begin? By the most brutal view, New York City is today a legislative pail of dismembered organs strewn from Washington to Albany. We are without a comprehensive function or a skin. We cannot begin until we find a function which will become our skin. It is simple: our city must become a state. We must look to become a state of the United States separate from New York State; the fifty-first, in fact, of the United States. New York City State, or the State of New York City. It is strange on the tongue, but not so strange.

Think on the problem of this separation. People across the state are oriented toward Buffalo or Albany or Rochester or Montreal or Toronto or Boston or Cleveland. They do not think in great numbers of coming to New York City to make their life. In fact the good farmers and small-town workers of New York State rather detest us. They hear of the evils of our city with quiet thin-lipped glee; in the state legislature they rush to compound those evils. Every time the city needs a program which the state must approve, the city returns with a part of its package — the rest has been lost in deals, compromises, and imposts. The connection of New York City to New York State is a marriage of misery, incompatibility, and abominable old quarrels.

While the separation could hardly be as advantageous to New York State as it would be for the city, it might nonetheless begin the development of what has been hitherto a culturally undernourished hinterland, a typically colorless national tract.

But we will not weep for New York State — look, rather, to the direct advantages to ourselves. We have, for example, received no money so far for improving our city transit lines, yet the highway program for America in 1968 was $5 billion. Of this, New York State received at least $350 million for its roads. New York City received not a dollar from Washington or Albany for reconstruction of its six thousand miles of streets and avenues.

As a city-state we could speak to the federal government in the unmistakable tones of a state. If so many hundreds of millions go to Pennsylvania and Oklahoma and Colorado and Maine for their highway programs, then we could claim that a comparable amount is required for our transportation problems, which can better be solved by the construction of new rapid transit. Add the moneys attainable by an increased ability as the fifty-first state to press for more equitable return on our taxes. Repeat: we give to Washington and Albany almost five tax dollars for every dollar which returns; Mississippi, while declaiming the virtues and inviolability of states' rights, still gets four federal dollars for every income-tax dollar she pays up.

As the center of the financial and communications industries, as the first victim of a nuclear war, the new state of the City of New York would not have the influence of one state in fifty-one, but rather would exist as one of the two or three states whose force and influence could be felt upon every change in the country's policy. With the power implicit in this grip, it may not be excessive to assume that divorce from Albany would produce an extra billion in real savings and natural efficiency, and still another billion (not to mention massive allocations for transit problems) could derive from our direct relation with the federal government: the first shift in our ability to solve our problems might have begun.

It would not, however, be nearly enough. The ills of New York cannot be solved by money. New York will be ill until it is magnificent. For New York must be ready to show the way to the rest of Western civilization. Until it does, it will be no more than the first victim of the technological revolution no matter how much money it receives in its budget. Money bears the same relation to social solutions that water does to blood.

Yet the beginning of a city-state and the tonic of a potential budget of eight or nine or ten billion dollars would offer a base on which to build. Where then could we take it? How would we build?

We could direct our effort first against the present thickets of the City Charter. The Charter is a formidable document. There are some who would say it is a hideous document. Taken in combination with the laws of New York State, it is a legal mat guaranteed to deaden the nerve of every living inquiry. The Charter in combination with the institutional and municipal baggage surrounding it is guaranteed to inhibit any honest man from erecting a building, beginning an enterprise, organizing a new union, searching for a sensible variety of living zone, or speaking up for local control in education. It would strangle any honest mayor who approached the suffocations of air pollution or traffic, tried to build workable on-the-job training, faced the most immediate problems of law and order, attacked our shortage of housing or in general even tried to conceive of a new breath of civic effort. There is no way at present to circumvent the thicket without looking to power brokers in the trade unions, the Mafia, and real estate.

Only if the people of New York City were to deliver an overwhelming mandate for a city-state could anything be done about the thicket. Then the legal charter of the new state could rewrite the means by which men and women could work to make changes in the intimate details of their neighborhoods and their lives.

Such a new document would most happily be built upon one concept so fundamental that all others would depend upon it. This concept might state that power would return to the neighborhoods.

Power to the neighborhoods! In the new city-state, every opportunity would be offered to neighborhoods to vote to become townships, villages, hamlets, sub-boroughs, tracts, or small cities, at which legal point they would be funded directly by the fifty-first state. Many of these neighborhoods would manage their own municipal services, their police, sanitation, fire protection, education, parks, or like very small towns, they could, if they wished, combine services with other neighborhoods. Each neighborhood would thus begin to outline the style of its local government by the choice of its services.

It may be recognized that we are at this point not yet vastly different from a patch of suburbs and townships in Westchester or Jersey. The real significance of power to the neighborhoods is that people could come together and constitute themselves upon any principle. Neighborhoods which once existed as separate towns or districts, like Jamaica or New Utrecht or Gravesend, might wish to become towns again upon just such a historic base. Other neighborhoods with a sense of unity provided by their geography like Bay Ridge, Park Slope, Washington Heights, Yorkville, Fordham Road, Riverdale, Jackson Heights, Canarsie, or Corona might be able without undue discussion to draw their natural lines.

Poorer neighborhoods would obviously look to establish themselves upon their immediate problems, rather than upon historical or geographical tradition. So Harlem, Bedford-Stuyvesant, and the Barrio in East Harlem might be the first to vote for power to their own neighborhoods so that they might be in position to administer their own poverty program, own welfare, their own education systems, and their own — if they so voted — police and sanitation and fire protection for which they would proceed to pay out of their funds. They would then be able to hire their own people for their own neighborhood jobs and services. Their own teachers and communities would, if they desired, control their own schools. Their own union could rebuild their own slums. Black Power would be a political reality for Harlem and Bedford-Stuyvesant. Black people and, to the extent they desired, Puerto Rican people, could make separate but thoroughgoing attacks upon their economic problems, since direct neighborhood funding would be available to begin every variety of economic enterprise. Black militants interested in such communal forms of economic activity as running their own factories could begin to build economies, new unions, and new trades in their neighborhoods.

Power to the neighborhoods would mean that any neighborhood could constitute itself on any principle, whether spiritual, emotional, economical, ideological, or idealistic. Even prejudicial principles could serve as the base — if one were willing to pay. It could, for example, be established in the charter of the city-state that no principle of exclusion by race or religion would be tolerated in the neighborhoods unless each such neighborhood was willing to offer a stiff and proper premium for this desire in their taxes.

In reaction to this, each and every liberal, Negro and white, who would detest the relinquishment of the principle that no prejudice was allowed by law, might also consider the loss of the dream of integration as the greatest loss in the work of their lives. They would now be free to create neighborhoods which would incorporate on the very base of integration itself — Integration City might be the name of the first neighborhood to stand on the recapture of the old dream. Perhaps it might even exist where now is Stuyvesant Town.

On the other hand, people who wished anonymity or isolation from their neighbors could always choose large anonymous areas, neighborhoods only in name, or indeed could live in those undifferentiated parts of the city which chose no neighborhood for themselves at all. The critical point to conceive is that no neighborhood would come into existence because the mayoralty so dictated. To the extent that they had been conditioned for years by the notion that the government was the only agency large enough and therefore effective enough to solve their problems, so to that extent would many people be reluctant to move to solutions which came from themselves.

To the degree, however, that we have lost faith in the power of the government to conduct our lives, so too would the principle of power to the neighborhoods begin to thrive, so too would the first spiritual problem of the twentieth century — alienation from the self — be given a tool by which to rediscover oneself.

In New York, which is to say, in the twentieth century, one can never know whether the world is vastly more or less violent than it seems. Nor can we discover which actions in our lives are authentic or which belong to the art of the put-on. Conceive that society has come to the point where tolerance of others' ideas has no meaning unless there is benumbed acceptance of the fact that we must accept their lives. If there are young people who believe that human liberty is blockaded until they have the right to take off their clothes in the street — and more! and more! — make love on the hood of an automobile — there are others who think it is a sin against the eyes of the Lord to even contemplate the act in one's mind. Both could now begin to build communities on their separate faiths—a spectrum which might run from Compulsory Free Love to Mandatory Attendance in Church on Sunday! Grant us to recognize that wherever there is a common desire among people vital enough to keep a community alive, then there must be also the presence of a clue that some kind of real life resides in the desire. Others may eventually discern how.

Contained beneath the surface of the notion is a recognition that the twentieth century has lost its way — the religious do not know if they believe in God, or even if God is not dead; the materialist works through the gloomy evidence of socialism and bureaucracy; the traditionalist is hardly aware any longer of a battlefield where the past may be defended; the technician — if sensitive — must wonder if the world he fashions is evil, insane, or rational; the student rebellion stares into the philosophical gulf of such questions as the nature of culture and the student's responsibility to it; the Blacks cannot be certain if they are fundamentally deprived, or a people of genius, or both. The answers are unknown because the questions all collide in the vast empty arena of the mass media where no price has ever to be paid for your opinion. So nobody can be certain of his value — one cannot even explore the validity of one's smallest belief. To wake up in New York with a new idea is to be plunged into impotence by noon, plunged into that baleful sense of boredom which hints of dread and future violence.

So the cry of "Power to the Neighborhoods!" may yet be heard. For even as marriage reveals the balance between one's dream of pleasure and one's small real purchase upon it, even as marriage is the mirror of one's habits, and the immersion of the ego into the acid of the critic, so life in the kind of neighborhood which contains one's belief of a possible society is a form of marriage between one's social philosophy and one's private contract with the world. The need is deeper than we could expect, for we are modern, which is to say we can never locate our roots without a voyage of discovery.

Perhaps then it can be recognized that power to the neighborhoods is a most peculiar relocation of the old political directions. It speaks from the Left across the divide to conservatism. Speaking from the Left, it says that a city cannot survive unless the poor are recognized, until their problems are underlined as not directly of their own making; so their recovery must be based upon more than their own private efforts, must be based in fact upon their being capitalized by the city-state in order that the initial construction of their community economics, whether socialist or capitalist or both, can begin.

Yet with power in the neighborhoods, so also could there be on-the-job training in carpentry, stonemasonry, plumbing, plastering, electrical work, and painting. With a pool of such newly skilled workers, paid by the neighborhood, the possibility is present to rebuild a slum area *room by room.*

Better! The occupant of an apartment who desires better housing could go to work himself on his own apartment, using neighborhood labor and funds, patching, plastering, painting, installing new wiring and plumbing — as the tenant made progress he could be given funds to continue, could own the pride of having improved his housing in part through his own efforts.

So power to these poor neighborhoods still speaks to conservative principles, for it recognizes that a man must have the opportunity to work out his own destiny, or he will never know the dimensions of himself, he will be alienated from any sense of whether he is acting for good or evil. It goes further. Power to all neighborhoods recognizes that we cannot work at our destiny without a contest — that most specific neighborhood which welcomes or rejects our effort, and so gives a mirror to the value of our striving, and the distortion of our prejudice. Perhaps it even recognizes the deepest of conservative principles — that a man has a right to live his life in such a way that he may know if he is dying in a state of grace. Our lives, directed by abstract outside forces, have lost that possibility most of all. It is a notion on which to hit the campaign trail.

Which is where we go now — into the campaign: to talk in the days ahead of what power to the neighborhoods will mean. We will go down the steps of the position papers and talk of jobs and housing and welfare, of education, municipal unions, and law and order, finance, the names of laws, the statistics of the budget, the problems of traffic and transportation. There will be a paucity of metaphor and a taste of stale saliva to the debates, for voters are hardworking people who trust the plain more than the poetic. How then can Mailer and Breslin, two writers with reputations notorious enough for four, ever hope to convince the voting hand of the electorate? What would they do if, miracle of political explosions, they were to win?

Well, they might cry like Mario Procaccino, for they would never have a good time again; but they would serve, they would learn on the job, they would conduct their education in public. They would be obliged to. And indeed the supposition could remain that they might even do well, better than the men before them. How else could they have the confidence to run? They might either have supposed that the Lord was not dead but behind them or they must have felt such guilt about the years of their lives that only the long running duties of office could satisfy the list of their dues.

As for the fact that they were literary men — that might be the first asset of all. They would know how to talk to the people — they would be forced to govern by the fine art of the voice. Exposed by their own confession as amateurs they might even attract the skill of the city to their service, for the community would be forced to swim in full recognition of the depth of the soup. And best of all, what a tentative confidence would reign in the eye of New York that her literary men, used to dealing with the proportions of worlds hitherto created only in the mind, might now have a sensitive nose for the balances and the battles, the tugs, the pushing, the heaves of that city whose declaration of new birth was implicit in the extraordinary fact that *him,* Mailer! and *him,* Breslin! had been voted in.

Sweet Sunday, dear friends, and take a chance. We are out on the lottery of the years.

Two Mayoralty Speeches

At the Village Gate

(*May 7, 1969*)

Now, look, let me talk, because it's my evening and you know it. I listened to you a long time, and I'll tell you why I listened to you. I'll tell you why there are no Black people here tonight — it's a simple reason. It's because Adam Clayton Powell has not decided whether he's going to declare yet or not, and the Black people know they would be foolish to declare for a maverick candidate until Adam Clayton Powell has made up his mind. It's as simple as that.

All right, now look, let me have your attention, really. Let me try something. Can you hear me without the mike? All right now, let's get into a couple of very simple small bags, which is — one, we're in the Village Gate, which has the worst psychedelic acoustics in the whole world. The acoustics in this place are hooked, (yea, fuck you)* are hooked out of Art D'Lugoff's beard. And I love Art, cause he is an ogre just like me, and Art decided a long time ago that he was expendable, but he said to the whole world and New York, "To hell with you; shove it up your screw. I'm here, I'm running the Village Gate. You cannot stop me unless you come in here and wipe me out." And they never came in, and Art created a neighborhood.

Now the reason I hate talking into this mike is because it sets up a hypnotic trance which is full of the weaker bullshit in our continuing relationship. Now get away from me, everybody. Now look, look, let's be sensible for a little while. You're just nothing but a bunch of spoiled pigs — and there ain't a cop in the house! And yesterday I went up to the Police Academy and talked not to the cops first, but to the students at the John Jay Criminal Justice Academy or whatever it is called. (Please get away from me, and stop all this dull bullshit. I'm onto it — I'm onto it. Don't interrupt me when I'm talking, I'll be interrupted soon enough.)

(From audience: Norman, talk about the fifty-first state, you're among friends.) Hey, I'll tell you something. Shut up. You're not my friend if you interrupt me when I'm talking 'cause it just breaks into the mood in my mind. So fuck you, too. All right, I said you're all a bunch of spoiled pigs. You're more spoiled than the cops. I'll tell you that, I'll tell you that. You've been sittin' around jerkin' off, havin' your jokes for twenty-two years. Yeah! And more than that — more than that. You all want to work for us? You get in there, and you do your discipline, and you do your devotion. You get in there, and you do some dull work. Don't come in there and help us because "we're gonna give Norm a little help." Fuck you! You help us or don't come near us. I'll tell you why — 'cause we can win this thing. We can win it, if we're very good. We

* Parentheses are response to audience heckling.

can win it with all of you angels and devils. But we can't win it, we can't win it if you come in here with your dull little vanities. The cops I talked to yesterday were a more impressive group of people than all of you. I'll tell you that.

Now is there anybody here who is not familiar with our program by now? No one? All right, then this I say to you. This I say to you. You are all gonna go through a tremendous hour of horror, panic, and vomit if you start to work seriously for us, because you know I'm not the only nearsighted crazy man in America, and some of you could get hit. Get it straight. If you're gonna come in and work for us then work, but leave your ego at the door. If you think I'm in this for fun, then I feel sorry for you, 'cause I might have to pass on you after I have gone through. Got it? Got it? All right. Then fuck you. Got it? If you're gonna help me, then help me. But I don't want any of those dull mother-tired ego trips. Work.

Now, to prove to you how good this mayoralty is gonna be . . . I didn't quit while I was ahead, I'm about to reinvest my winnings and see if I can capture some of the more delicate spirits in the house. The point to what we're up to is that we are either running in fun or not. Since the neighborhood assembled here has only one thing in common, which is that they have a ticklish little liver and anus on the notion of who is putting who on, they think, they think that we are running in fun. Some of our own people put out campaign buttons like "Mailer-Breslin Seriously." Let me point out to you one quick little notion. Anybody who is runnin' in fun in the mayoralty election in New York deserves to run in fun.

Now I wanna finish with a small story, which you can shove down your throats. Years ago, I went out with the distinguished novelist, Mr. Ralph Ellison, to Iowa for a schlock magazine called *Esquire* run by a martinet and tyrant named Harold Hayes, who wouldn't know a good piece of writing until the Pulitzer Prize kicks him in the back of the ear. One of my dearest friends! And we went out there. A little fellow named Mark Harris — he's a little Jewish fellow with a big cigar which he blew in everyone's face, he's a tiny version of Groucho Marx, and Dwight MacDonald looking as though he was gonna die of asthma and apoplexy twenty-two years ago, and Ellison, and myself. And we went out there to Iowa and we said — this is back in 1959 — over and over again that the country is in a terrible time. It is full of the worst disease. You don't begin to know how bad this country has become. You people in Iowa have to recognize this is a marvelous state, Iowa, but it really doesn't begin to know how awful things are outside. And we got this marvelous applause, and we kept saying people in Iowa — we didn't know the word "turned on" — we kept saying people in Iowa are marvelous, until we found out they all were graduate students from Michigan and, ah, places like, ah, Philadelphia. So when it was over, like a high-school team that fought a very good game and finally lost in the last quarter, I turned to Ellison in the dressing room — we were having some drinks with some marvelous-looking Republican women — and I said, "Ralph, what the hell do we do it for? Why do we work so hard?" And he said, "Well, we're expendable."

So get that into your head. There's a very simple little notion going on, which is, we're all going to run and we're gonna do our best, and we'll go on for eighty-two years or more. But the notion to get through your heads is to get over your silly little ego-tired trips. If you have a lot of money and that's the way that you turn on to workin' for us, then thank you very much. We can use that money if you give it to us, and you can give it to us any way you want — publicly, privately, quietly, at large or small. If you have other ways of working for us, work for us.

What we really want is to get out into the neighborhoods. I want to go out and talk in every neighborhood before I'm done. I'll talk in the sweetest neighborhoods and the worst neighborhoods. But I'm running on the notion that New York can't begin to become the incredibly absolute and magnificent city that it is until there is power to the neighborhoods. Two weeks ago at the end of a long evening of campaigning, speaking at a marvelous, to me, Irish Club in Park Slope — overcome with happiness, I said, "I am running on everything from Black Power to Irish Self-Righteousness," and the good Irishmen in that place laughed and applauded, and I thought I had a victory until I read in the *Village Voice* that the smell of political death was upon us. I know what the fellow was up to. He was saying — "Get out of this campaign. You're just a little Jewish fellow from Brooklyn, and you don't know what's up." Well, let me tell you something. I know what's up because the greatest Jewish paper in New York, the despicable *New York Post*, won't print a word of what we're up to. And let me tell you what that means — let me tell you this — I am proud of my people. Very few people understand the Jews, but I do, 'cause I'm one of them. Fuck you, let me talk. The Jews are an incredible people at their best. At their worst they are swine. Like every Wasp I ever met, at their worst they are awful. All people are awful at their worst. Some are worse than others. But the Jews are sensational at their best, which is rare enough, given Miami and a fur coat. No, don't laugh, because you don't know what you're laughing at. Think about it. Whenever a people loses its highest race, there's nothing funnier going on in the world.

What we're running on is this: that this town has come to the point where this town, that many of us grew up in, the greatest city in the history of the world conceivably, is now some sort of paralytic victim in an orphan asylum. This city must be saved by vigorous activity by everybody within it, and I'm not just talking in my cups. But as the people of New York turn on and become fantastic, which we all are because I've met more interesting people in New York, per capita, than anywhere else in the world . . . Come on, let's not spend any time on applause, let's get to the point. The point is simple. Unless this city turns on and becomes fantastic, it'll become the first victim of the technological society — you know what that means? That means that the smog, the dead, dull air of oppression will be upon us first, and we will destroy each other first, because we all have too much within us to be able to bear the unendurable dullness of our days in New York when we all know we're capable of so much more.

So this I say to you. If we don't save our city, our city will become that little ward, that ward of eight million. There'll be a fifty-mile bypass around us, and they'll say, "We understand there are three divisions of Marines in there to keep the populace down." (No, keep quiet! Let me finish 'cause I'm talkin' very hard. Look — don't come here to be entertained), we're into somethin' that's deep. Don't kid yourself on this. We're running on the notion of power to the neighborhoods. What we're saying is very simple. We're saying — (Shut up and fuck you! Let me talk) — we're here on something very simple, which is that nobody knows any longer which idea has more validity than another, because there's no ground, there's no content, there's no situation for an idea. We're running on one notion — let the Left and the Right have their neighborhoods. Let them each see what kind of society they can create and then decide on the basis of a thousand contests and a hundred bloody encounters which particular neighborhood, or style, or conception of life is more interesting than another. Let people at least be ready to begin to put their notion of existence behind themselves, in front of themselves, within themselves. Let them begin to work for something they believe in.

Nobody in this city can begin to work for anything they believe in, 'cause it just isn't there, it just doesn't exist.

This city is controlled from without. That's why everybody is going crazy in this city, because they have no objective correlative, which I remind you literary people is a remark first coined in twentieth-century cultural history by Mr. T. S. Eliot, of all people. There is no objective correlative in this city, but we say power to the neighborhoods would give an objective correlative that would give a notion of where everybody is. We are running on one profound notion. Free Huey Newton, end fluoridation. We're running on another profound notion — compulsory free love in those neighborhoods which vote for it along with compulsory church attendance on Sunday for those neighborhoods who vote for that. What we are running on is one basic, simple notion — which is that till people see where their ideas lead they know nothing; and that, my fine friends, is why I am running. I want to see where my own ideas lead. Thank you very much.

To the Time-Life Staff

(June 3, 1969)

If I win the primary on June 17, I am — as Breslin always says — in trouble. I'm in terrible trouble. I will then have to go on and work in the mayoralty campaign all summer and earn not a sou. And after that point, if I win, I'll be in the paltry position of entering the mayoralty a tremendous number of bucks in debt. How will I ever keep from becoming corrupt? So you have to assume my candidacy is a prima facie case of seriousness. No man runs to win in such a way as to pauperize himself, unless he is either the victim of a *grande idée* or paying his debt to society. I submit that I'm paying my debt to society, and that is why I'm running for mayor.

Since I have brought the mood of this audience down

to zero in my feisty* little way, let me present the simple campaign notions upon which we're running. They are several. One, that New York has become a city so sick, so wracked with pain, so torporous, feverish, edemic, pandemic, and miserable that, as my running mate, James Breslin, says: "To run frivolously in a city as mortally ill as New York would be a sin." The city is suffering from every disease that sets upon America, including the disease cf bad reportage. None of us, by now, has an accurate notion of what is going on anywhere at all. We have the most extraordinary network of communications in the history of Western civilization, and we have less sense of where reality resides than perhaps at any time in our history. And the reason is that we are a divided nation. But we are a nation divided within the soul of each man and woman alive in the country, because we are racing forward, on the one hand, at a great rate toward the most extraordinary adventures in the history of man, and on the other hand, we find ourselves each year, each season, virtually each month, more and more unable to solve our most fundamental social problems. And in New York the diseases of America settle, and develop, and fester, and finally begin to burn and suggest that eventually they may even explode. We live in a city which has an enormous welfare roll. We have more than a million people on welfare in this city. The figure is actually one million two hundred thousand people. The moneys that we spend for welfare are over a billion and a half dollars a year now — they're larger than the amount we spend for education. Yet that welfare roll we support in this city — not through direct payments — although more than directly we support it, as I will try to suggest a little later, that welfare roll is not even of our own creation.

There have been extraordinary developments made by

* There had been a reference to the candidate as "feisty" in the preceding issue of *Time*.

the kind of corporations who produce farm machinery. They have discovered ways to mine the bottom lands of great cotton states like Mississippi. And in the course of that, whole hordes of tenant farmers who'd been buried in a miserable existence but nonetheless a cultivated one, because they at least partook of a culture down South, were uprooted and came here to the North, where they immediately were drawn by the fact that New York was a city with a mildly liberal tradition, a city which sought to pay people on welfare a little more than people were being paid in other cities. So a disproportionate number of dispossessed farm workers came to New York, and our welfare rolls began to grow, and grew at a huge rate.

We had, at the same time, a series of powerful unions in this city, who would not let Black or Puerto Rican people into those unions. So the people who came here went on welfare and stayed on welfare, and their condition deepened until it became a way of life. And as it became a way of life, so it became a way of criminal life; and criminality became attached to the edges of welfare, so that many a hardworking woman lived on her welfare check and brought up her children, legitimate or illegitimate, and the young boys who grew up in this environment began to look more and more for purposes in crime. Because crime, for a man who is poor and landless and disenfranchised and living on a government dole, is finally a witty activity. It is the one way in which he may express himself.

So the crisis of the city deepened. It was like a boat waterlogged with welfare. On the other hand, all sorts — to use the worst word for crime — all sorts of rats were feeding on the cargo. This ship has been staggering along and getting into worse condition year after year after year, until now there's grave question whether it can really be saved, short of a federal takeover of the economic necessities of this city. Now in this situation, any man who runs for mayor has good cause to examine his motives, if he's interested in attacking the problem on the old basis. To wit, running for mayor in such a way that he would be elected: making the old deals in the old ways, coming into power with an administration and a bureaucracy and a set of municipal unions who are all waterlogged themselves, all corrupt themselves, all full of crime themselves. Trying to work and accomplish anything in such a city — no matter how brave or honorable or worthwhile or even noble he may be in his own mind and to others — his hands are tied, he is manacled to the oppression of his condition because he too is oppressed. He has to deal with an administrative system which is impenetrable. So, at that point, he may be a man as well-intentioned as our honorable John V. Lindsay and still fail. He can work like a Trojan for four years and go down to abysmal defeat after defeat. The difficulty in the situation is that there is no way to solve the problems of New York, because the most fundamental problems of New York are not only aggravated by the farm machinery, but by the legislative morass of the north in Albany.

So over the last year, as must have been suggested to a thousand men in this city, many people came to me time and again to say, "Well, why don't you run for mayor? If Bill Buckley could run for mayor, you certainly can run for mayor." And I kept saying it was impossible. It was hopeless. One would not even begin to think of running for mayor. It is too terrible a job to contemplate if you ever won.

Until that marvelous day, and I blush to admit this, when a magazine editor talking to me said: "Norman, have you ever thought of the fifty-first state, of New York becoming a separate state?" And at that moment I said, "Good Lord, I've now found a way to pay my enormous account to you. I can work, I can campaign, I can serve. I can run on a notion that makes sense to me, which is that if New York can become the fifty-first state, it can begin to attack its incredible problems." Because if I run, and win a primary, and go on from there to win a mayoralty election against the extraordinary opposition of forces by stealing a primary election, then indeed a small miracle would have happened in this city; and the people of this city would have voted for a set of ideas which would be unheralded in previous political history. To wit, they would not have voted for their immediate security, but for setting out on an adventure whose end could not be foreseen. Because at that moment when the people would vote to become the fifty-first state, which as I say would be embodied in our candidacy, at that moment the city would have declared that it had lost faith in the old ways of solving political problems, that it wished to embark on a new conception for politics.

Now this new conception would revolve around the second point in our platform, which is power to the neighborhoods. And what indeed could that possibly mean? It means something unheralded in American politics. It means that, because a state had been declared by majority vote of the citizens of this city and I can say in parenthesis that if the mayoralty election were won in a three- to four-cornered race, and one did not have a majority, there would be no recourse but to throw the city open to a referendum, where the people of the city would vote on whether they wished to have a fifty-first state or not, because one could not begin to proceed without a majority of the people in the city voting to become the fifty-first state — one could not steal or trick such an election. At that point, having won such a majority, one could then call into being a constitutional convention, which might be one of the most remarkable moments in the history of this city or of any city, because the talent and the dedication and the hard consciousness of people in this city is remarkable. There's more talent waiting on line in this city, there's more energy bottled up and pent waiting to express itself in this city than perhaps in any city in

America — and that's possibly a way of saying any city in the world. The people in this city have been disenfranchised from any kind of power, any kind of approach to the problems before them which could have political issue for twenty years. It is impossible for any man, even a man of power, to get anything done in this city, and it has been impossible for many, many years. So, at this moment, we might assume that an extraordinary amount of intelligence and experience might collect to write a constitution which would be a remarkable document, because it would have to contend with the age-old problems — no, the two-centuries-old problems of the constitution. It would have to deal with checks and balances, the proportion of power. It would have to contend primarily with the notion, upon the one hand of power to the neighborhoods, and on the other hand that power which is due in respect to the Constitution of the United State, to the Supreme Court, the decisions of the Supreme Court, and to the power of the new state. Under the umbrellas of the Constitution of the United States, the Supreme Court, and the powers allocated to the new state, power to the neighborhoods could have its expression. It would begin by neighborhoods voting themselves into existence in the new state, declaring that they wish to become neighborhoods incorporated, small towns, small cities, hamlets, villages — whatever. These neighborhoods would have powers to deal with their own immediate problems in a way they cannot deal with them now. And so a great variety of neighborhoods would soon begin to flourish, one might hope, in this city. At the very least, if the acrimony, if the sense of combat and strife in these neighborhoods was fierce, people living in these neighborhoods would have a sense of whether they adhered to the principles of the neighborhood, or if they really, literally, wished to move out and move on. But the one virtue of this, it seems to me, is that the energies of the people of New York, which at present have no purchase or power — no purchase on their own natural wit or intelligence — no purchase other than to watch with a certain grim humor, a gallows humor, the progressive deterioration of this city, those energies could now be attached to working for their deepest and most private and most passionate ideas about the nature of government, the nature of politics, the nature of man's relation to his own immediate society. And it's possible that out of this interaction of these neighborhoods — which would be like small towns only in one sense, which is that they be small — these people might produce extraordinary results. So I present to you this notion: that we might begin to discover the nature of our reality as men and women in this seventh decade of the twentieth century. We might begin to discover which political ideas had validity, the power to continue themselves and nourish themselves, and those ideas which, finally, were surrealistic, nihilistic, excessive, and destructive to the ultimate aims of society, which finally is to find some balance in the lives of men and women.

Now, on this notion, I would like to throw some time open to you for questions and I will do my best to answer them, and then proceed with a peroration, if that still remains within our possibility. Thank you.

What makes you think you could get the fifty-first state?

I would ask you to use your imagination. We are not talking about the city as it exists today. We're talking about the city after Mailer and Breslin — forgive me for talking like a conventional politician — after Mailer and Breslin succeed in stealing a primary election in the Democratic Party from Meade Esposito, Mario Procaccino, and a few other people. Now, at that point, that is an extraordinary moment in the history of the city, nothing less. If we then go on, but I would submit that is easier to do than win the mayoralty election, because at that point the time is so surrealistic that people might just say, "Oh, the hell with everyone. Let's just vote them in. Vote them in, so we'll have some amusement." Well, at that point, we then have four months to run through a hot summer through September and October, working under the long shadow of John Lindsay, who will seem more viable to leftists, liberals, conservatives, and reactionaries alike each day that they come face to face with the fact that if they vote for us, they are voting for an embarkation upon an unknown journey, which may end with the city of New York being cut loose from the mainland of America and being shipped out to sea. So I say to you, at that point, when we win the mayoralty election, this city will have gone through a transformation so extraordinary that the questions with which we engage ourselves today are not likely to be nearly so alive and pressing.

If you were mayor or governor of New York would you be able to continue writing?

I think, since I pay great attention to my betters, that would be a small sacrifice to make. I would merely have confirmed the fond opinion that *Time* magazine has of me, which is "this fella better stop writing or none of us will benefit." Seriously, I would not be able to continue writing, dear lady.

What are the legal steps necessary to achieve statehood?

There are three steps. A constitutional convention would have to be called; it would doubtless take months for a constitution to be written. At that point, it would be submitted to the state legislature in Albany for ratification; once Albany had ratified it, it would go to the Congress of the United States for ratification, and on that happy day we would be a state. Now, if you say how is that possible, how would Albany ever begin to pass it, let me point out to you, sir, that something like forty-two or forty-three percent of the legislators, I think it's actually more than that, forty-four percent of the legislators in Albany come from New York City. And one would assume that the large majority of those men and women would be prepared to vote for statehood about the time we had gotten in, for that would be the shock from which no one could recover. It would mean that people who felt they really understood the political game would have to recognize they didn't understand it at all, and so they would be inclined to go along with the winner. Politicians keep that as their last resort. If you can't figure out what else to do, go along with the winner. I think we could find another five or ten or fifteen percent in the upstaters who are proud and feel that we in New York City have been dragging them down for one hundred and eighty-two years. On top of that, I think that President Nixon might go to the phone and talk to Rockefeller and say, "Now look, there's not much else you can do. Are you going to put on your tin hat? Are you going to go at the head of the state militia and cross at Yonkers?" He'll be worse than that; he'll say, "Will you defile through the hills of the Bronx? Cross the Harlem River? Move south? You will never reach Central Park!"

Do you have political ambitions beyond becoming the mayor of New York City?

It's precisely because I have the stature I have that my ambitions are limited. I wish to be mayor of New York. Lindsay, who's a tall fellow, looks further.

You've put forward a very provocative idea, the fifty-first state. Do you feel anyone is listening to this at all?

When we go down the street, we find that more people have heard of this idea than have heard of us, when we get out in the neighborhoods. They say, "Oh yeah, you're the fellows who are running with the ah — what is it — the fifty-first state." And I get the feeling, maybe, that I have nothing but candidatitis; but I also get the feeling that people are particularly excited by this idea. Of course, I have an interest in thinking that way.

Why did you support the dual admissions policy for CCNY?

Well, I was the only candidate who supported the dual admissions plan, and I was pleased to find myself in such a position because it meant that I was living well, since it's almost impossible in a mayoral primary in which you have five men running in one election and two in another to find yourself on one side of an issue . . . well, you're all very serious about CCNY, aren't you? All right, I'll talk particularly straight about CCNY. It gives no one any pleasure, who has grown up in this city as I have, in Brooklyn, to enjoy seeing the pearl of the free higher educational system in New York having its standards adulterated. But the fact of the matter is simply this: we really don't know. One, we have no idea at all what's going to happen after two or three years; in other words, the students who succeed in being admitted without academic standards to CCNY will have much more life experience, presumably, than the students whose marks are a little better, because they've grown up in an environment which is near criminal for many of them. So I would just suggest that a great many of the people — among them the candidates who have been bleating about law and order and getting the crime off the streets — are acting like unconscionable hypocrites. Would they rather have those young people out on the streets, unemployed, living on welfare and looking for extraordinary varieties of mischief or would they rather have some of them going through the Draconian steps of trying to reorient themselves into an educational system, and conceivably some of them even wrestling with books at night to catch up? So to begin with, what was marvelous about the dual admissions system is that it would have opened the system to the kids who are presently wrecking and sacking the high schools and running through them with only one sort of expertise, which is, whoever is most adept at disrupting the educational system in the high school because there is no future past these high schools. They know their marks are so poor that they can't begin to contemplate getting into a university. Having them now being able to contemplate the fact that, yes, they can get into universities, they will feel that first moment of fear — of what happens if I go to a university and I'm completely ill-equipped? Some of them might even begin to start studying in high school, which opens up the possibility that the high schools may be seeded by this first seeding and may begin to improve a little bit, so that the morale of the teachers may begin to improve at that point also. Now, all these matters, I think, are more substantial than the fact that the educational standards at CCNY may be lowered for a period. It's my optimism and my hope that Black and Puerto Rican students who enter CCNY will end up being fine students, and the academic standards of CCNY, after a few years, will become as high as they are now or even higher. But even if that does not happen, we have to recognize that we are merely paying our dues, because the history of the treatment of Black people in this city is not an honorable history or an agreeable one. They've been kept from getting into any of the powerful unions of this city, so they have not been able to enter the working class and the middle class in any numbers. And now that they've been shut out from all other opportunities, now that they are pushing into the colleges, we bleat when we discover that white boys who are qualified are not going to get into these colleges. Well, I say fine, because that's the point when you're going to begin to have community colleges in this city built to fulfill precisely that need. The moment white boys can't get a free education, then you're going to get the community colleges, not before.

So long as Black boys can't get it, you're going to keep having the same buck-passing and the same complaining about expenses, and so that was why I supported the dual admissions system.

Wouldn't communities set up along geographical lines tend to freeze in present racial and economic distinctions very poor cities or very poor mini-cities that couldn't afford the police, the sanitation, and the fire departments that they would need . . . ?

I think you'd have to begin with the notion that the fifty-first state would be able to command more moneys than New York City. We've had people working on it, and they can't come up with any figure that's really sufficiently satisfactory to present to a technical audience or even a critical audience, because there are too many fluctuations in too many of the figures. We estimate that, immediately, it would be worth between two and three billion dollars more a year to New York City, if it were a state. For instance, there are all sorts of taxes that we would be able to collect directly, like the cigarette tax, the gasoline tax, the tax on registered automobiles, the take on pari-mutuels — and if off-track betting were legalized, there would be a tremendous amount of money there. There would be any number of funds available that we don't have now, so we would have more money to deal with immediately. It seems to me that you would have to make some sort of estimate of the funds that are going into each neighborhood now. For example, when you take poor neighborhoods you would have to estimate how much of the money that goes into those poor neighborhoods is spent on police. After the neighborhoods were constituted block to block, you could figure out what the administration of those neighborhoods had cost in the past, and these moneys would be passed over to the neighborhoods so they could elaborate their own forms of administration. They might wish to save money on one service or another in order to have more money available for other purposes. But on top of that, this could be any place in the city, and this is why I call myself a left-conservative, we would have to recognize that the history of these communities is not a fair nor an equitable history, and they are not capable of solving their problems through their own human agency nearly so well as we are in more fortunate communities. And so a majority of the new moneys in the new state would have to go toward economic funding in these communities. Now the difference between that and federal funding, which is going to happen anyway, is a great one, I think — because these particular poor neighborhoods would now be administering the funds themselves. So when people working in these programs began to cheat and swindle the programs they'd be cheating and swindling their own people rather than the federal government, and that I think would make a noticeable difference. I don't mean that all crime and all corruption and all embezzlement would stop; but I do think that it would make a big difference, because not only would they be cheating their own people, which might give great pause, but also they would have to face their own people, which might give even greater pause. So I think that would make for a more lively basis for economic funding for economic self-development in the poor communities.

Even more than financial problems you might have the freezing of racial enclaves and the polarization of communities which I think we've got to try to correct in New York.

Well, I think what you'd find is that you'd have a certain freezing into racial enclaves, as you put it, although I would suggest that that's exactly what we have today in the city, because there are few white people, for instance, who are going to just travel on the loose through Harlem after dark — just as a small example. So, as a practical

matter, Harlem and the rest of Manhattan are more separated, I'd say, than East Berlin and West Berlin. But
apart from that, what you also could recognize is to the
extent that certain neighborhoods declared themselves
for this sort of separation, other people who had been
rather tolerant, fairly noncommittal liberals up to that
point might say, "This is a disgrace, now we've really got
to work for integration because we're about to really lose
it." They might recognize that integration is something
that has been given to us from above, and if they really
wish to work for it, they now have to work for it directly.
So I think you would have communities that would
form themselves on principles of integration and collaboration and tolerance. And on top of that, you've also got
to recognize that New York is a particularly curious city,
and there are any number of blocks in this city and small
neighborhoods in this city where you have a mix of six,
eight, ten minority groups, and they all get along together reasonably well. Sometimes there's a historic tradition for it. There's one neighborhood, Park Slope in
Brooklyn, that's marvelous, and I think one of the reasons
for it is that architecturally it's a superb neighborhood.
So even though people live there who are rich, poor, of
all minority groups and races, the architecture — the
character of the neighborhood — is lovely. So there's a
certain possibility for getting and living together.

*Are you worried about hurting Badillo's chances in the
primary?*

Let's take it head on. One, I don't think Herman Badillo
has the chance of a snowball in hell of winning the primary, whether I'm in it or not. That's because I don't
think he's a winner. I think he's a congressman, and I'm
prepared to support him for Congress on that happy day
he runs. Two, if Herman Badillo ever did win the primary he would hurt Mr. Lindsay's chances, because you
would then have Lindsay running against Badillo, and

you could be certain that you would have Marchi or Procaccino running on some other ticket. In fact, you certainly would have Marchi running against them, and you would have two liberals running against a conservative at that point. You would have an unhappy situation for yourself if you were a liberal. So I don't think I'm hurting anyone's chances because, since I'm running as a left-conservative, I'm to the left and right of every man in the race.

If elected to the Harvard Board of Overseers, would you undermine Nathan Pusey's position as president?

I think Nathan Pusey undermined his position on the campus many years ago when he put up that building on Mount Auburn Street, that Medical Health Center which is fourteen stories high and expresses a style in architecture known as brutalism, which is unfinished gray concrete. That building is one of the six ugliest buildings in the United States. And the campus at Harvard, no matter what you might have said about it in the past, was not a disagreeable campus, and Mount Auburn Street was one of the pleasanter streets in our vast vanishing Western world. I think on that day that Dr. Pusey permitted that building to be put in, one could read the future. He would do something precisely so idiotic as calling up the Cambridge cops to get the kids out of University Hall. So whether I'm elected to the Board of Overseers or not, I can't say that I have a high opinion of the ongoing potentialities of Dr. Pusey's presidency.

Primary odds?

Breslin figures he's an odds-on two-to-three favorite. I think I'm running as a twenty-to-one shot. But in the handicap, the mayoral handicap we set up the other day at Aqueduct, we did say that while I was by Amateur out of Statehood and it was my first start, I was out of a good barn. So the handicapper put stars after my entry and said "Best Bet." Of course, the handicapper was my campaign manager. Would you like to hear the rest of the handicapping? Well, it was the mayoral handicap, and in post position one was Wagner, a twelve-year-old gelding by Meade Esposito out of Machine. The handicapper's comment on him was "Knows the track." The odds were eight to five. In the second post position was Procaccino, a Bronx ridgling. Now a ridgling, for the ladies I must say to you, is a horse of evil disposition. In fact, the Italian word *vellano* is the only way to describe the disposition of a horse — what you do with a horse or a man who's *vellano* — I'll leave the man out of it — but in any case what you do with a horse who's *vellano* is you're obliged to perform a curious testicular operation — ah — which leaves the fellow with one nut. A ridgling. There was Procaccino, a Bronx ridgling. This is the one argument I had with my handicapper, who wrote this particular sheet. He had "By Fear out of Law and Order." I said to him after, "You should have had 'By Prunes out of Law and Order.' " Anyway, the comment on him was "Moves up on a sloppy track." Then there was Badillo and Scheuer. They were an entry. They were both "By Liberal out of Loser," eleven to one. And finally there was our own entry. "Best Bet."

So the notion that we're running on, finally, is that everybody in this city suffers from the same disease that everyone in America suffers from — that we suffer from it doubly, triply, and in exaggerated form, which is, we do not have a proper sense of our own identity. So, we argue that statehood, the quality of statehood, once achieved would perform several wonders for this city. Not because we would get more money, although I think we would, and I think that money would be terribly necessary, but because the citizens of this city would have embarked upon an adventure in voting for that statehood particularly since we're the candidates, at the moment, who embodied that desire. So to get to statehood at that point, they would have to vote for us, which means they would be voting for amateurs, which means they would be deserting their belief in expertise because we run on one notion over and over again, which is that the experts have driven this city right into the ground. And we run on the notion, finally, that politics is philosophy and that one cannot begin to solve the problems of a city without engaging in philosophical arguments with oneself and with one's neighbor.

And the particular small continuing event which gives me most pleasure since I've been campaigning is I find that I can give my speeches at the level at which I wish to give them, I never try to talk down, I say what I wish to say to an audience, trying to pick up the mood of that audience, talking at my best to reach that audience, and I find that the philosophical density of the argument never bothers them one bit. I've talked to left-wing audiences, to right-wing audiences, to all sorts of audiences, and they all listen. The right-wing audiences listen even more carefully than the left-wing audiences because, perhaps, our words are fresher to them. At any rate, the powerful notion in it, which I think is appealing to all people in degree, is that if each group of people, each interest, each force in this city can begin to think in terms of neighborhoods, then it can begin to think in terms of discovering whether its own ideas have validity, have savor, give energy to others, give energy to oneself, or don't.

The tragedy of this city and the tragedy of this country is that we all live in a situation where none of us know what the reality is, and we explore for it and we explore for it — we spend our lives exploring for it — and we never find an objective ground where we can begin to locate whether some pet idea of ours or some profound idea of ours is partially true or partially untrue.

To talk about the situation, even briefly, people on the right wing feel that the Black people are lazy, spoiled, ungrateful, and incapable of managing their own society. Black people feel, I would guess on the one hand, that they have extraordinary possibilities and that they are great people. On the other hand, they have to feel that they can't possibly know, because they never had an opportunity to express that desire. So, if nothing else, Black communities working with their own power in their own neighborhoods could show to other neighborhoods one of two things, which is either that Black people were right about their potentiality for the future or that they were wrong and that, finally, they are incapable of making those extraordinary steps. And so that even right-wing people would have, at the end of that time, the confidence of knowing that they were seriously right or seriously wrong about some extraordinary matter. In turn, right-wing neighborhoods would discover in living with their principles whether their principles were nourishing and could maintain a society against all of the nihilistic tides of the twentieth century, or whether, finally, their principles were not sufficiently flexible to meet the extraordinary quality of the age. And on top of that, we would have the marvelous, if somewhat comic, alternatives of considering all those magical LSD communities where you would have children living on LSD for five years. At the end of that time they would either be creating castles, or they might be two-thirds dead of liver disease.

The notion that we're running on, then, is that until we begin to know a little more about each other — not through the old-fashioned New Deal governmental methods of tolerance — but through the quality of human experience in societies, small societies and somewhat larger societies, founded upon various principles — philosophical, spiritual, economic, geographical, territorial, historical, or whatever — we know nothing at all. And that's why I feel a certain optimism about this candidacy. Because what I think it offers to all the people of the city of New York is a chance to turn this city around and make it what it once was — the leader of the world. Thank you.

Acknowledgments

The author gratefully acknowledges permission to include the following previously copyrighted works in this collection: "King of the Hill." Copyright © 1971 by Norman Mailer. First published in *Life*, March 19, 1971. Also published by New American Library Inc.

"Homage to El Loco." Copyright © CBS Records, 1967. Published by the CBS Legacy Collection.

"The Playwright as Critic." Copyright © 1967 by Norman Mailer. A portion of the introduction was first published in the *New York Times Book Review* in 1967. The entire piece was first published as an introduction to *The Deer Park*, published by the Dial Press in 1967.

"Some Dirt in the Talk." Copyright © 1967 by Norman Mailer. First published in *Esquire*, December 1967.

"A Course in Film-Making." Copyright © 1971 by Norman Mailer. First published in *New American Review* #12.

"Up the Family Tree." Copyright © 1968 by Norman Mailer. First published in *Partisan Review*, Spring 1968.

"Introduction to *The End of Obscenity*." Copyright © 1969 by Norman Mailer. First published in the British edition of the book, published by André Deutsch Ltd. in 1969. Not published in the American edition.

"An Imaginary Interview." Copyright © 1967 by Norman Mailer. First published in the *New York Times Book Review*, September 17, 1967.

"Lament for Ignacio Sánchez Mejías." Copyright © 1955 by New Directions Publishing Corp. Translation copyright © 1967 by Norman Mailer. Translation first published in *The Poetry Bag*, Volume 1, Number 6, Winter 1967–68.

"Excerpts from *Playboy*." Copyright © 1967 by *Playboy*. First published in *Playboy*, January 1968.

"To the *New York Review of Books*." Copyright © 1966 by Norman Mailer. First published in the *New York Review of Books*, April 28, 1966.

"To the *Saturday Review*." Copyright © 1971 by Norman Mailer. First published in the *Saturday Review*, April 20, 1971.

"To the *New York Times*." Copyright © 1971 by Norman Mailer. First published in the *New York Times Book Review*, June 20, 1971.

"An Appreciation of Henry Miller." Copyright © 1966 by the Delacorte Press. First published as a contribution to *Double Exposure* by Roddy McDowall, published by Delacorte Press in 1966.

"An Appreciation of Cassius Clay." Copyright © 1967 by Norman Mailer. First published in the *Partisan Review*, Summer 1967.

"Two Oddments from *Esquire*." Copyright © 1963 by Norman Mailer. First published in the October and November 1963 issues of *Esquire*.

"*Rush to Judgment* by Mark Lane." Copyright © 1966 by Norman Mailer. First published in the *Village Voice*, September 1, 1966.

"Looking for the Meat and Potatoes." Copyright © 1969 by Norman Mailer. First published in *Look*, January 7, 1969.

[364]